A Linguistic History of English Poetry

Bringing together the emphases and techniques of modern linguistics and literary criticism, the author applies these to a range of poems from Shakespeare to the present day. The author argues that poetry is uniquely and intrinsically different from other linguistic discourses and non-linguistic sign systems.

Looking at a variety of approaches, including those of the New Critics, Formalists, structuralists and poststructuralists, he reveals how poetic structure and poetic signification have changed since the sixteenth century, and offers new interpretive models and methods for criticizing poetry. Particular emphasis is placed on the texts' contexts, both in relation to literary history, and social, cultural and aesthetic considerations.

The texts covered include poems by Donne, Herbert, Marvell, Milton, Pope, Thomson, Wordsworth, Coleridge, Blake, Keats, Shelley, Tennyson, Browning, Arnold, Hopkins, Pound, Eliot, William Carlos Williams, Dylan Thomas, Auden, e.e. cummings, Larkin, and E. J. Thribb.

The book contains detailed readings of individual texts, worked examples and exercises, and a glossary, and is ideal for under-graduate courses in English, Stylistics and Linguistics.

Richard Bradford is Lecturer in English at the University of Ulster at Coleraine.

The INTERFACE Series

A linguist deaf to the poetic function of language and a literary scholar indifferent to linguistic problems and unconversant with linguistic methods, are equally flagrant anchronisms. – Roman Jackobson

This statement, made over twenty-five years ago, is no less relevant today, and 'flagrant anachronisms' still abound. The aim of the INTERFACE series is to examine topics at the 'interface' of language studies and literary criticism and in so doing to build bridges between these traditionally divided disciplines.

Already published in the series:

NARRATIVE
  A Critical Linguistic Introduction
  Michael J. Toolan
LANGUAGE, LITERATURE AND CRITICAL PRACTICE
  Ways of Analysing Text
  David Birch
LITERATURE, LANGUAGE AND CHANGE
  Ruth Waterhouse and John Stephens
LITERARY STUDIES IN ACTION
  Alan Durant and Nigel Fabb
LANGUAGE IN POPULAR FICTION
  Walter Nash
LANGUAGE, TEXT AND CONTEXT
  Essays in Stylistics
  Edited by Michael J. Toolan
THE LANGUAGE OF JOKES
  Analysing Verbal Play
  Delia Chiaro
LANGUAGE, IDEOLOGY AND POINT OF VIEW
  Paul Simpson

The Series Editor
Ronald Carter is Professor of Modern English Language at the University of Nottingham and was National Coordinator of the 'Language in the National Curriculum' Project (LINC) from 1989 to 1992.

A Linguistic History of English Poetry

Richard Bradford

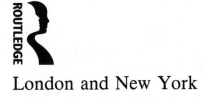

London and New York

First published 1993
by Routledge
11 New Fetter Lane, London EC4P 4EE

Simultaneously published in the USA and Canada
by Routledge Inc.
29 West 35th Street, New York, NY 10001

Phototypeset in 10 on 12 point Times by Intype, London

Printed in Great Britain by TJ Press (Padstow) Ltd, Cornwall

British Library Cataloguing in Publication Data
Bradford, Richard
   Linguistic History of English Poetry. –
   (Interface Series)
   I. Title II. Series
   821.009

Library of Congress Cataloging in Publication Data
Bradford, Richard,
   A linguistic history of English poetry/Richard Bradford.
      p. cm. – (Interface)
   Includes bibliographical references and index
      1. English poetry – History and criticism – Theory, etc. 2. English
   language – Versification. 3. Literary form. I. Title. II. Series: Interface
   (London, England)
   PR508.V45B73 1993
   821'.009 – dc20 92–40118
                        CIP

ISBN 0–415–07057 0
ISBN 0–415–07058–9 (pbk)

To Measham, Coleraine
and Jan

Contents

Series editor's introduction to the Interface series

There have been many books published this century which have been devoted to the interface of language and literary studies. This is the first series of books devoted to this area commissioned by a major international publisher; it is the first time a group of writers have addressed themselves to issues at the interface of language and literature; and it is the first time an international professional association has worked closely with a publisher to establish such a venture. It is the purpose of this general introduction to the series to outline some of the main guiding principles underlying the books in the series.

The first principle adopted is one of not foreclosing on the many possibilities for the integration of language and literature studies. There are many ways in which the study of language and literature can be combined and many different theoretical, practical and curricular objects to be realized. Obviously, a close relationship with the aims and methods of descriptive linguistics will play a prominent part, so readers will encounter some detailed analysis of language in places. In keeping with a goal of much work in this field, writers will try to make their analysis sufficiently replicable for other analysts to see how they have arrived at the interpretative decisions they have reached and to allow others to reproduce their methods on the same or on other texts. But linguistic science does not have a monopoly in methodology and description any more than linguists can have sole possession of insights into language and its workings. Some contributors to the series adopt quite rigorous linguistic procedures; others proceed less rigorously but no less revealingly. All are, however, united by a belief that detailed scrutiny of the role of language in literary texts can be mutually enriching to language and literary studies.

Series of books are usually written to an overall formula or design.

In the case of the Interface series this was considered to be not entirely appropriate. This is for the reasons given above, but also because, as the first series of its kind, it would be wrong to suggest that there are formulaic modes by which integration can be achieved. The fact that all the books address themselves to the integration of language and literature in any case imparts a natural and organic unity to the series. Thus, some of the books in this series will provide descriptive overviews, others will offer detailed case studies of a particular topic, others will involve single author studies, and some will be more pedagogically oriented.

This range of design and procedure means that a wide variety of audiences is envisaged for the series as a whole, though, of course, individual books are necessarily quite specifically targeted. The general level of exposition presumes quite advanced students of language and literature. Approximately, this level covers students of English language and literature (though not exclusively English) at senior high-school/upper sixth-form level to university students in their first or second year of study. Many of the books in the series are designed to be used by students. Some may serve as course books – these will normally contain exercises and suggestions for further work as well as glossaries and graded bibliographies which point the student towards further reading. Some books are also designed to be used by teachers for their own reading and updating, and to supplement courses; in some cases, specific questions of pedagogic theory, teaching procedure and methodology at the interface of language and literature are addressed.

From a pedagogic point of view it is the case in many parts of the world that students focus on literary texts, especially in the mother tongue, before undertaking any formal study of the language. With this fact in mind, contributors to the series have attempted to gloss all new technical terms and to assume on the part of their readers little or no previous knowledge of linguistics or formal language studies. They see no merit in not being detailed and explicit about what they describe in the linguistic properties of texts; but they recognize that formal language study can seem forbidding if it is not properly introduced.

A further characteristic of the series is that the authors engage in a direct relationship with their readers. The overall style of writing is informal and there is above all an attempt to lighten the usual style of academic discourse. In some cases this extends to the way in which notes and guidance for further work are presented.

In all cases, the style adopted by authors is judged to be that most appropriate to the mediation of their chosen subject matter.

We now come to two major points of principle which underlie the conceptual scheme for the series. One is that the term 'literature' cannot be defined in isolation from an expression of ideology. In fact, no academic study, and certainly no description of the language of texts, can be neutral and objective, for the sociocultural positioning of the analyst will mean that the description is unavoidably political. Contributors to the series recognize and, in so far as this accords with the aims of each book, attempt to explore the role of ideology at the interface of language and literature. Second, most writers also prefer the term 'literatures' to a singular notion of literature. Some replace 'literature' altogether with the neutral term 'text'. It is for this reason that readers will not find exclusive discussions of the literary language of canonical literary texts; instead the linguistic heterogeneity of literature and the permeation of many discourses with what is conventionally thought of as poetic or literary language will be a focus. This means that in places as much space can be devoted to examples of word play in jokes, newspaper editorials, advertisements, historical writing, or a popular thriller as to a sonnet by Shakespeare or a passage from Jane Austen. It is also important to stress how the term 'literature' itself is historically variable and how different social and cultural assumptions can condition what is regarded as literature. In this respect the role of linguistic and literary theory is vital. It is an aim of the series to be constantly alert to new developments in the description and theory of texts.

Finally, as series editor, I have to underline the partnership and cooperation of the whole enterprise of the Interface series and acknowledge the advice and assistance received at many stages from the PALA Committee and from Routledge. In turn, we are all fortunate to have the benefit of three associate editors with considerable collective depth of experience in this field in different parts of the world: Professor Roger Fowler, Professor Mary Louise Pratt, Professor Michael Halliday. In spite of their own individual orientations, I am sure that all concerned with the serious would want to endorse the statement by Roman Jakobson made over twenty-five years ago but which is no less relevant today:

A linguist deaf to the poetic function of language and a literary scholar indifferent to linguistic problems and unconversant with linguistic methods, are equally flagrant anachronisms.

Richard Bradford's *Linguistic History of English Poetry* provides a useful and much-needed guide to the language of poetry from both an historical and a linguistic perspective. Working with particular attention to the innovative theory of double articulation, the book contains detailed stylistic analysis of syntax, vocabulary and rhythm and metrics. It is supported by a valuable range of exercises and questions for further study which should made the book of value and utility in a wide range of courses in language and literary studies. It provides a necessary complement to Waterhouse and Stephens' *Literature, Language and Change* in the Interface series, which covers a number of different literary genres. Throughout the book Richard Bradford demonstrates the value of systematic stylistic analysis not simply in and for itself but with constant reference to social, cultural and historical contexts of innovation and development in poetic language. In this respect the book is an important contribution to a genuinely 'contextualised' stylistics.

Acknowledgements

I am grateful to the Humanities Faculty of the University of Ulster for providing me with the funds and the time to finish this book.

Permission has been granted by Faber & Faber to reprint Larkin's 'An Arundel Tomb' and Auden's 'In Memory of W. B. Yeats'; by Penguin for sonnet 2 of Geoffrey Hill's 'Funeral Music'; by W. W. Norton for e. e. cummings's 'No. 9' from *No Thanks*; by New Directions for extracts from W. C. Williams's 'The Corn Harvest' and 'The Red Wheelbarrow'; and by Oxford University Press for Charles Tomlinson's 'Lines'.

Professor Robert Welch, my head of department, deserves some thanks, and Professor Ron Carter of Nottingham University has been an encouraging and helpful editor. Nothing at all would have been possible without Louie and Bill Bradford. Jan Elliott was, as usual, tolerant and valuable in the true Ulster tradition.

Introduction
How to Use the Study

The principal problem in any attempt to find a fruitful and cooperative pattern of contacts between linguistics and literary criticism is depressingly simple: where do you begin? Should the study of syntax structure precondition your encounters with sentences in a poem? If so how do you classify and respond to deviations from normal structure? Perhaps these should not be regarded as deviations; perhaps poetry should be categorised as an autonomous linguistic system, maybe even an independent sign system, with its own rules and conventions.

Two assumptions will govern the structure and methodology of this study: firstly, poetry is different from other linguistic discourses and non-linguistic sign systems. Its difference is not, as many current cultural theorists claim, a product of the reader's a priori cultural, aesthetic and ideological expectations; its uniqueness is an intrinsic feature of its structure. The key to our understanding of poetic difference is the 'double pattern' – in its simplest form the relation between the line and syntax – and this will be more fully explained in Chapter 1. Secondly, distinctions between the form, the objectives and the meaning of individual poems can best be understood in terms of the different historical and generic categories that constitute the canon of post-sixteenth-century literature, and Chapters 2–6 will follow this traditional format.

The study is intended to be accessible enough for those whose familiarity with the terms and methodology of linguistics is slight and uncertain, and its format will provide the student with a means of contextualising each poem in terms of the major historical and aesthetic categories of literary studies – metaphysical, Romantic, modernist and so on. But it is not offered as a mechanical 'reader's guide' to conventional perceptions of poetry and interpretation. As well as explaining concepts, terms and effects it also invites the reader to challenge literary and critical norms.

Each specialised interpretive tool – deictics, cohesion, structural versus functional elements, text versus context, etc. – will be briefly defined at its point of introduction, and this system will be supplemented by a glossary of terms, including pointers to uses within this study and to recommended background reading. The Appendix, 'Using the Double Pattern and the Sliding Scale' is a brief guide to the methods employed in the book.

With the exception of Chapter 1, each chapter will conclude with an Exercise section in which the reader will be asked to test issues raised against other texts from the same generic–historical category.

The bibliography will include publication details of every text referred to in the study. If I cite a proper name in the main text or refer to a permutation of surname, title, date and page number, the source will be found in the bibliography.

1 Theory

INTRODUCTION: THE DOUBLE PATTERN

The question of how poetry might be described and defined as a linguistic structure has troubled readers since . . . well, since we have been able to keep records of what critics have said about literature. Regarding English poetry, this quest can be divided roughly into three stages: the classical sources (Aristotle, Plato, Longinus, etc.); the sixteenth–nineteenth centuries, in which critics both drew upon classical precedent and developed theories to account for the types, methods and objectives of modern English poetry; and the twentieth century, in which literary criticism has become an academic discipline and has found itself encountering, sometimes harmoniously and sometimes not, the non-literary practices of historicism, semiotics, sociology, politics and, most significantly, linguistics.

Apart from sharing the objective of defining poetry, the critics of these periods have one other, more paradoxical, thing in common. They already know what in purely abstract terms poetry is, but they remain uncertain about what exactly it does to and for the reader, precisely how these effects are achieved and to what extent such effects can be identified as purely poetic, rather than as elements drawn from the signifying procedures of other linguistic discourses. I can tell you in crude but accurate terms how to recognise a poem: it is a structure whose formal common denominator – that which separates it from non-poetic discourse – is its division into lines. The title of that rare and briefly fashionable phenomenon, the prose poem, testifies to the validity of my definition – the text calls itself a prose poem in order to warn the reader of its claims to be something that in basic empirical and formal terms it is not. The problem, or the paradox, faces us when we attempt to state how, apart from being divided into lines, the poem employs linguistic structures and exhibits effects that are essentially different from those found in other discourses.

The most widely debated literary device is the metaphor, or, in a more general sense, the trope. We use metaphors – comparing or contrasting two or more linguistic elements in relation to a pre-linguistic impression or fact – in all forms of speech and writing. How do we identify the essentially poetic qualities of metaphor? We could argue that by submitting this commonplace device to the compositional and interpretive restraints of metre, rhyme and lineation we change its effects.

Consider the following line from Wordsworth's *Resolution and Independence*:

The sky rejoices in the morning's birth

The metaphor is fairly easy to decode. The vehicle, to rejoice in birth, and the tenor, the sky and the morning, draw upon shared contextual correspondences – beginnings, optimism, new starts, and so on. The question we have to ask is how the copresence of metaphor and the structure of the iambic pentameter make this effect uniquely poetic? Consider the difference in effect between Wordsworth's line and the same metaphor transplanted into a form that might open a novel:

The sky seems to rejoice in the birth of the morning.

We could argue that in Wordsworth's line the unstress–stress pattern of the pentameter succeeds in foregrounding those words which effectively govern the metaphoric correspondences: sky, rejoices, morning's, birth. But this argument could be countered by pointing out that although the prose version is not metrically regular, the same words maintain their rhythmic and thematic priority in the sentence. Does the fact that we hear a regular iambic undertow in Wordsworth's line affect the way that we perceive the metaphor? If so, how can we claim that metre – which does not in itself create meaning – can influence meaning? Even if we could make such a claim, it would bring us up against even more troubling questions about the form of poetry that has effectively dominated twentieth-century poetic writing, free verse. If we succeed in identifying the essentially poetic qualities of Wordsworth's line, then by implication the prose line is unpoetic. Yet it bears a close formal resemblance to lines that we will come across in the 'poetry' of Eliot, Pound and Williams for example. We will consider the problematic relation between regular and free verse later in this chapter and in Chapter 6, but for the moment let us return to the question of whether elements such as metre can influence, perhaps even create, meaning.

It would be useful to specify the terminology and the limitations of our enquiry. Linguistics can provide us with the tools and the methodology to analyse syntactic structures, semantics and patterns of sound, but what is lacking is a single term or method which allows us to fully consider the interrelationship between the structures of language as a whole and the specific details of what is variously known as metre, prosody or, in its broader sense, versification. I shall call this area of interaction the double pattern. A brief definition is required: in all forms of linguistic discourse some kind of pattern emerges. At its most basic it is the pattern of comprehensibility, which is a function of grammar, syntax, semantics, and the interlocking of the syntagmatic and paradigmatic chains. We understand and create linguistic statements because we know that some words should and some words should not follow one another in order to create intelligible meaning. To use a term made famous by Noam Chomsky, it is the deep structure, the abstract framework of rules and conventions, that allows us to create and decode the specific and complex meanings of a chain of individual words. Occasionally, and often by accident, this referential, syntactic pattern of discourse will create surface patterns of rhythm and sound which draw upon the materiality of language but which do not relate directly to its conventions of meaning and signification. The double pattern occurs when this secondary, surface pattern is deliberately deployed as a regular and persistent feature of the text. The unit by which we measure and classify this secondary pattern is the poetic line. The key issues in our use of the double pattern as an analytical framework are first, the means by which we classify and interpret the relation between individual lines and second, the relation between lines and the pattern of syntax. The first task can be dealt with and addressed from within the sphere of versification.

1 Some poems will consist of lines that do not vary in their syllabic length or metrical pattern, the most widely used in sixteenth-twentieth-century poetry being the iambic pentameter. Thus the framework of the secondary pattern is regular and repetitive. If the poem uses rhyme this will create a counterpattern of relationships between individual lines. The most basic rhyme–metre formula will be found in the couplet, the smallest and simplest example of the stanza. Rhyme is important in regular verse because it allows poets

to vary the length and metrical structure of their lines while maintaining their distinct identity. The most important and widely used
form of unrhymed regular poetry is blank verse, in which the regular
metrical structure of each pentameter is the single factor which
distinguishes the line from interlineal movement of syntax. Free
verse is a phenomenon that, unlike its counterparts in regular
poetry, avoids abstract definition. The free verse poem might deploy
an irregular and unpredictable rhyme scheme, the lines themselves
might exhibit a variable pattern of rhythmic and metrical sequences.
Or they might not. The only definitive component of the free verse
poem is its division into lines which do not necessarily correspond
with the patterns of syntax – the double pattern is thus preserved,
but the means by which the reader distinguishes between these two
formal structures (perhaps only by seeing the poem on the page)
is, a century after the arrival of free verse, still a matter of conjecture
and opinion. This problem brings us to the second point, the relation
between the two components of the double pattern, and this, as we
shall see, will feature as the point of departure for the more varied
and complex issues of signification, interpretive conflict and literary
history that will concern us in this study.

2 In purely technical, descriptive terms the relationship between
the two components of the double pattern is easy to document. For
instance, the most obvious case of conflict or interaction between
the two can be categorised as enjambment. This occurs when the
fundamental unit of versification, the line, literally cuts into the
structure and movement of syntax. A line might divide adjective
from noun, verb from subject or object. The degree of tension
between the two components depends partly upon the type of verse
and partly upon questions of interpretation and vocal performance.
If the dangling adjective also incorporates a rhyme-word then a
sense of what we can term poetic counterpoint will be evident no
matter how the verse is interpreted or read aloud. But if the poem
does not rhyme (blank or free verse) it would be possible in oral
performance to close the gap between the lines, maintain the timing
and rhetorical structure of the syntax and effectively marginalise the
prosodic component of the double pattern. What we see on the
page might not correspond with what we hear.

Such questions might seem to limit themselves to the now dated
spheres of metrical pedantry and localised close reading, but they
actually provide us with a productive axis between our mastery of

the technical jargon of poetic form and the far more problematic issues of how our technical definition of poetry corresponds with the essentially poetic generation of effect and meaning.

Let us return to enjambment. If the performer or the critical interpreter chooses to acknowledge the break between an adjective and a noun, what does this tell us about the intentions of the poet and the textual patterns of signification? We could argue that the poet exploits the double pattern as means of foregrounding a contextual issue, a particular mimetic effect: hesitation or uncertainty on the part of the speaking presence. In written prose discourse this would be impossible without the use of a stage direction ('speaker pauses') or in a novel the interpolation of ellipses or the interjection of the narrator ('John paused, before proceeding with his account'). In the poem such an effect can be achieved by, to use a term made familiar by the Russian Formalists, 'the baring of the device'. In this case the device is the poetic line, which, instead of maintaining a parallel correspondence with the structure of syntax, effectively interferes with it. Thus the material, non-signifying component of the double pattern succeeds in becoming part of the means of signification. But having reached this conclusion we have hardly begun to answer the questions it engenders.

The formula that underpins the methods and assumptions of structuralism, semiotics and linguistics is the distinction and relation between system and event, or in the terms used by Ferdinand de Saussure, the founder of structuralism, *langue* and *parole*. These might refer to the structure, conventions and rules of a particular language in relation to an individual statement or text, or they might encompass a broader network of linguistic and non-linguistic sign systems – colours, cars, buildings, clothes, food, and so on. One of the most contentious issues to emerge from the various uses and investigations of the structure–event formula is in the threat it presents to the notion of originality, individuality, or in current phraseology, the autonomy of the subject. If, when using language, we need to draw upon the vast impersonal structure of the system in order to be understood, then it would seem that what we say or write is by no means unique to our personal, prelinguistic experiences or perceptions; rather it is something made available from a shared system of enabling conventions which constitute and delimit the varieties of discourse. If we accept that a sentence in English can have meaning only by virtue of its relations to other sentences and abstract deep structures within the conventions of the language, then when we supplement syntactic structure by imposing upon it the arbitrary code of rhythm, metre, rhyme and lineation, we are imposing even more limitations upon the identity and individuality of the subject represented within or speaking through poetic language. So when we praise poetic discourse for allowing us to represent hesitation and uncertainty within the text, without contextual interjections, we also face the contention that this imagined speaker who pauses and hestitates becomes more a function of the text itself and less an individual who inhabits the world outside the text.

This question does not arise only from the special instance of enjambment. Most poems, whatever their immediate provenance or concern, will at some point engage with issues of perception, truth and identity that we would usually associate the non-literary spheres of philosophy, psychology, theology and sociology. Within these discourses it is permissible to use devices that are more self-consciously foregrounded in poetry: metaphor, allegory, analogy, symbolism, irony, parody. But the one feature of poetry that will not be found in the philosophic theorum or the essay on psychology is the use of metre, rhyme and lineation. So when in the 'Immortality Ode' Wordsworth states that,

> The sunshine is a glorious birth;
> But yet I know, where'er I go,
> That there hath past away a glory from the earth,

we can accept that he is making a profound statement about his own existential vision. But had Kant or Wittgenstein made such a statement in rhyme and metre we would assume that they had taken a day off from their more serious philosophic conjectures. Why? There are several interrelated responses to this. We could claim that if Wordsworth's single objective was to communicate his model of mortality and existence, then there are surely better ways of clarifying such issues than dressing them up in metre and rhyme. Why then did he choose poetic form? It might be that the 'music' of metre and rhyme have some almost subliminal, persuasive effect upon the addressee. If so, this is not so much a statement, but more an exercise in deception. To complicate matters, we find that in adopting this traditional perception of what poetic form is and does, we have further compromised the equally traditional notion of the poet as the source, the originator of a thought or an image. If his message registers as an impressive vision of life and reality, particular to Wordsworth, it does so at least partly because of its ability to draw upon the same system of conventions and techniques shared by other poets and other poems. Northrop Frye observed that

'Poems are made out of other poems', and if we accept that the prosodic material of construction plays some part in the generation of specifically poetic meaning we would also have to concede that the poetic identity of William Wordsworth is similarly 'made out of other poems'.

Before testing these issues and questions against the work of a number of eminant linguists and critics, we should remind ourselves of what they actually are.

1 **The double pattern** All poems consist of two linguistic patterns, one which corresponds with and organises the structure of the poetic line, and one which poetry shares with other linguistic discourses, the structural keystone of which is the sentence, and the broader signifying functions of which (the generation of metaphor, the use of irony, the employment of grammatical deviation, etc.) are unlimited.

2 **The relation between the two patterns** This problem can be approached in two ways: first, we can, using linguistic and prosodic terminology, classify the points at which the metrical or even the visual identity of the line, interacts with, controls, submits to, the structures of syntax; second, we can consider the extent to which each dimension of the double pattern influences the other in the production of meaning: to introduce another currently problematic term, we can examine how the tensions created by the double pattern play some part in the way that we naturalise poems or extracts from poems.

3 **Text and system** All linguistic statements must draw upon a system of rules and conventions. The double pattern means that poetry must draw upon two of these at the same time: first, the structural terms and conditions of syntax, metaphor and, in a broader sense, literary stylistics; second, the conventions of metricality and unmetricality, rhyme and non-rhyme, that constitute the fluctuating identity of the poetic line.

Clearly, none of these three categories of analysis is entirely immune from the others, but it is the third that will effectively dominate this study. After this chapter our emphasis will be determined by the chronology of literary history, from the sixteenth century to the present day. Literary history provides us with an index to our late-twentieth-century understanding of the two codes or systems of the third category. For instance, the decentred narrative and unstructured rhetorical play of Eliot's 'The Love Song of J. Alfred Prufrock' represents an extension, even a violation, of the metaphoric and narrative codes that governed earlier examples of the dramatic monologue by Browning. However, its use of a variable metrical structure and an irregular rhyme scheme would find a precedent in the Romantic ode or in short narratives such as Coleridge's 'Christabel'. Wordsworth's 'Tintern Abbey' bears no thematic resemblance to Milton's *Paradise Lost*, yet its form and, consequently, its effect upon the reader pay allegiance to Milton's success in establishing the unrhymed pentameter as a vehicle for non-dramatic poetry.

The two elements of the double pattern certainly do not follow parallel lines of change and development through literary history. What we will do in Chapters 2–6 is to examine the changing and unpredictable relation between these two codes as a basic framework for the examination of much broader questions about poetry, its relation to other literary and non-literary discourses and its position within different cultural, social and political contexts. Before relating these and other questions to individual texts we shall, for the rest of this chapter, examine a number of ways in which the double pattern, the relation between the formal identity and the broader signifying function of the poem, have been dealt with by different individuals and interpretive schools.

ROMAN JAKOBSON

Roman Jakobson (1896–1982): linguist, structuralist, semiotician and, according to David Lodge, 'one of the most powerful minds in twentieth-century intellectual history'. If critical guides and anthologies of critical essays are a reliable index, Jakobson's most significant contribution to the relation between linguistics and literary studies occurred in his 'Closing Statement' delivered at a conference on stylistics at Indiana University in 1958. The proper title of this much reprinted and discussed essay is 'Linguistics and Poetics' (1960), and it is important for two reasons. It brings together the techniques and objectives of the Eastern bloc linguists, structuralists and Formalists, the groups with which Jakobson is most readily associated, with the less easily definable methods of Anglo-American New Criticism. It can also claim to be the most precise and comprehensive attempt, within this broad international and cross-disciplinary context, to arrive at a scientific definition of poetry. Its dealings with the double pattern are as we shall see at once enlightening and problematic. Jakobson's argument is difficult to summarise, but the following quotation holds the key.

The poetic function projects the principle of equivalence from
the axis selection into the axis of combination.

(1960, 39)

It is upon the relationship between these two axes that post-Saussurian linguists have based their investigations of the precise functional
properties of the *langue* and the *parole*. The selective axis also
encompasses the designations of the paradigm, similarity and metaphor and the combinative those of the syntagm, contiguity and
metonymy, and the two axes work in the following way.

When we construct a sentence – the basic organisational unit of
any *parole* – we draw both upon the rules and conventions of the
syntagmatic chain, in basic terms grammatical rules, and upon the
more flexible dimension of paradigmatic choices available at each
stage in this process. For example, in 'His car moved along the
road', the syntagmatic chain consists of a main verb 'moved along',
two nouns 'car' and 'road', and a pronoun and connective 'his' and
'the'. If we wanted to offer another version of the same message
we could maintain the syntagmatic structure but make different
choices from the selective–paradigmatic axis at each stage in the
combinative sequence. For instance, 'The man's motor vehicle progressed along the street'. The only substantive difference occurs in
the substitution of street for road, suggesting as it does an urban
environment, and indeed such changes as the above are generally
made in order to clarify the message. In this context we might
substitute 'sped' for 'moved' or 'progressed' to indicate that the car
is moving faster than we would normally expect.

So far we have not made use of the metaphoric element of the
paradigmatic axis, and we might do so by stating that 'His car flew
along the road'. This is an, albeit unexciting, metaphoric usage
because although we have maintained the conventions of the syntagm ('flew' is a verb) we have also drawn upon an unexpected
choice from the paradigmatic–selective axis. Cars do not fly, but
since the flight of birds and aeroplanes is generally associated with
degrees of speed and unimpeded purpose we have offered a similarity between two otherwise distinct fields of perception and meaning. We have used the relation between the two axes to move
beyond the mode of clarifying the event and have intervened as an
active perceiver, and offered an impression of the event – the movement of the car reminds us of the progress of a bird or an aeroplane.
Such a shift in perceptual status has been designated, by Emile
Benveniste, as a distinction between *histoire* (objective) and *discours*

(involving the participation of the perceiver in the account of the event). To return to Jakobson's formula, we have also engaged in the poetic function. By 'equivalence' he means the relation between the imperatives of the syntagm and the choices available within the paradigm, and by 'projects' he claims that the usual conventions of non-poetic language have been subtly disrupted by the imposition of the axis of selection upon the axis of combination. In short, we don't expect the relation between a car and a road to involve flight, but by drawing upon an apparently unrelated context of active verbs we have created a productive tension between linguistic usage dominated by the progressive logic of the syntagm (we expect 'cars' to 'move' or 'progress' along the 'road') and the purposive, and indeed poetic, use of the paradigmatic bag – a car flying along the road gives emphasis to the perceiver's imaginative use of the selective axis.

We should now consider the relation between the metaphoric dimension of the paradigmatic–selective axis and the metonymic dimension of its syntagmatic–combinative counterpart. Metonymy had usually been considered by conventional literary theorists to be an element or subdivision of metaphor, but Jakobson regarded it as a dimension of the progressive logic of the syntagm. A metonymic version of our sentence could be 'His wheels moved across the tarmac'. Here an element has been substituted for the whole (wheels for car, tarmac for road). This might seem metaphoric but in effect we have only deleted one element of the original word for another. To have metaphorically selected or substituted one for another we might have replaced 'wheels' with 'his last refuge' or 'his heart's delight' which tells us something about, at least in our view, the man's relationship with his car but is not directly related to its physical or contextual dimensions.

Jakobson does not claim that by giving emphasis to the syntagmatic–combinative axis we will always construct metonymic effects. Rather he cites metonymy as one example of how the logic of the combinative axis will restrict and delimit the choices available from the paradigmatic bag. He associates this compositional imperative with prose. However, when he says that 'in poetry, where similarity is superinduced upon contiguity, any metonymy is slightly metaphorical and any metaphor has a metonymical tint'(49), Jakobson's point is that the poetic function draws upon the two axes in a way that deliberately and self-consciously foregrounds the interrelation between them. So when we read genuine poetry we become uncertain about the balance between the logical and the irrational, the flatly informative and the wildly imaginative.

As a way of concentrating attention on the inherent structure and condition of poetry Jakobson's proposition resembles the theories of such Anglo-American New Critics as William Empson and Cleanth Brooks who respectively identified 'ambiguity' and 'paradox' as the definitively poetic uses of language. It could similarly be submitted to the danger of removal from its object, since if a prose sequence were disguised as a poem it might be possible for a competent reader to suggest that it possesses a poetic blend of metaphor and metonymy. For instance figurative reference to the human conditions of 'disguise' and 'possession' in the previous sentence could, potentially, be turned into a version of the poetic process defined by Jakobson. It would seem that any attempt to specify the inherent qualities of poetic language is insufficient without an accompanying and acceptable verification of its target. And this is what Jakobson provides:

> The principle of similarity underlies poetry; the metrical parallelism of lines, of the phonic equivalence of rhyming words prompts the question of semantic similarity or contrast . . . Prose, on the contrary, is forwarded essentially by contiguity. Thus for poetry, metaphor, and for prose metonymy is the line of least resistance.
>
> (*Fundamentals of Language*, 1956, 95–6)

What Jakobson means is that the formal element of the double pattern provides a method of foregrounding or framing the metaphor–metonymy tension; and since its prosodic or metrical identity is a feature it does not share with prose we find ourselves with a formidable definition of the poetic.

Even Jonathan Culler, a critic who has submitted the New Critics Empson and Brooks to the merciless procedures of structuralist scepticism, respects the validity of Jakobson's thesis.

> As Jakobson has stressed, in poetic discourse equivalence becomes the constitutive device of the sequence, and phonetic or rhythmic coherence is one of the major devices which distances poetry from the communicative functions of ordinary speech.
>
> (1975, 163)

Both Jakobson and Culler invoke the double pattern as the signal to the reader to engage with the complex and intrinsically poetic intensifications of meaning.

But there are a number of problems with this formula that remain unresolved. When Jakobson claims that formal structure 'prompts' the question of semantic complexity does he mean (i) that there is a causal relation between the deployment of metre and sound pattern and the resulting blend of metaphor and metonymy, or (ii) that this formal framework operates as a contextual signal for the reader to concentrate on and centralises linguistic effects that might just as easily be found in prose?

If we examine the examples used by Jakobson in the 'Linguistics and Poetics' essay and, more significantly, in his other much debated interpretive pieces we will find that he favours (i). In his famous (1970) analysis of Shakespeare's 129th sonnet he describes how the grammatical parallelism of the text effectively organises its complex metaphoric–metonymic shifts between mortal instinct (metonymic) and the notion of life as a mirror image of heaven and hell (metaphoric). His anatomical division of the text into grammatical structures and strophes is grounded upon his awareness that the fundamental organising principle of the sonnet, that which effectively governs the interaction between grammar and semantics, contiguity and similarity, is the abstract structure of the sonnet itself. In theory, the syntactic and stylistic structures identified by Jakobson might well be possible within a text that does not adhere to the prosodic formula of three pentameter quatrains concluding with an heroic couplet, but in fact there is a 'cogent and mandatory unity of its thematic and compositional framework'. What he means by this is that it is impossible, or more accurately incorrect, to regard any of the signifying structures of the sonnet as immune from each other. For instance, when he considers the phonological parallelism of the final couplet he is also aware that the repetition of /ɛ/, *heaven* /heɛvn/ – *men* /mɛn/ – *hell* /hɛl/, draws upon and intensifies the broader thematic subject of the sonnet and that the position of each phoneme within the syntactic structure cannot be fully analysed without giving equal attention to the fact that this structure is organised by the abstract formula of the iambic pentameter.

Jakobson's analysis of the sonnet is a practical demonstration of the thesis of 'Linguistics and Poetics':

> In poetry, any conspicuous similarity in sound is evaluated in respect to similarity and/or dissimilarity in meaning . . . In referential language the connection between *signans* (signifier) and *signatum* (signified) is overwhelmingly based on their codified contiguity . . . The relevance of the sound-meaning nexus [in

poetry] is a simple corollary of the superposition of similarity upon contiguity.

(1960, 51)

He refers here specifically to rhyme, but this model of analysis extends to all systems of organisation which foreground the materiality of the signifier – metrical sequences, alliteration, assonance, etc. His central claim is that in Saussurian terms the *parole* (event) of the poetic text draws upon two separate dimensions of the *langue*; the first will involve techniques and formulations that will feature both in poetic and non-poetic texts – syntax, grammatical deviation, the stylistics of metaphor–metonymy; the second will consist of abstract formulae – metrical sequences, line lengths, rhyme schemes – which are founded not upon the syntactic or semantic designation of words but upon their material existence as signs. The genuinely and definitively poetic effect is achieved when these two systems are seen to interact. However, Jakobson does not attempt to provide a set of descriptive formulae which account for the possible types of interaction, the way in which these will be affected or determined by different verse forms or different historical periods, and the role of the reader in responding to, processing and classifying these clashes between distinct compositional and signifying codes. He does cite individual examples and it is from these that we can consider how his essay functions as a nexus for a series of otherwise distinct strategies and fields of interpretation.

THE SLIDING SCALE

Jakobson cites free verse as an exception to his model of the double pattern, but he takes the case no further: 'Except in the varieties of the so-called "vers libre" . . . any meter uses the syllable as a unit of measure at least in certain sections of the verse'. The question of what free verse actually is will be considered in more detail in Chapter 6, but for the moment it would be useful to examine the way in which free verse has been used by critics as a means of validating their thesis that the methods by which we naturalise poems are not, as Jakobson argues, entirely responsive to intrinsic textual and linguistic structure but are, at least to some degree, a consequence of our ability to construct or impose meanings from within a shared interpretive framework.

Reader-centred criticism is a complex and varied phenomenon, but it would not be an overgeneralisation to claim that it involves a shifting of the system–instance, *langue–parole* relationship away from the author and the techniques and conventions of composition toward the reader, who will draw upon a similar formula as a means of classifying and interpreting texts. Jonathan Culler (1975) demonstrates how this shift in emphasis operates, by changing the context within which we would usually interpret the opening sentence from W. V. O. Quine's philosophic essay 'From a logical point of view'.

> *From a Logical Point of View*
> A curious
>   thing
> about the
>   ontological
> problem
>   is
> its
>   simplicity.

The typographical arrangement produces a different kind of attention and releases some of the potential verbal energy of 'thing', 'is' and 'simplicity'. We are dealing less with a property of language (intrinsic irony or paradox) than with a strategy of reading, whose major operations are applied to verbal objects set as poems even when their metrical and phonetic patterns are not obvious.

(Structuralist Poetics, 163)

This type of exercise became something of a habit with the new generation of structuralist/reader-response critics of the 1970s and 1980s, and holds a number of implications for the way we perceive and analyse the double pattern. Clearly with free verse the relation between the metrical and syntactic structure of the text is infinitely flexible, and as a consequence it becomes the duty of the reader to impose an accepted framework of interpretive conventions – such as the possibility that typographic spacing is a signal to the reader to foreground elements of the syntactic structure – that in the interpretive context of prose would not be invoked. Culler concedes that where formal patterns are a regular and intrinsic feature of the text the notion of a strategy of reading is balanced against our perception of linguistic phenomena that are verifiably there, but he maintains that these operate as sequence of interpretive signals: 'the essence of poetry lies not in the verbal artifice itself, though that serves as a catalyst, but more simply and profoundly in the type of reading . . . which the poem imposes on its readers'(164). Thus, he shifts the critical model of the double pattern away from Jakobson's notion of both elements as a cooperative and intrinsic feature of signification toward a reader-centred model in which elements such as metre, sound pattern and line endings motivate a particular attitude to the poetic as opposed to the prosaic use of, for example, metaphor.

I would argue that this thesis contains a number of flaws. If a poet chooses to write within the regular rules and conventions of the pentameter or the sonnet – and before the twentieth century, poets, with a few rare exceptions, had no choice – then it becomes difficult to distinguish between what Samuel Levin in 'The Conventions of Poetry' (1971) has called the 'cognitive' and the 'conventional' dimensions of the double pattern. Consider again the closing couplet of Shakespeare's sonnet,

> All this the world well knows yet none knows well,
> To shun the heaven that leads men to this hell.

The cognitive features of this couplet are determined essentially by its correspondence with the rules of grammar, while its conventions are determined by the abstract formula of two rhyming iambic pentameters. In this instance the cognitive rules are not violated, but in the second line there is a case of what is known as stress reversal. In the iambic pentameter the seventh syllable should receive a lower stress value than the sixth and the eighth. Clearly to grant the word 'to' a higher stress position than 'men' would be inconsistent with the rhetorical pattern of the sentence. A form of tension has been created between the cognitive and the conventional patterns, and as a consequence we are invited to respond to the foregrounding of 'men' at this point of interaction, and to follow this perhaps by noting that the sonnet concludes by re-emphasising the active, predatory and dangerous function of lust as part of the male condition ('men' rather than the collective, asexual noun 'man'). The positioning of 'men' at the point of interaction between the cognitive and the conventional dimensions of the text seems to produce the same 'release of verbal energy' as Culler identifies in the typographical positioning of 'thing', 'is' and 'simplicity'. But there is a difference. Consider Levin's definition of poetic conventions:

> the essential fact about the conventions [rhyme, meter, etc.] is

that even though they comprise patterns or structures of language elements, the patterns or structures so constituted have no *linguistic* significance. Another way to put this is to say that a structure has linguistic significance if it figures in a grammatical or phonological rule, and that the structures entered into by the conventional features figure in no such rule.

(1971, 177)

In the abstract, Levin has a case, since neither an iambic pentameter nor a rhyme scheme can be regarded as grammatical formula, but the actuality of the sonnet makes his distinction more uncertain and problematic. The sonnet demands the most disciplined and intense coordination of the cognitive and the conventional dimensions of language, to the extent that in reading the text the two become effectively inseparable. Following Levin's formula we could claim that the foregrounding of 'men' causes no violation of a grammatical rule. But we might also claim that in the sonnet the metrical rule *is* the grammatical rule: the syntactic structure of the text is determined by its abstract conventional structure to a degree that any disjunction of this parallelism becomes just as apparent and has the same effect upon signification as an instance of grammatical deviation.

With Culler's 'rewritten' piece of free verse Levin's formula transfers more easily from the abstract to the particular, in the sense that the free verse line effectively follows the rules of grammar and operates only as a secondary pattern of conventions which foreground elements already present in the grammatical pattern.

We should now pause to consider how the problems raised by Jakobson, Culler and Levin affect our understanding of the double pattern.

Jakobson holds that poetic form or convention plays an active, purposive role in the creation of meaning, but Levin and Culler argue that it provides a framework which prompts and accommodates specific interpretive strategies through which the reader imposes, rather than discloses, meaning. The disagreement is complicated by the examples of the sonnet and free verse, because the Jakobson model appears to be more valid in the case of the former and the Levin–Culler model in the latter. If we accept that the conventions that constitute poetic form operate as a *langue* which governs and effectively defines each poetic *parole*, how is it that the relation between the two can change radically with two different texts?

In order to address, if not to entirely resolve, this question I shall propose an analytic framework which will allow us to compare, and indeed judge, interpretive models against individual texts. I shall call this the sliding scale. This is a comparative index against which we can consider the interactive relation between the two dimensions of the double pattern, to adopt Levin's terms, the cognitive and the conventional. Interaction is the key term because to qualify for inclusion the text must create a distinction and consequently an interpretive tension between the cognitive and the conventional. The two basic phenomena that will allow us to identify and then to judge the relation between the two are the sentence (cognitive) and the line (conventional). At one end of the scale we will find forms such as the sonnet which involve a thickening and a foregrounding of the purely conventional features of poetry to the extent that form can never remain immune from meaning. At the other we will encounter forms such as free verse where in some cases the lines of the poem correspond neither to an abstract metrical formula nor to a particular pattern of conventions operating within the poem itself. In such cases the line is no longer entirely a function of an abstract metrical code, but more the point at which the readers' perceptions of what the structure of free verse is plays some part in the way that the poem is naturalised. To see how the sliding scale might assist us in judging and understanding the questions raised in the conflict between Jakobson and Culler/Levin we should consider the relation between poetic form and the protocols of naturalisation (see Appendix for a brief guide on how to use the double pattern and the sliding scale).

NATURALISATION

Naturalisation is a precise definition of the process of critical exegesis. We naturalise literary texts by first identifying their formal features and classifying their genre (poem, novel or short story, or more specifically regular or free verse) and then by considering how this particular form of linguistic organisation can absorb and restructure meaning. The conventional features of poetry are naturalised when we translate our initial impression of the multi-dimensional effects of a poem – its rhyme scheme or its metrical pattern in conflict with its syntactic structure for instance – into a prose description of how these effects occur and of the variety of meanings generated from them.

One major distinction between poetic and non-poetic writing

exists in the relation between the textual object and the metalanguage of criticism and understanding. When we engage with prose either in discursive critical language or by employing the precise descriptive formulae of transformational and generative linguistics, we are closer to the stylistic and referential pattern of the text than we can be with poetic writing. With poetic writing there is an uneasy relationship between (i) the materiality of the poem, (ii) the mental register of our initial response and (iii) the subsequent process of naturalisation. Criticising and naturalising poetry involves a literal demystification of the text, in the sense that we are obliged to strip its 'meaning' from the interwoven patterns of rhythm, sound and lineation. But there are a number of, mostly tacit, conventions which allow us to effect this procedure without causing us to feel that any serious injustice has been done to our initial impression of the text.

Consider the opening lines of Pope's 'Epistle to Dr. Arbuthnot',

> Shut, shut the door, good John! fatigued I said
> Tye up the knocker, say I'm sick, I'm dead.

Reading those lines we can discern a peculiar tension between the progressive, syntactic movement of the couplet and the extra-syntactic echo of 'said' in 'dead'. Logically there should be no correspondence between Pope's straightforward order to his servant and the potentially disruptive juxtaposition of life (speech) and death. How do we naturalise this phenomenon? W. K. Wimsatt in his seminal article on rhyme 'One Relation of Rhyme to Reason' (1944) offers a formula, preempting Jakobson's sound–meaning thesis:

> The words of a rhyme, with their curious harmony of sound and distinction of sense, are an amalgam of the sensory and the logical, or an arrest and precipitation of the logical in sensory form; they are the ikon in which the idea is caught (p. 163).

The key term here is the 'arrest and precipitation of the logical in sensory form'. Following Wimsatt's advice we might comment on how the said/dead amalgam of the phonological and the semantic add an extra dimension of signification to the message of the couplet: the fact that Pope is able to vocalise his own posthumous condition imbues what might otherwise be an unengaging problem of domestic order with a degree of dark comedy. But naturalising the tension between device and meaning in this way necessarily involves the imposition of the linear format of prose criticism upon the simultaneity of the initial impression. In other words when we naturalise – or in more basic terms understand – poetry we effectively translate one form of linguistic organisation into another. When we decode, analyse or interrogate all non poetic forms of signification we participate in a shared condition of composition and understanding. For instance when I state that NP (noun phrase) plus VP (verb phrase) underlies all English sentences, I should be aware that this formulaic concept of deep structure underlies the sentence that I'm using to describe it, all other sentences that I might use to clarify my statement and any sentences that my addressee might use to enquire about my statement. But when I consider the signifying pattern of Pope's couplet I would have to account for relations between words and their consequent meaning in a way that cannot be dealt with through the methodology used to describe all other non-poetic structures.

So, we face a paradox. Poetry, being language, will communicate meaning by employing the enabling conventions of the syntactic deep structure, but its total meaning cannot be accounted for through the techniques of analysis used to describe the relation between structure and text in all non-poetic uses of language. The paradox lies in the fact that, according to linguists such as Chomsky, we communicate with one another through linguistic competence, a shared, perhaps intuitive, awareness of how sentences work. Yet poets seem able to communicate effects to us through techniques that stand outside linguistic competence. This second level of understanding has been described (by Stanley Fish and others) as literary competence: we learn the grammar, the codes, of literature as a supplement to their counterparts in non-literary language. It is this notion of literary competence that enables Culler to claim that we, at least if we are 'educated', carry with us a recipe of interpretive techniques that are activated by such signals as rhyme and metre.

But this contention becomes problematic when we consider the hypothetical reader equipped with linguistic competence yet lacking the interpretive skills of literary competence. It is implausible to claim that such a person would not notice the chiming of rhyme words at every tenth syllable, the rhythmic pattern of unstress–stress or even, reading from the page, the curious typographic format of a free verse text. The disagreements we have considered so far have arisen because critics remain uncertain about how such encounters with poetic phenomena are transformed into understanding. Culler, Levin and Fish would argue that formal conventions are not in themselves linguistic phenomena but that we have constructed an arbitrary aesthetic code which draws upon the methods of linguistics and which will allow us to construct this second level of literary understanding. Jakobson and Wimsatt would argue that this second level of understanding is intrinsic to the structure of the text, and that although metre, rhyme and lineation are not in themselves linguistic elements they react with these elements to cause intensifications and deviations that literary competence enables us to name.

Who is correct? In effect both, and to account for this we should call upon the sliding scale. Consider again the case of the sonnet and free verse. Free verse must be regarded as the final episode in a long running conflict between poets and the prescribed *langue* of poetic conventions. Most of the early free versifiers offered a challenge both to themselves and their readers by presenting texts which did not correspond with the then accepted definition of poetry. But less than a century later the works of Pound, Williams and Eliot rest easily in the same anthologies and on the same 'Poetry' bookshelves as the works of Pope and Wordsworth. This is possible because readers and critics have developed methods of inscribing the techniques of free verse within an extended version of the interpretive programme of regular verse. They have done so, mostly, though not entirely, by identifying the salient formal features of free verse – at its most basic its division into lines – and adapting the well-established principles of reading regular verse to the new methods of naturalising these more tenuous formal elements.

This does not mean that Culler's contention that we supply meaning to the type of free verse that he cites is comprehensively justified – as we shall see in Chapter 6 free verse can be shown to possess its own intrinsic structure – rather that there is some truth in his attendant argument that poetic structures require the active participation rather than merely the passive reception of the reader. But the degree and method of participation will depend largely upon the position of the text on the sliding scale. Sonnets require us to participate in and to mediate the active, purposive transactions between grammar, metre, rhyme scheme, semantic transference and metaphor (the relation between the formal density of the text and the role of the reader is the subject of a much debated exchange between Jakobson and Michael Riffaterre – see Chapter 3). Free verse requires us to draw more upon our knowledge of the broader poetic *langue* in order to account for the ways that the formal gaps, discontinuities and improvisations that replace cohesive structure relate to the total signifying purpose of the text. The sonnet and free verse are useful binary poles for formal analysis, but as we shall see the sliding scale can operate as a starting point, or to be more accurate an entry point, for investigations of questions of how the study of literature and language interrelate, and of how the post-sixteenth-century history of English poetry can be charted and analysed both as a progressive and developing *langue* within which each text reproduces, extends or violates the conventions of others, and as a function of how textual experiment and diversification can be related to broader changes in aesthetic affiliation and judged as reflections or critiques of their social, cultural and political ethos. In the two concluding sections of this chapter we will consider briefly the history of the study of versification and look at how this corresponds with our perceptions of what poetry is and of how it relates to non-poetic writing and pre-linguistic events.

HISTORIES

The study of versification can claim to be the oldest and most enduring branch of English literary criticism. The language and methodology of George Gascoigne's 'Certayne Notes of Instruction concerning the Making of Verse or Rhyme in English . . .' (1575) might superficially seem to have little in common with Paul Kiparsky's 'Stress, Syntax and Meter' published, exactly four centuries later, in 1975. But both share the same objective of determining how the stress patterns of ordinary language can be organised into the phenomenon known as metre. Consult T. V. F. Brogen's excellent bibliography *English Versification 1570–1980* and you will find that hardly one of the four hundred years between these essays passed without someone writing something about the metres of English poetry. Such proliferation is both intriguing and depressing. Intriguing because each of these studies will, if only by implication, be grounded upon the phenomenal status of the poetic line, and this testifies to the claim that poetry, like non-poetic language, is founded upon a shifting yet self-perpetuating concept of a *langue*, a system, a grammar: for the sentence, substitute the line. It is depressing because for all the precision, ingenuity, innovation and scholarly foot-slogging (no pun intended) exhibited in these writings the majority of them suffer from a severe case of self-limitation. For all the time and effort spent in inventing newer and more accurate ways of documenting the stress pattern of the iambic pentameter only a small percentage is given to examining such questions as why poets might or might not want to use the pentameter as the appropriate vehicle for what they want to say and why some of them felt the need to violate the abstract norms of this structure in order to allow them to free the syntactic or metaphoric dimensions of language for a more productive engagement with life.

I shall attempt to justify this criticism by briefly examining the encounter between the ancient science of prosody and the twentieth-century techniques of linguistics.

The encounter began in 1951 with the publication of a monograph by G. L. Trager and H. L. Smith. Their structural–linguistic description of English phonology and morphology identified four discrete levels of stress (primary, secondary, tertiary, weak), pitch (highest, high, normal, low) and juncture (internal, and word-, phrase-, clause-terminal). Trager and Smith did not refer specifically to poetry but their model provided the basis for what has come to be known as linguistic metrics. In studies of metre since the sixteenth century the unit of measurement of the poetic line had been the foot, itself composed of the theoretically indivisible unit, the syllable. This system derived from the study of classical, quantitative metres, with the principle change being that each foot was in English principally determined by the stress or accentual value of its syllables rather than, as in Latin and Greek, the length of time taken to pronounce it. An iambic pentameter consists of five iambic feet with the higher stress falling upon the second syllable of each foot. Trager and Smith offered a potential challenge to this model because if there were four degrees of stress and pitch it might be possible to identify an 'unstressed' syllable at say the fifth syllable of a line with a higher stress value than the supposedly 'stressed' syllable at the second. This would not mean that the line is no longer iambic, rather that prosodists must reexamine their perceptions of what an iambic pattern actually is. Consider the following pentameter from Book IV of Milton's *Paradise Lost* describing Satan's contemplation of Eve.

Sŭch pleás / ŭre tóok / t̂he sérp / ȇnt tó / b̂ehóld.

This is a traditional scansion of the line, dividing it into five iambic feet. No-one would quarrel with the contention that each even syllable is more prominently stressed than those immediately preceding and following it, but does this inflexible binary opposition of unstress–stress give us an accurate account of its full rhythmic movement? If we conflate Trager and Smith's distinction between pitch and stress and convert their four types into a numerical gradation from 1 to 4, a reading of the line might well appear as follows:

2   4   1   3   1   4   1 2   1   4
Such pleasure took the serpent to behold.

The syllables 'Such' and 'to' occupy unstressed and stressed positions in the pentameter yet it is possible to judge their stress/pitch values as equal; indeed, given the context of the line, it is possible to claim that the particular, in fact unique, form of pleasure felt by Satan in his contemplation of Eve promotes the syllable 'Such' to a level of emphasis above that of a number of subsequent syllables occupying stress positions.

Such a reading does not destroy the iambic pattern, since the immediate relation between low–high, unstress–stress is maintained, but it discloses the limitations of the foot system as a means of measuring the broader peaks and troughs of the rhythmic pattern. Moreover, it provides us with a more accurate means of classifying the relation between the cognitive (syntactic–rhetorical) pattern and its conventional counterpart (the iambic pentameter).

The legacy of Trager and Smith's model is vast and complex, and I shall attempt a very selective summary (see pp. 290–318 of Brogan's bibliography for a summary of texts, theories and controversies).

A symposium published in the *Kenyon Review* in 1956 represented the first attempt to implement a literary–linguistic programme based on Trager and Smith's observations. Seymour Chatman proposed an analytic technique founded upon the identification of two systems: the abstract, usually iambic, metrical pattern and the more contingent stress, pitch and pause variations of spoken language. His chief point is that the study and indeed the performance of a line should incorporate both. A succinct description of this thesis is provided by Roger Fowler in 'Structural Metrics' (1967):

> Structural metrics could be said to be concerned with the reconciliation (through phonemics) of two extremes of analysis. On the one hand is the old belief in two fixed degrees of stress alternating with perfect regularity and uniformly disposed in time. At the other extreme is the instrumental revelation that each of the syllables in a line is realised differently by various complexes of intensity, pitch and length (p. 156).

The question exactly of how we might 'reconcile' the abstract with the actual pattern (Jakobson in his 1960 article named these phenomena, verse design and verse instance) became the central concern of linguistic metrists through the 1960s and 1970s.

Morris Halle and Samuel Keyser (1971) developed a system of 'correspondence rules' to chart the relation between the abstract pattern and variations caused by syntactic and lexical stress groupings, their objective being to establish the limits and flexibility of metricality and unmetricality, but the most celebrated and widely debated analytical system was proposed by Paul Kiparsky.

In two seminal essays (1975, 1977) Kiparsky adapted the techniques of transformational-generative syntax to account for the metrical structure of the line. To offer a very crude definition, transformational-generative syntax is employed to establish what is universal to all linguistic statements (the system–event model at its most specific and practical). We can start by identifying the abstract formula of NP and VP as the basic phrase structure of the sentence and go on to examine how different statements are generated from this structure. The transformational element of this technique allows us to show how we transform one syntactic structure into another (passive to active for example) in relation to these abstract models. The abstract model through which we chart and document different syntactic instances is generally termed the deep structure. What Kiparsky did was to show how the abstract deep structure of, say, the iambic pentameter can generate very different patterns of stress, pitch and pause. For instance the weak–strong abstract pattern of the following sequence (labelled beneath it) can be seen to anchor the more dominant lexical relation of strong–weak in each word (labelled above).

```
            /\        /\        /\
   w      s   w     s   w     s   w
   or    summer,   winter,   autumn
   w      s   w     s   w     s   w
            \/        \/        \/
```

Kiparsky employed the so-called tree diagram of TG analysis to show how the immediate contiguous relation between strong and weak syllables could generate much broader patterns of stress and pause. The chief benefits of this system are that it grants us a broader overview of the line. Just as TG syntax show us that grammatical structure is not entirely determined by the relation between contiguous words, so Kiparsky's technique shows us that the traditional notation of unstress–stress cannot fully account for the complex pattern of the line.

But the self-imposed limitations of linguistic metrics can, I shall argue, outweigh its benefits.

The work of the linguistic metrists, and indeed of their more traditional forebears, can be of use in the documentation of localised formal structures and in the comparing of different techniques between individual poems and poets, but only if such work is supplemented with facts and suppositions gained from our broader knowledge of the social, political and aesthetic contexts of literary writing. Context is a problematic term, with various functions and uses, but for the purposes of this study it can be divided into three types: the intertextual and the historical, which I shall now briefly summarise, and the situational which will be dealt with in the following section.

The intertextual context is not entirely ahistorical. Since the sixteenth century poets have either imitated, transformed or self-consciously rejected the formal precedents set by their forebears. For example, Milton's *Paradise Lost* maintains many of the conventions set in the use of blank verse by dramatists but also effectively alters the accepted convention that blank verse should be used only in dramatic rather than non-dramatic poems. To appreciate this combination of continuity and innovation we cannot simply rely upon precise documentations of the syntactic and metrical distinctions between Milton and Shakespeare. We must also consider such issues as why the subject and purpose of his Christian epic demanded such a shift between generic and formal categories, how this shift would have affected the expectations of contemporary readers, and, in a broader sense, how Milton's own experience of the social and cultural condition of the late seventeenth century would have prompted him to disrupt the established balance between form and interpretive expectation. Hence intertextuality can never remain immune for the historical context of a particular poem. To give another example, it is possible to fully document the structural differences between the regular eighteenth-century closed couplet of Pope and its more irregular uses by early-seventeenth-century poets, but such details are virtually useless without our consideration of how the status and function of poetic writing in society and in relation to non-poetic discourses underwent a radical change between the 1620s and the 1720s.

The first serious challenge to the role and function of linguistic metrics occurred in Wimsatt and Beardsley's essay 'The Concept of Metre: an Exercise in Abstraction' (1959). Wimsatt and Beardsley argued that in attempting to construct a 'grammar' of the double pattern the linguistic metrists further isolated the function of poetic form from its interaction with such effects as metaphor, and implied that their programme would encourage the widespread image of poetic studies as a hermetic and specialised field. But since the late 1950's their warning has remained largely unheard. On the one hand linguists have extended and intensified the work of Trager and Smith, Halle and Keyser, Chatman and Kiparsky, and on the other, 'conventional' literary critics have remained generally immune from these developments and have drawn upon the methods of traditional and contemporary prosody more or less at random. It is the purpose of this study to offer a productive analysis of the minutiae of poetic form – the principal topic of linguistic metrics – in relation to its broader aesthetic, linguistic and historical contexts, and we might begin by giving some attention to a formula developed by Jakobson in 'Linguistics and Poetics'.

HISTORY, CONTEXT AND TEXT

This takes the form of two diagrams that seek to represent, respectively, the relationship between the intrinsic and contextual properties of any linguistic message and the specifically literary properties of a single message.

1

	context message	
sender addresser	——————————————	receiver (addressee)
	contact code	

2

	referential poetic	
emotive	——————————————	conative
	phatic metalingual	

The first diagram is a relatively straightforward model of any act of linguistic communication. Consider our present circumstances. The assumed context of my message is the field of linguistics and literary criticism, a field whose aural and written exchanges are usually limited to the more specific context of higher education. The context will often determine the code, and, in this instance, I the sender, assume that you, the receiver, have become innured to the stylistic and disciplinary codes of talking and writing about language and literature. Contact is a further subdivision of context and code: in this case it is written rather than aural, with the likely and probably unfortunate condition that you cannot interrupt me to seek further clarification of my message. These six designations could be easily adapted to, say, the purchase of a railway ticket. I, sender will speak to (contact) the receiver within the usually self determined context of the station. The code is variable, within a number of agreed limitations, so that 'Ticket, return London' would preserve the message, but would deviate sufficiently from the usual locutionary format to indicate impoliteness or urgency on the part of the sender.

For the purposes of this study the first diagram refers principally to the historical, social and cultural contexts of the poem. The three functions of context, contact and code depend largely upon the receiver's role as a competent literary reader, a person sufficiently equipped to recognise invocations and signals that link the text in question to conditions that it shares with other texts. And this role will often be determined by the prevailing interpretive expectations of a particular historical period. The second diagram refers to the intrinsic properties of the text itself and to the more immediate communicative context created by these properties, the latter being variously termed the speech act or the situation of the utterance. The transposition of the sender–receiver relation with emotive and conative effects can be explained in terms of the generally agreed communicative function of poetic language. If I were to ask for my ticket in metre and rhyme I would not necessarily change the meaning of my message, but I would create an incongruous relation between the contact–context codes (practical, utilitarian transparent) and my use of specifically and recognisably poetic devices which would signal a more personal, enclosed circuit in which the emotive (sender oriented) and conative (receiver oriented) elements of the message bind the two presences together in a way that reminds us more of John Donne addressing his lover or Wordsworth imparting his visionary experience to the reader than they do of commuter addressing ticket seller.

Clearly there are patterns of interdependency between these two sets of terms that are far more complex than their diagrammatic separation would lead us to expect. The referential function of 2 and the message of 1 might appear interchangeable, but the former is effectively split between the degree to which the poem can be said to have a paraphasable meaning (the objective of naturalisation) and the way in which the phatic, metalingual and poetic functions enclose this message within the internal patterns of the text. In poetry the least significant of these three functions is the phatic. For example the repetition of 'shut' in the opening line of Pope's 'Epistle to Dr. Arbuthnot' is an instance of phatic usage (it emphasises the informality of the exchange). But the phatic utterance in poetry is usually a subsidiary element of more powerful stylistic determinants. These are the metalingual and the poetic. The metalingual function is that which explicitly draws our attention to the fact that the utterance is poetry. For example in 'The Relique' John Donne refers to 'this paper' in order to remind the reader that the emotive–conative transference is taking place within the artefact of the poem. Jakobson defines the poetic function as something that promotes 'the palpability of signs, deepens the fundamental dichotomy of signs and objects'. In other words, the use of metre, rhyme, sound pattern and the extra-syntactic deployment of lines. The metalingual and the poetic are two sides of the same coin, the former depending largely upon the signifying processes of syntax and semantics and the latter upon the materiality of language. In poetry the one will never remain immune from the other, and their pairing corresponds with my model of the double pattern.

We should now return to the question of why Jakobson distinguishes between these two communicative circuits. I would argue that he does so to draw our attention to the two most important stages in the process of poetic naturalisation. When we interpret, naturalise or demystify a poem we effectively attempt to reconcile the effects created by its intrinsic structural properties (the situation of the utterance, diagram 2) with our much more complex awareness of how this specific poem is similar to or different from others and, more significantly, of how these features correspond with the socially and historically determined conditions of linguistic communication (diagram 1). A number of examples are necessary.

Wordsworth's use of the ballad form in *Lyrical Ballads* involves, as we shall see in Chapter 4, a disorientating confluence of the intertextual and historical axes, respectively distinguished by diagrams 2 and 1. At the end of the eighteenth century the ballad was an icon of popular culture and consequently the contemporary reader would be uncertain as to whether to give prominence to the context–contact, popular–cultural modes of diagram 1 or whether the intrinsic properties of each ballad should override these broader contextual considerations.

When Culler rewrote Quine's prose as free verse he clearly invoked the poetic–metalingual signal of line divisions and used these to link the 'poem' with the cultural mode (poetry) and its related counterparts in the contact–context modes. In order to do so he drew upon 'real' precedents such as William Carlos Williams's 'This Is Just To Say' whose referential function (it is a note on the kitchen table apologising for eating the plums from the fridge) seems to shift it outside the poetic sphere (to diagram 1), yet whose deployment of line divisions draws the reader back to the poetic and metalingual signals of diagram 2. To further complicate matters, we should also acknowledge that the acceptable designations of the poetic and metalingual functions had changed radically between 1915 and 1975, since many of the early reviewers of free verse poems regarded the unmetrical, unrhymed line as a meaningless echo of its regular counterpart. Consequently they would not have been inclined to recognise the signals of diagram 2 as sufficiently 'palpable' to qualify the text for interpretation as a poem (cultural code, diagram 1) or as capable of promoting the practical, utilitarian contact–context codes to the status of the enclosed and specifically poetic realm of the emotive and conative.

From these examples alone it would seem that any reliable causal relation between the socio-historical axis of diagram 1 and its textual counterpart in diagram 2 is subject to a constantly shifting pattern of terms and conditions. But a framework of stability can be found in the correspondence between the sliding scale and the fluctuations of literary history, and this will be the primary focus of the following chapters. Our working method will consist of a number of inter-related assumptions and emphases. The opposing dimensions of the sliding scale correspond firstly with the constituent elements of the double pattern, in Levin's terms the cognitive and the conventional constituents of the text. These in turn betray allegiances, respect-ively, to the broader linguistic, historical, social and cultural deter-minants of diagram 1 and to the internal, intertextual features of diagram 2. Consequently any change in the relationship between these elements must signal a desire on the part of the poet to readdress the conventionally accepted function of the poem. For example the eighteenth-century programme of maintaining a parallel and unitary correspondence between the two elements of the double pattern cannot be fully appreciated without our understanding that this objective was inspired by the trend toward poetry as an access-ible and productive contribution to the broader network of social and political discourses. The desire of the Modernists to move poetry away from the dense and self-referential patterns of formal regularity toward a structure which pays closer allegiance to the spontaneous nature of the speech pattern (a shift from the conven-tional to the cognitive element of the sliding scale) can only be fully understood in relation to the widespread aesthetic articulation of the anxious relationship between the individual and the accelerating institutional, intellectual and political determinism of the early twentieth century. On the sliding scale the archetypal free verse poem foregrounds the specific circumstantial nature of the speech act rather than its deference to stylistic convention.

But we should not forget that to whatever extent the double pattern and the sliding scale are influenced by the overarching patterns of social, political and cultural change, their primary function is to distinguish the reader of the poem, the poem and the poet, from all other functional and structural elements of linguistic discourse. One of the objectives of this book, while respecting the contributions of semiotics, cultural studies and socio-linguistics to the study of literature, is to establish poetry as an independent self-determined sphere in which language, aesthetics, gender distinction, politics and social convention are continuously addressed but in which none of these can displace or marginalise the mysterious yet undeniably tangible function of the poetic.

2 Shakespeare and the metaphysicals

MEASURE FOR MEASURE

Measure for Measure is generally regarded as one of Shakespeare's 'problem' plays. The principal problem for the reader or member of the audience is that it offers a series of questions that remain largely unanswered. It does not inscribe a reliable formula against which we can properly judge the violation of moral norms or the subversion of political, religious or social absolutes. How should we judge Isabella's decision to preserve her own code of virginity and consequently to endanger her brother's life? Is Angelo merely a disagreeable individual or a symptom of a more widespread form of social and moral corruption? Is the Duke obliged to temporarily abdicate, disguise himself and engage with the murky practices of his fiefdom because autocratic monarchy is no longer a practical institution?

Like many of Shakespeare's more problematic dealings with the state and the individual the context is shifted safely to a time and a place that are not early-seventeenth-century London. However the problems of government and of administering the judicial system faced by the Duke bear a more than accidental resemblance to a number of ideas addressed by James I (before whom the play was first performed) in his tract *Basilicon Doron*. The image of Vienna as a city-state threatened by criminality and incipient moral anarchy could just as easily apply to the expanding capital of the new trading and mercantile powerhouse of England. By examining the use of language in the play we will not immediately find solutions to the questions of whether Shakespeare is indulging a taste for dark comedy or offering a complex political allegory, but we will provide ourselves with a framework within which such questions can be more clearly addressed. First, some general observations about the language of the play.

Like all of Shakespeare's plays it consists of two primary linguistic patterns, blank verse and prose. There are different types and forms of prose style, but its principal distinction from verse is that it adheres to a single pattern of grammatical rules and conventions. Blank verse supplements these with a secondary pattern of iambic decasyllabic units. Before Milton's *Paradise Lost*, blank verse was regarded as a dramatic form which, because it lacked rhyme, did not fully qualify for use in non-dramatic verse. However, it offered a sufficient foregrounding of the poetic function to make the reader aware of a distinction between the poetic and the non-poetic. Three questions should be considered: What effect did Shakespeare intend to create by shifting the text between these two patterns? What effect do such changes have upon our perceptions of the speaker? What does this splitting of discourse tell us about contemporary attitudes to the functional as well as the formal distinction between poetic and non poetic language?

We can offer a number of fairly straightforward propositions. The distinction between blank verse and prose mirrors the distinction between the social patterns and the behavioural patterns of the characters. Isabella, Angelo, Claudio and the Duke communicate with one another and conduct their own introspective discourses mainly, though not entirely, in blank verse. Pompey, Mistress Overdone, Elbow, Lucio and Froth communicate mostly in prose – and do not generally reflect upon their own condition. When individuals from these two groups, representing the upper and lower ends of the social scale, communicate with one another, it is generally the case that the latter will shift into prose while the former will seem either incapable or unwilling to use blank verse. We might thus conclude that Shakespeare maintains the status of poetry as part of a complex series of sign systems – including dress, demeanour, names, occupations – that allow us to recognise strata within a particular social hierarchy. Poetry is culture; it is a linguistic form which disposes a collective identity upon its users. In sharing a particular code they can be seen as sharing a particular set of privileges, responsibilities, intellectual and moral concerns. Spoken, prose discourse does not even demand literacy. It is a means of exchange, dependent upon circumstance and contingency. Crucially it is not a discourse whose users seem capable of fully addressing; it is not something that they at once possess and inhabit, whereas the possessors and inhabitants of poetry are able to use the form as a means of contemplating the universals of their own and the human condition (see Isabella's reflections upon Angelo's proposition, II iv, 171–88; and Claudio's confrontation with death, III i, 115–30). But as such socio-cultural distinctions become evident they are also threatened by attendant distinctions between patterns of commitment and behaviour. Angelo (ruler, aristocrat, blank verse) proves to be even more dangerously corrupt than Lucio (criminal, pimp, prose). Isabella (novitiate nun, embodiment of purity and piety, blank verse) finds herself submitted to the same conditions of bodily trading as Mistress Overdone (prostitute, victim of contingency and circumstance, prose).

To address this paradoxical relation between text and context we should return to Jakobson's models of the speech act. Throughout the play the contact-code functions are thrown into a state of continuous change and interplay. In the exchanges between Angelo and Isabella both seem to be addressing the same fundamental issues of life and justice (II ii and II iv), from, necessarily, different perspectives. But at the same time their adherence to the same pattern of compositional and performative rules compromises their claims upon separateness and individuality and reduces them to components of a single text. In Act II scene ii Isabella finds herself in the difficult position of, on the one hand, arguing with Angelo about the ethical and judicial validity of her brother's death sentence, and on the other listening to Lucio's asides which prompt her to play the emotional, indeed the physical card, against the movement of what is apparently a purely intellectual exchange.

Isabella	We cannot weigh our brother with ourself:
	Great men may jest with saints; 'tis wit in them,
	But in the less foul profanation.
Lucio	(*Aside to Isabella*) Thou'rt i' th' right girl: more o'that.
Isabella	That in the captain's but a choleric word
	Which in the soldier is flat blasphemy.
Lucio	(*Aside to Isabella*) Art advis'd o' that? More on't.
Angelo	Why do you put these sayings upon me?
Isabella	Because authority, though it err like others
	Hath yet a kind of medicine in itself
	That skins vice o' the top. Go to your bosom;
	Knock there, and ask your heart what it doth know.
	(126–37)

Lucio speaks in unpoetic prose while the exchanges between Isabella and Angelo take place in blank verse. To return to Jakobson's model it could be claimed that the related functions of contact and code effectively determine the reception and outcome of the message. Lucio is in the peculiar position of being both commentator upon the code – the poetic disposition of her argument for mercy – and the manipulator of contact and context – he knows that as a woman she will have a different effect upon Angelo than would a man, and that Angelo's position of impersonal arbitrator will consequently be compromised.

From this tripartite exchange we might reexamine Shakespeare's deployment of the relation between language and the situation of the addresser–addressee. Consider the following statement by Robert Graves and Laura Riding on the political significance of regular poetry (1925).

> Metre considered as a set pattern approved by convention will stand for the claims of society as at present organised: the variations on metre will stand for the claims of the individual (p. 24).

They are addressing the phenomenon of free verse, but their distinction between set pattern and variation might also apply to the blank verse and prose tensions of *Measure for Measure*.

Consider the relation between the linguistic (code) and phenomenological (referential) elements of the Isabella–Angelo exchange. In each instance the speaker attempts to situate his or her problem within a broader framework of moral, ethical and concrete sign systems. Isabella moves easily through the unusual paradigmatic correspondences between her brother's condition, saintliness and profanity, the otherwise separate imperatives of martial combat (captains, soldiers) and the physical and theological demands of choler and blasphemy; and she maintains this extravagant metaphoric pattern with her association of authority (moral and political) with the more contingent physical images of medicine, skin, bosom, heart. Angelo is prone to very similar metaphoric excursions, while Lucio on the other hand addresses only the actual circumstances of the utterance, rather than the linguistic power of the utterance itself. Consider the following:

Ay touch him; there's the vein

Ay well said

That's well said

O, to him to him, wench! He will relent:

(70, 89, 109, 124)

Lucio allows his discourse to be determined by the circumstances of each utterance and in this sense he operates as the paradigm for the prose utterances and their speakers in the rest of the play. The prose sequences are driven by external context and to a large extent their signifying function depends upon the reader's understanding of this broader contextual meaning. The verse sequences are similarly prompted by circumstantial conditions but they also draw upon a much more elaborate pattern of signification. They create patterns of correspondence between the personal and immediate situation and broader abstract and universal themes that the speaker feels able to use either as strategies of persuasion or consolation. We should also note that Lucio's interventions create formal as well as thematic disturbances in the Isabella–Angelo exchange. If you listen to the passage as a whole you will find that Isabella is struggling to reinstall herself within the self-contained circuit of addresser-addressee and their shared poetic code. Here the Graves and Riding passage is particularly relevant because Isabella and Angelo attempt to address 'the claims of society' within the 'set pattern' of verse while Lucio's prose interjections are indeed prompted by 'the claims of the individual'. The question we should now ask is of whether there is an intrinsic element of poetic and non-poetic structures that effectively determines their situational context or the purpose of their message?

Jakobson again: 'Prose . . . is forwarded essentially by contiguity. Thus for poetry, metaphor, and for prose, metonymy is the line of least resistance'. Consider the Provost's attempt to persuade Pompey that he might be suited to the post of assistant executioner (IV ii, 6–15). Here the cohesive structure of the sequence focuses upon the axis of combination and contiguity – 'tomorrow morning', 'prison', 'executioner', 'helper', 'assist him', 'if not', 'your deliverance'. The prose sequence is effectively determined by the perceived pressures of external circumstances. Language becomes the lever by which individuals are prompted to respond directly to external circumstances. Compare this with Claudio's contemplation of death (III i, 116–26).

Ay, but to die, and go we know not where;
To lie in cold obstruction and to rot;
This sensible warm motion to become
A kneaded clod; and the delighted spirit

To bathe in fiery floods, or to reside
In thrilling region of thick-ribbed ice;
To be imprison'd in the viewless winds,
And blown with restless violence round about
The pendant world; or to be worse than worst
Of those that lawless and incertain thoughts
Imagine howling: 'tis too horrible!

In this passage the temporal and spatial immediacy of death is transformed into a manic sequence of shifts between the empirical and the spiritual, the sensual and the intellectual – 'rot', 'sensible', 'clod', 'spirit', 'floods', 'imprisoned', 'pendent world', 'incertain thoughts'. Claudio has projected himself, via the selective, paradigmatic axis, into a purely linguistic realm where what in the real, contingent world would remain separate concepts are suddenly thrust together. As Jakobson says: 'the poetic function projects the principle of equivalence from the axis of selection into the axis of combination'. In other words the speaker's use of the selective axis allows him to project into the contiguity axis of circumstance a wildly speculative, poetic pattern of causes and effects.

It would be wrong to base a general judgement upon a single comparison, but it will be seen in the following extracts that in the blank verse sequences the speaker attempts to situate his/her problem within a broader framework of images and concepts (the paradigmatic chain projected on to the syntagmatic and the effect foregrounded by the metrical pattern) while in the prose sequences structure will become a function of context and contingency (the progressive order of the syntagm will dominate the individual's use of both axes): the opening exchanges between Angelo and the Duke on the future of the city (I i, 4–84, blank verse) and the Duke's encounter with Lucio (III ii, 46–204, prose); the exchange between Claudio and Isabella on his fate and her decision (III i, 52–146, blank verse) and the Duke's suggestion to Isabella of a blackmail solution (III i, 181–283, prose).

The second comparison is particularly important because context here seems to determine code. Isabella and Claudio speculate on their individual perceptions of the meaning of choice, submission and death, while Isabella and the Duke address the more immediate practical solutions to the same problems. Note particularly how the use and effect of pronouns becomes a function of the poetic and prosaic codes. After Isabella addresses Claudio as 'O you beast / O faithless coward' she seems able to shift easily to a use of the first person that at once involves her exchange with her brother and her more introverted, lyrical contemplation of the existential condition of 'I': 'What should I think' . . . 'Might but my bending down / Reprieve thee from thy fate' (138–43). In the prose exchange with the Duke the use of the first person pronoun is more clearly limited by its direct dialogic function. When Isabella says 'I am now going to resolve him' (193), 'I have spirit to do any thing' (211) and 'I have heard of the lady' (218) she addresses the previous proposition or statement made by the Duke. Unlike the blank verse sequence each verb or noun phrase dependent upon the personal pronoun of the prose sequence is contrained by the circumstantial progress of the dialogue. She ('I') must respond to the details of the Duke's propositions and is never given the opportunity to enclose the 'I' within a more personal disquisition on her condition. This distinction should be kept in mind for our encounters with the early-seventeenth-century lyric poem, whose dialogic function must be specified by its internalised terms of reference rather than validated by an external context.

To summarise, there would seem to be intrinsic structural differences between the prose and verse passages of the play which correspond both with their contextual and purposive functions. In the verse sequences emphasis is shifted away from the dialogic function of language toward a more internalised, reflective realm. The contextual prompter to each verse utterance becomes the correlative, the point of comparison, from which the speaker will spin out complex metaphoric patterns, drawing more upon their own command of the linguistic system rather than submitting that system to the pressures and demands of the situation. In the prose passages, the syntagm, the combinative sequence is as Jakobson puts it, 'the line of least resistance'. The thematic focus and the internal structure of each passage become functions of a progressive causal relation between the events and imperatives of the context.

A troubling question persists: can it be argued that Shakespeare presents a natural, instinctive correspondence between individuals, their circumstances and their choice of linguistic pattern? Yes and no. Clearly the play shifts between formal mimesis and the self-referential conventions of literary art. A member of a contemporary audience, be they bawd or monarch, would recognise that the prose sequences are much closer to the formal structures of their own exchanges than are the complex prosodic and metaphoric designs of blank verse. The blank verse sequences, though often part of a dialogic exchange, bear a much closer resemblance to the contemporary discourse of the lyric: speaker, circumstances and events and objects mediated, become functions of a self-determined structure of metrical, syntactic and metaphoric patterns. Here mimesis begins to merge with allegory and symbolism. One of the functions of the contemporary lyric poem (consider Shakespeare's and Sidney's sonnets) was to situate the speaking presence as the focus for linguistic syntheses of otherwise disparate elements of existence and representation, the most common being the relation between the immediate and contingent and the universal and absolute. It is the relation between these, more specifically the conflict between human instinct and the demands of circumstance and the overarching transcendent concepts of order, law and justice, that constitute the plot of *Measure for Measure.* And the characters whose function and identity are shaped by their use of verse before prose are those whose social and judicial positions oblige them to effectively control the balance between these two types of existential condition. Shakespeare seems to claim that culture, high art, writing, the imaginative engagement with and command of the discourse correspond with power, privilege and responsibility. But if this is his mimetic–symbolic schema its attendant message is disturbing. The blank versifiers, although in admirable command of the medium of representation, are no more able to control their own baser instincts or the broader situation that their language mediates than are their counterparts whose language reflects the combinative, contingent patterns of their lives. So if we were to argue that *Measure for Measure* addresses itself primarily to the circumstances and responsibilities of the inhabitants and rulers of London in 1604, we must also concede that it offers an equally troubling challenge to the linguistic and cultural codes within which these individuals situate themselves. How might we reconcile the two potentially conflicting purposes of this address to linguistics and politics?

During the 1920s and 1930s a group of Soviet linguists and critics attempted to develop an interpretive model based on the linguistics of history and ideology. The work of Mikhail Bakhtin focuses mainly on the nineteenth-century novel, but his contention that literary texts embody but do not directly reflect the social tensions and interactions of their period corresponds closely with the issues raised by *Measure for Measure.* In his *Problems of Dostoyevsky's Poetics* (1973), Bakhtin introduced a notion of 'metalinguistics', based not merely upon the location of a text as an instance of a broader system of linguistic and cultural rules but upon the study of a dynamics of interaction between two or more voices in the same text, such an interaction often occurring in the single, apparently third person, voice of the novel's narrator. In his later work, *Rabelais and His World* (1968) he located the primary source of such interactions in the relation between the 'carnivalesque', the festivities, practices and locutionary forms which constitute the unrecorded substance of pre-twentieth-century sub-culture, and the rules and conventions of the cultural, social hierarchy, otherwise known as high art. Texts which allow the free play of the former (i.e. Rabelais) to influence or even subvert the orderly protocols of the latter are, he argues, indicative of those points in history where changes in what Marxists call the base of society (its fundamental economic and political structure) begin to cause disturbances in its superstructure (the social norms, the judiciary, high art etc.). This model would seem to provide us with an intriguing interpretive framework for the linguistic, cultural and political tensions of *Measure for Measure*. We might argue that the Duke is the dramatic counterpart for the authorial presence of the novel (a model perhaps for Prospero in *The Tempest*). For much of the play he is literally and linguistically in disguise; he mediates between the different levels of the social and cultural hierarchy, and in doing so he displays an impressive ability to shift between the two patterns of linguistic discourse that define and prescribe the roles of the characters (at one point he even adopts the rhymed couplet). The political message to James I that mediation rather than autocracy is the role demanded by contemporary conditions seems clear enough, but the play's engagement with broader issues of signification and represen-tation is even more intriguing. The Duke could also be seen to represent both the figure of the poet and the personae constructed by the poet. Unlike the other characters, he is able to enclose himself within the self-determined structure of the poetic function yet release his speaking presence from these constraints to allow his and his addressee's discourses to be driven by the pressures and imperatives of contingency and the pragmatics of the real world.

As Bakhtin observed, it is wrong to treat language and its generic distinctions as a thing, an object, rather than as a medium for social and personal interaction. When we analyse and document different linguistic formulae we run the risk of not paying sufficient attention to the elements that actually prompt and determine the structure of each utterance. In more recent debates on linguistics, Michael Halliday (1973, 1978) has taken against the transformational-generative systems of Chomsky and others and argued that what is intrinsic to a particular sentence or broader textual *parole* can never remain immune from its immediate or social and political context. In short, he argues that the *langue* is by no means a purely linguistic system, that the way in which it is drawn upon and deployed becomes a function of the situation of the utterance and the social/ political status of the addresser and addressee. What Shakespeare provides us with is a fictive model of the actual circumstances in which we distinguish between poetic and non-poetic language. In the blank verse sequences we might regard each speech act as the dramatic counterpart to an isolated non-dramatic lyric, in the sense that we must attend both to the known and inferred circumstances in which the utterance takes place and to the rules and conventions of verse that each statement shares with others. In the prose sequences our attention will shift toward the non-textual circumstances that determine each statement and away from their intrinsic formal and stylistic characteristics. In both instances we find that structure (metre or non-metre, the foregrounding of the syntagmatic or the paradigmatic axis) corresponds with context and genre. The question we will have to address as this chronological study proceeds is whether these correspondences are determined by contemporary perceptions of poetic and non-poetic discourses or whether they reflect an instinctive, natural correspondence between language and experience. For the moment let us consider how our reading of *Measure for Measure* can influence our understanding of the non-dramatic poetry of the early seventeenth century.

THE METAPHYSICALS

The first issue to consider is how we begin to distinguish between the terms and conditions of poetic form within the dramatic text and within the isolated structure of the poem. Here we will encounter a phenomenon that is vitally important in our discriminations between text, context and meaning: 'deixis' and 'deictics'. Deixis, the Greek word for 'pointing' refers to the orientational features of a particular statement. The principal deictic features of a sentence will refer to the conditions of the speaker (first or third person pronoun) and will involve the use of locatives, the time, place and circumstances of the utterance (the use of second person pronouns, the indication of objects and concepts and their spatio-temporal relation to the speaker). In non-dramatic poetry deictics/deixis is particularly important because we will rarely encounter the actual circumstances, fictional or real, that brought the poem into existence, so we will need to construct these circumstances from the deictic evidence within the poem itself. Clearly in dramatic texts our need to use deictics is limited by the fact that we know who the speaker is, who the speaker is addressing and in what circumstances this exchange takes place. Even with the soliloquy, the closest dramatic counterpart to the non-dramatic lyric, we have a good deal of background information. So with the non-dramatic lyric we will construct an absent addressee from the addresser's discourse, and, more significantly, we will be obliged to resolve the distinction between the formal and stylistic allegiances of the text – it will have a great deal in common with other poems that deploy rhyme, metre and metaphoric strategies – and its more specific reference to particular circumstances and conditions.

We will start with 'The Flea', a lyric by John Donne, published in 1633, but written within a decade of Shakespeare's play.

The Flea

Mark but this flea, and mark in this,
How little that which thou deny'st me is;
Me it sucked first, and now sucks thee,
And in this flea, our two bloods mingled be;
Confess it, this cannot be said
A sin, or shame, or loss of maidenhead,
 Yet this enjoys before it woo,
  And pampered swells with one blood made of two,
  And this, alas, is more than we would do.

Oh stay, three lives in one flea spare,
Where we almost, nay more than married are.
This flea is you and I, and this
Our marriage bed, and marriage temple is;
Though parents grudge, and you, we are met,
And cloistered in these living walls of jet.
 Though use make you apt to kill me,
  Let not to this, self murder added be,
  And sacrilege, three sins in killing three.

Cruel and sudden, hast thou since
Purpled thy nail, in blood and innocence?
In what could this flea guilty be,
Except in that drop which it sucked from thee?
Yet thou triumph'st, and say'st that thou
Find'st not thyself, nor me the weaker now;
 'Tis true, then learn how false, fears be;

> Just so much honour, when thou yield'st to me,
> Will waste, as this flea's death took life from thee.

The most prominent and distinctive deictic features of this lyric are its interpersonal references – the density and almost obsessive emphasis upon personal pronouns, I, thee, you, we, and its use of very specific locative phrases, this flea, it sucked, now sucks. The locative phrases are temporal as well as spatial determinants in that they consistently relocate the immediate past and future in the present; everything done both by the flea and the addressee takes place within seconds of the speaking voice's response to them. By identifying the main deictic features of the poem we provide ourselves with a framework to chart the metaphoric strategies of the speaking presence. The two people – male addresser and female addressee – and the flea function as the three principal components of the vehicle. Stanza 1 maintains an allegiance to the metonymic rather than the metaphoric pole. The key phrase is 'our two bloods mingled be'. This statement of verifiable fact allows the speaker to propose a daring but somehow logical connection between one form of physical union, the flea bite, and another, the sexual act. In stanza 2 metaphor replaces metonymy with the flea proposed as at once a token and symbol of their relationship, 'marriage bed and marriage temple', 'living walls of jet', and, more disturbingly, as a kind of contractual joining of their fate, 'three sins in killing three'. In stanza 3, after the woman has succeeded in swatting his vehicle, the male voice has to reinterpret his own metaphoric propositions and return to a more metonymic pattern – the flea bite and the death of the flea are both physical acts which neither harm nor dishonour their perpetrators and nor, he argues, would the proposed sexual act.

Donne deliberately and self-consciously foregrounds the apparently spontaneous and improvisational nature of the utterance and in doing so he creates a paradox. The reader constructs the situation of the utterance by locating the temporal–spatial relation between the deictic features, and we should note that the speaker's imagined existence is given greater psychological plausibility by his almost desperate deployment of extravagant metaphor in the second stanza, the point at which the vehicle for his pseudo-logic is most seriously threatened. The paradox exists in the fact that it is entirely implausible to imagine that the deployment of such a complex structure of rhyme and metre is spontaneous. In *The Literary Work of Art* (1973), Roman Ingarden distinguishes between aesthetic objects which are iconic and non-linguistic, in the sense that their form incorporates elements of pre-representational experience (painting and sculpture, for instance), and the linguistic text which is a 'purely intentional object'.

> In comparison with the ontically autonomous object, the intentional object is an 'illusion' that draws its illusionary existence and essence from the projecting intention . . . of the intentional act. The purely intentional object is not a 'substance' . . . Some of the elements assigned to it fool us with the outward appearance of a 'carrier'; they seem to play a role which according to their essence they are truly not capable of playing (122–3).

What Ingarden means by 'fooling us' is that in order to naturalise a poem we must suspend our awareness that there is likely to be an incongrous relation between the 'carrier' and the 'intentional act'. Human beings do of course attempt to seduce other human beings and are often given to reflect verbally upon their existential condition, but they do not, in normal circumstances, do so in rhyme and metre. When we naturalise poems we strip the intentional object of its textual 'essence' and demystify, or in basic terms explain, the intentional act. Donne seems to be fully aware of this paradoxical relation between the 'carrier' and the 'intentional act' because he contrives to deliberately subvert the process of demystification and naturalisation.

In our readings and our naturalisations of all poems there is an uneasy relationship between our interpretation of the 'carrier' and our creation of an 'intentional act'. To return to Jakobson's diagrams, we depend entirely upon the textual features of the message – deictics, metre, syntax, etc. – for our perception of context and contact. The former are properties of language whereas the latter are elements of an imagined non-linguistic situation. We can usually reconcile this somewhat paradoxical relation between the textual and the real by reminding ourselves that poetry demands that, in Coleridge's words, we suspend disbelief. But with Donne's poem every significant textual feature seems designed to remind us that text and world are irreconcilable.

In the second stanza we encounter an instance of grammatical deviation,

> Though parents grudge, and you, we are met,
> And cloistered in these living walls of jet.

The second person pronoun and its conective, 'and you', are shifted outside the more conventional grouping of second and third person forms antecedent to the verb, 'though you and your parents grudge'. We might explain this as a mimetic effect, a paratactic slippage betraying the sense of pressure felt by the speaking presence as he attempts to rescue his linguistic strategies from the woman's act of rejection. In doing so we would have drawn upon the contact–code functions to explain one element of the message, but we would then have to remind ourselves that it is only through our explication of features within the message that we are able to construct the contact–code functions. To complicate matters even further the deviation occurs only within the syntactic (real) rather than in the metrical (textual) element of the double pattern; 'and you' fits easily into the iambic/octosyllabic structure of the line (we can assume that 'we are' is, in contemporary fashion, elided as a single unstressed syllable). This tension between elements of the poem anchored to the contextual situation of the utterance and elements that function as constituents of the text is continuous and unremitting. We should, for example, consider the rhyme scheme.

The semantic–phonemic–syntactic syntheses are quite dazzling. On two occasions the locative term 'this' rhymes with the emphatic 'is', and there is an habitual almost urgent configuration of the speaker's projected ideal, 'be', and the pronouns that allow the reader to construct the situation of his utterance: 'sucks thee', 'mingled be'; 'kill me, added be', 'killing three'; 'fears be', 'to me', 'life from thee'. The pattern is complicated by the use of 'flea' as an internal counterpoint to 'be', 'thee' and 'me'. We might argue that the speaker's ingenious interpolation of the materiality of language, its phonic signifiers, with their semantic–syntactic functions is part of his rhetorical strategy – an attempt to persuade the woman, perhaps subliminally, that there is a natural correspondence between 'flea', 'thee', 'me' and 'be'. This argument would depend upon an interpretive conflation of textual and contextual features, and again its validity is by no means secure. When reading the poem we are continuously aware that its structure and the development of its argument is responsive to contextual circumstances and events: between stanzas 1 and 2 the woman attempts to swat the flea, between 2 and 3 she succeeds. But we are also aware that this foregrounding of the context–contact functions is matched by an equally prominent foregrounding of self-evidently textual features. The fact that each stanza consists of a very complex system of three couplets of eight and ten syllables terminated by a triplet of two octosyllabic lines and one pentameter disrupts our attempts to naturalise the rhyme scheme. On the one hand we are invited to admire the complexity and precision of the design; on the other we have again to confront the paradoxical relation between self-evident preplanning and our use of its effects to construct a speech act based upon and determined entirely by unpredictable non-linguistic circumstances. We might argue that the mixture of regular and irregular patterns – octosyllabic and decasyllabic lines in the same couplet – is a concession to the contextual element of improvisation and spontaneity, but at the same time we would have to acknowledge that such a concession is made through the foregrounding of the double pattern, and the double pattern is anything but improvised or spontaneous.

To summarise, we, as readers, are caught between two separate and often conflicting models of the communicative circuit. We have to situate ourselves, at least partly, in the position of the addressee, whose silent non-linguistic responses determine the structure of the message, but we also maintain a commanding position outside this dramatic communicative circuit and find ourselves faced with a conflict between the internal structure of the text and the inferred but very real circumstances that created the text. As I have stated, no poem is entirely immune from some potential for conflict between its concentration of linguistic features and its ability to construct its contextual circumstances, but it would be difficult to find another text which so self-consciously and continuously foregrounds this conflict. In creating such effects Donne becomes the poetic counterpart to the Duke. The Duke could shift easily between the linguistic and circumstantial conditions of the poetic and non-poetic language; Donne asks us to consider this uneasy relationship as purposive elements of the same speech act. The consequent tension between the speaking presence within the text and our image of the controlling hand, the creator of the text, is a consistent feature of metaphysical poetry. Moreover, it operates as an element that can disrupt the protocols of linguistics and literary analysis.

Emile Benveniste (1971, 206–7) distinguished between two fundamental elements of linguistic representation, *histoire* and *discours*. *Histoire*, like history, involves an emphasis upon the story, the events, while any evidence of who the narrator is and of what his/her opinion of these events might be slips into the background. But with *discours* we are as much aware of the means by which the story is told and the circumstances in which the telling occurs as we are of the events narrated. The most obvious point of distinction between these two concepts is the use of third and first person narratives in prose fiction, but with poetry, particularly regular poetry, the distinction becomes virtually useless as a framework for naturalisation. With 'The Flea' we might safely assume that the text functions as an example of *discours*, but whose *discours* is it? In one sense we need to construct the presence of the addresser who weaves complex metaphoric patterns out of events and circumstances, yet at the same time we are made aware that addresser and addressee are as much functions of the texts as are its metrical and syntactic design.

This problem of identifying a speaking presence upon which we might base interpretive strategies is considered by Jacques Derrida, arguably the most incisive commentator on the fallacies of modern linguistics:

> What was it that Saussure in particular reminded us of? That 'language [which consists only of differences] is not a function of the speaking subject'. This implies that the subject (self-identical or even conscious of self-identity, self-conscious) is inscribed in the language, that he is a 'function' of the language. He becomes a *speaking* subject only by conforming his speech . . . to the system of linguistic prescriptions taken as the system of differences.

(Derrida, 1973, 145–6)

What Derrida does not acknowledge is that in texts such as 'The Flea' there are effectively two speaking subjects: one is indeed a function of the language, but the other, a.k.a. John Donne, has manipulated the ability of language to designate its own contextual circumstances and has deliberately and self-consciously 'inscribed' his poetic persona in the language of the text.

The sense of uncertainty as to who exactly is in command of the text, poet or persona, underpins the most widely discussed exchange on the value of metaphysical technique. Samuel Johnson (1779, 40–3) dismissed metaphysical technique as 'heterogeneous ideas yoked by violence together'. In short their metaphors, or more commonly their conceits, drew too readily upon the paradigmatic axis, and consequently shifted the message, the poetic function, too far from the terms and conditions of linguistic exchange in the real world. T. S. Eliot (1921, 2024) praised this same method: 'A thought to Donne was an experience. It modified his sensibility'. Thought and experience, whose relation parallels the unification of language and its referent, are, according to Eliot, the constituents of the poetic function, and their bringing by violence together is what should distinguish poetic from non-poetic discourse. The disagreement between Johnson and Eliot can be explained in terms of the historical/cultural circumstances of their judgements – eighteenth-century rationalist versus twentieth-century expressionist views. As we shall see in the next chapter, eighteenth-century poets and critics regarded poetry as the aesthetic counterpart to the practical and utilitarian functions of non-literary discourse. *Histoire* and *discours*, events and perceptual response should be balanced, and their differences acknowledged, within the structure of the text. For Johnson, Donne and his contemporaries moved too far toward the extravagant employment of *discours*: 'wit, abstracted from its effects on the hearer . . . a combination of dissimilar images, or discovery of occult resemblances in things apparently unlike' (1779, 40–3). In short the text had created its own world, in which linguistic effects and the situation of the addresser and addressee had become detached from the situation of 'the hearer' or more accurately the reader. But for Eliot this same effect registered as the copresence, rather than the separation, of addresser and poet: '[The ordinary man] falls in love, or reads Spinoza, and these two experiences have nothing to do with each other, or with the noise of the typewriter or the smell of cooking; in the mind of the poet these experiences are always forming new wholes'. In Eliot's opinion the linguistic text should effectively contain and transform the contextual and referential functions of non-poetic language and experience. To summarise the Johnson–Eliot disagreement: the former favoured a balanced relation between the syntagm–paradigm configurations of poetry and non-poetic discourse while the latter held that the imaginative and unexpected use of the paradigm should create a world within the text. The validity of either of these judgements still remains open to question, but for the moment we should note that the metaphysicals, Donne in particular, represented the test case for two very distinct perceptions of how the functions of addresser, addressee, message, contact and context operate in relation to one another.

'The Flea' corresponds with one of the primary characteristics of the metaphysical tradition in that in most cases the speaking presence will establish a fictive situation of immediacy. The metaphysical conceit, the metaphoric technique that maintains a single vehicle throughout the metaphoric excursions of the poem, is often founded upon what might be termed the deictics of verification. The selective axis that constitutes poetic metaphor will usually be linked directly to a person or a non-human object or concept that inhabits the situation in which the utterance occurs. For instance in Donne's 'The Sunne Rising' the speaker does not directly address his female companion; the notion of the addressee is split between the reader, the introspective reflections of the speaker himself and the fictive companion who functions both as a deictic element and the recipient of the speech act. The deictic configurations of the poem make it clear that the thoughts and ideas mediated occur in response to a particular morning on which the sun rises and the speaker's presence in a particular bedroom following a particular night of sexual activity. Again we confront a conflict between the notion of speaker/poet who employs the fictive situation of the utterance as a function of its linguistic effect and the speaker within the text who is balancing the temporal immediacy of experience against his own mental condition. As Eliot said, a thought to Donne was an experience! But how do we judge the extent to which thought (the use of the paradigmatic axis) constrains experience (the syntagmatic, combinative axis) or vice versa?

At the other end of the metaphysical spectrum we will encounter the religious poems of Vaughan, Herbert and the holy sonnets of Donne himself. Here the range of metaphoric associations will, by virtue of the context of man speaking to or about God, be both reflective and speculative but the poem will still be anchored to a particular situation in which the speaker finds that he needs to address God directly, and it is usually the case that abstract concepts such as the nature of eternity or redemption will be drawn back into a chain of more concrete associations – the archetype for this pattern of linkages is Herbert's *The Temple* in which the objects that inhibit his daily life become correlatives for his perceived relationship with God. Like their 'amatory' counterparts, in which addresser and addressee are usually man and woman, the religious poems create an uncertain relationship between the communicative circuit occupied by poet and reader and that which governs the addresser–addressee function of the text itself. The following is Donne's most famous 'Holy Sonnet':

X
Batter my heart, three-personed God; for, you
As yet but knock, breathe, shine, and seek to mend;
That I may rise, and stand, o'erthrow me, and bend
Your force, to break, blow, burn, and made me new.
I, like an usurped town, to another due,
Labour to admit you, but oh, to no end,

Reason your viceroy in me, me should defend,
But is captived, and proves weak or untrue,
Yet dearly I love you, and would be loved fain,
But am bethrothed unto your enemy,
Divorce me, untie, or break that knot again,
Take me to you, imprison me, for I
Except you enthral me, never shall be free,
Nor ever chaste, except you ravish me.

Like 'The Flea', the deictic interpersonal features of the poem allow
us to establish a projected blending of the features of the text and
the situation of the utterance (first and second person pronouns,
present tense – 'I', 'you', 'me', 'God'). Even though the poem opens
with a very precise and concrete use of verb, pronoun and noun,
the extra-grammatical, cultural significance of 'God' automatically
precludes the dialogic context of a shared experience at the moment
of the utterance. In an important sense the immaterial nature of
the addressee governs the curious, almost urgent, use of compound
metaphor: first God is transformed into a besieging force, then into
a suitor to whose enemy (Satan?) the speaker is betrothed and
finally, in the closing couplet, into a sexually purposive presence.
The effect of these manic shifts from one associative pattern to
another destabilises any firm relation between vehicle and tenor:
the tenor, the presence of God, is moved so rapidly through each
embodiment or vehicle that we are left with a foregrounding of
what is known as the ground of the metaphor – the usually syntactic
rather than semantic element that determines the relationship
between the two parts of the metaphor. These metaphors are
grounded upon the use of transitive verbs to present God as active
and the speaker as passive. This effect might be explained in terms
of Donne's obligation never to allow the tenor of the metaphoric
associations to come to rest upon a particular vehicle – it would
have been unwise to allow the transcendent, immaterial nature of
the deity to become associated with specific, and by definition
limited, human characteristics.

In prayers, hymns and psalms (and the seventeenth century was
particularly productive of all three) there are clearly established
zones of linguistic demarcation between the two pronouns 'I' and
'you', or more often 'thou'. In the best known, the Lord's Prayer,
the textual deictics ('our bread', 'our trespasses'; 'thy will', 'thy
name') are established as separate by the contextual determinates
of 'on earth' (as it is) 'in heaven'. Consequently the associations

between the images of God and humanity are metonymic rather than metaphoric: God as King and Father are versions of the orthodox theological dictat that human types of subservience and respect are transpositions of the overarching relation between God and man. For most of the sonnet Donne observes this convention (God as a military leader would be a metonym sanctioned by the Old Testament story of the 'battle' between God and Satan), but the concluding image of God and the speaker as sexual partners moves far beyond the more familiar religious associations. Sexual union, unlike leadership or the broader semantic connotations of love and subservience, is something that we find difficult to transpose from the mortal to the spiritual plane.

The question we should ask is why Donne feels confident enough to do with poetry what would have caused unease in non-poetic discourses? First of all we should note that he chooses to address God through the sonnet (there are nineteen holy sonnets in which God or other unverifiable entities such as the soul or death are directly addressed). The sonnet is arguably the most self-evidently conventional poetic structure. Unlike the couplet or stanza poem or blank verse, where the number of and the structural relation between each formal unit is controlled by the poet, the sonnet literally encloses and limits the duration and formal symbiosis of the message. Thus the degree to which the speaking presence becomes displaced from its contextual function and appears more as a construct of a system of conventions is increased. One might argue that the perennial desire to establish the 'real' identity of the speaker and dark lady of Shakespeare's sonnets is largely a consequence of their irritating enclosure within a textual world so separate from the usual balance between language and the pre-linguistic continuum. What Donne achieves in this holy sonnet is an effect closely related to the contextual–textual disjunctions of 'The Flea', though his methods and objectives are quite different.

In his amatory poems the tension between the textual function and the imagined relation between addresser and addressee is founded upon an almost infinitely flexible relation between the contingencies of existence and the ordering structure of language. With God as the addressee, emphasis is shifted further toward the relation between addresser and his own textual construction, and the sonnet provides Donne with the perfect safety net for his daring attempt to draw God into the behavioural and linguistic conditions of humanity. Again the key to our understanding of this strategy is the paradoxical interrelationship between the contact mode and the poetic function. The two octaves (abba, adda) followed by the quatrain (ef ef) and the couplet (g g) appear to determine the timing and the discrimination between the metaphoric excursions. The first octave consists almost entirely of transitive verbs whose subject and object are simply the speaker and God. The second maintains this verbal foregrounding while introducing the martial metaphor. The quatrain supplements this with the metaphoric images of divorce and betrothal, and the couplet transposes the two patterns of military and sexual conquest. On the surface the linguistic freedom of the speaking subject is constrained by the arbitrary metrical and syntactic rules of the sonnet, but in fact this textual determinism is matched by a more flexible pattern of semantic cohesion which provides us with an imagined presence outside the text, struggling with its perverse regulations. None of the figurative patterns remains immune from traces of the others: the 'weak' and 'untrue' viceroy in the besieged town prepares the thematic and phonemic ground for the internal rhyme 'love you' and the images of marriage and physical love carry with them traces of the earlier martial figure – 'enemy', 'imprison me', 'enthral' all maintain a double edged resonance of military and sexual activity. All the time we encounter the subject of the 'intentional act' attempting to negotiate the arbitrary structures of the 'carrier'; in this case the sonnet. This continuous conflict between text and speaking presence comes to a head in the closing three lines,

> Take me to you, imprison me, for I
> Except you enthral me, never shall be free,
> Nor ever chaste, except you ravish me.

The couplet makes use of a rhetorical device called chiasmus (a criss-cross arrangement of antithetical clauses and terms). The verb phrases 'enthral me' and 'ravish me' and the adjectives 'chaste' and 'free' occupy, respectively, caesural and terminal pause positions, and the binding mechanism of regular metre and rhyme overlays the semantic paradox with a kind of persuasive symmetry: a perfect instance of mutual collaboration between syntax and the metrical set. But the couplet is meaningless without the pronoun 'I', in this case left isolated at the end of the preceding quatrain. The contact mode (man addresses God) is again brought into conflict with the poetic function (the demands of the sonnet formula). Such an effect of textual and referential tension could not be achieved in non-poetic language because it is the double pattern that allows Donne to construct two communicative circuits: speaker addresses God within the arbitrary formal constraints of the sonnet, and at the same time speaker addresses reader on the subject of his own perceptions of the relation between man and God. The effect of Donne's use of the double pattern is significant both for our understanding of literary history and for our understanding of the relationship between linguistics and literary criticism.

As we shall see the poets of the early-seventeenth-century metaphysical school maintain an uneasy awareness that poetic writing is a discourse that allows them to create patterns of representation that would not be available in non-poetic writing. Donne demonstrates that by splitting the communicative circuit he is able to create an intriguing inbalance between language as a reflection and realisation of contextual conditions and language as something which transforms these into an enclosed systematic formula that detaches speaker and addressee from the terms and conditions of the real, or at least unpoetic, world. And we will encounter a more persistent foregrounding of this tension in the poems of Herbert.

Linguistics and its practitioners have maintained a somewhat defensive stance on how exactly a description of the linguistic features of a text can relate to an evaluation or interpretation of it as an aesthetic object. Roger Fowler (1975) writes:

> An urgent priority for contemporary stylistics is to determine just what additional fields of knowledge are relevant to literary discourse, how they relate to the diversification of language outside of literature and, perhaps most fascinating of all to the linguistics-inclined critic, how these systems of literary knowledge are coded in the structure of language (p. 122).

In our own, perhaps limited, field of the relation between poetic form and signification, the 'additional fields' of enquiry will be determined by our perception of how the prevailing conventions and imperatives of a particular historical period can affect the way that poets adjust the balance between the internal structure of the text and its relationship with the aesthetic, political, social and existential mood of its compositional and interpretive circumstances. We will defer a judgement on the contextual pressures felt by the metaphysicals until the end of this chapter. For the moment we will consider a poet who represents the archetype of the metaphysical obsession with textuality and its relation with the speaking presence.

Within each school or generic subdivision of literary history it is often possible to identify a poet whose work not only contributes to the collective stylistic whole but which exaggerates and foregrounds one or more element of its particular poetic *langue*. One could cite Blake as the Romantic manifestation of this tendency and Hopkins and e. e. cummings as his Victorian and Modernist counterparts, while the difficulties in identifying a similarly innovative or even eccentric individual in Augustan poetry testifies to the power of stylistic codification in that period. With the metaphysicals George Herbert most clearly fills this role. *The Temple*, published posthumously in 1633, is a sequence of lyric poems which draw upon the contemporary trends in rhetoric and image-making and which attempt in a very individual way to make verse do the work of prayer and devotion. In practice he establishes his work as the first continuous foregrounding of, in Jakobson's phrase, poetic metalanguage. Each poem in the collection is as much about the experience of constructing poetic artefacts as it is about George Herbert and his relationship with God and the world – the poetic and metalinguistic functions are given equal prominence with the referential. The self-referential concentration within the author–text–reader circuit is continuous and unremitting: his self-imposed condition of never repeating the same stanzaic/metrical formula is as much a component of the message as are his deictic positionings of 'I' and 'my Lord'.

Jakobson claimed that the principles of metrical parallelism 'underlie' and 'prompt . . . semantic similarity and contrast', but with Herbert we often find it difficult to disentangle these two elements of the double pattern.

> *Our Life is Hid with Christ in God*
> *Coloss. 3.3*
> *My* words and thoughts do both express this notion,
> That *Life* hath with the sun a double motion.
>   The first *Is* straight, and our diurnal friend,
>   The other *Hid*, and doth obliquely bend.
> One life is wrapped *In* flesh, and tends to earth:
> The other winds towards *Him*, whose happy birth
>   Taught me to live here so, *That* still one eye
> Should aim and shoot at that which *Is* on high:
>   Quitting with daily labour all *My* pleasure,
>   To gain at harvest an eternal *Treasure*.

We could naturalise this poem much as we would Donne's 'The Flea' or his 'Holy Sonnet'. The governing metaphor, the conceit which resonates through the texture of the whole poem, is founded upon the notion of doubling. The vehicle of the sun's double motion underpins the complex tenor of the speaker's double perception of the empirical world and its spiritual counterpart. But the poem actively resists such a process of demystification. We could, of course, reconcile the more conventional elements of the metrical/ poetic function with the referential: the double rhymes of the opening and closing couplets are all nouns whose semantic relations correspond closely with the more prominent thematic motifs of the poem. These two closed couplets effectively enclose the freer movement of the three central couplets, and from this we might claim that his intention was to create an effect of speculation and enquiry bounded by certainty. But how do we deal with the syntactic unit that cuts diagonally through the entire text? We might be tempted to dismiss this as marginal to the signifying structure of the text, a decorative embellishment, and claim that it functions only as a visual effect. This is not strictly true, since when we hear the poem we do indeed hear this sentence. But it is meaningless until we connect the implied aural register of the iambic, syntagmatic pattern with its visual foregrounding. Our process of searching and disclosing is consistent with the theme of things 'hidden' from humanity, and this effect of transposing the tactile materiality of the text, an element of its poetic function, with its referential keynote becomes a motif in the collection. A similar use of aural–visual correspondences occurs in his widely anthologised 'pattern poems', 'Easter Wings' and 'The Altar'. In both instances the resemblance between the iconic shapes of the texts and their referential themes is interactive rather than discrete. When we hear 'Easter Wings' the ab ab rhyme scheme makes us aware of a closing and opening pattern of line lengths and traces out aurally the visual shape of the two stanzas as two pairs of wings, and this visual–aural supplement to the double pattern is entirely consistent with its central metaphor of birds, angels, rising and redemption. In 'The Altar' the narrow central column of the altar shape consists of short, quatro-syllabic couplets, whose theme is appropriately enough, a play on the double signification of 'heart' as both the centre of the text-icon and the emotional centre of its human source.

There is rarely a poem in the collection which does not draw the reader's attention both to the process of signification and its referential function. 'Jordan I' and 'Jordan II' address the continuous sense of doubt felt by Herbert that the ingenious and infinitely complex patternings of poetic discourse are purely self-referential and consequently incapable of accommodating the pre-linguistic experiences of faith and worship. His closing lines of stanza 2 from 'Jordan I' could be read as a desperate acknowledgement of Jakobsonian linguistics.

> Must all be veiled, while he that reads, divines,
>> Catching the sense at two removes?

And in 'Jordan II' he contemplates what might be regarded as the combined paradox and manifesto of the entire metaphysical school.

> As flames do work and wind, when they ascend,
> So did I weave my self into the sense
> But while I bustled, I might hear a friend
> Whisper, 'How wide is all this long pretense!'

The enjambed phrase 'hear a friend/Whisper' foregrounds the tension between the arbitrary structure of the discourse and the pre-linguistic experience that it seeks to communicate. The metaphor of 'weaving my self into the sense', of combining presence with textuality, is literally contained within the ironic textual correspondence between the speaker's 'sense', and its echo in the friend's accusation of 'pretense'.

Herbert's collection addresses the same problem that we encountered with Donne: the tension, apparently unresolvable, between presence and textuality. Clearly the principal difference is that whereas Donne created continuous tensions between context, message, contact and code, and consequently foregrounded the uneasy relation between the poetic and the referential functions of language, Herbert gives far more prominence to the arbitrary codes of his discourse and effectively designates the referential function (George Herbert, his beliefs, his experience) as being governed and determined by the metalingual and the poetic.

Andrew Marvell is regarded as a second-generation metaphysical. It could indeed be argued that he is the sole member of that generation. His best-known lyric poems were written in the early 1650s, two decades after the death of both of the major practitioners of metaphysical technique and of that technique's status as the dominant poetic code. Consequently many of his poems exhibit an exaggerated degree of tension between the metalingual and the poetic function – he displays a self-conscious awareness of the particulars of his inherited discourse. Consider one of his most quoted and widely anthologised lyrics, 'To His Coy Mistress'.

Prosodically the poem anticipates a number of formal conventions that would come to dominate poetic writing in the Restoration and eighteenth century. It is written in octosyllabic couplets and the structure of his argument consequently shifts from the metaphoric dimension of a stanzaic pattern toward the progressive, sequential dimension of the metonymic. The localised effect of moving consecutively from one couplet to the next – as we might from one sentence to the next – is supplemented by the poem's framework of three verse paragraphs, each following the formulaic relations of a philosophic syllogism: 'Had we . . .', 'But . . .' 'Now therefore . . .'. But, as we shall see in the next chapter, it would be wrong to impute to this text the imperatives of Augustan order and formal logic. It would be more fruitful to regard it as indicative of the gradual redisposition of the hierarchy of formal codes that took place between the Civil War and the closing decades of the seventeenth century. The most intriguing point of comparison is Donne's 'The Flea'. It is almost as though Marvell has set himself the task of engaging with the same contextual and referential conditions that attend Donne's poem. The addresser–addressee relation similarly shifts the context away from poet and reader toward a more enclosed dramatic situation of male and female personae, and there is the same density of first and second person pronouns: I, my, our, your, thy. The deictics of the utterance move beyond the immediate and specific instance of a flea bite to the broader metaphoric range of time and space: 'Ganges', 'Humber', 'before the Flood', 'the Conversion of the Jews', 'Deserts of vast eternity'. The principal difference between the two texts is in Marvell's arguably deliberate invocation of the contact mode. In Donne's poem the deictic features of each shift between stanzas indicate that the speaking presence is improvising rhetorical strategies in response to the silent imperatives of the addressee. With Marvell we find that the same division into three verse paragraphs indicates calculation and planning. First we encounter the fantastic realm of space/time transcendence, working as a kind of softening-up procedure to heighten the shock of the more concrete and disagreeable conditions of the second section. Here the spatial/temporal deictics move towards the facts of human existence – decay, the loss of beauty, the termination of such encounters that prompt this utterance, and death. The third section, the 'therefore' closure of the syllogism, seems to offer the only consolation possible, through the hedonistic exploitation of what remains of their mortal tenure.

Could it therefore be argued that Marvell is involved in a rejection of the metaphysical tendency toward textuality – the containment of the speaking presence within the varied conventions of poetic discourse – in favour of a more strategic, purposive deployment of poetic devices? To address this question we should first remind ourselves that Marvell does not entirely abandon the characteristic metaphysical device of textual foregrounding. Just as we are aware that the contact mode has shifted from improvisation to calculation so we should recognise that this shift occurs within the terms and conditions of the poetic function. The couplet presents the opportunity for the foregrounding of syntactic components, the use of the double pattern to supplement the compositional and interpretive conditions of syntax. Note, for example, how the metrical determinants of the couplet form are used to promote the more purposive and indeed threatening elements of the time/space deictics by placing them within the inexorable movement of the aa bb cc rhyme scheme. 'Time' and 'crime' in the first couplet remain in the mind to be supplemented by related semantic–acoustic correspondences between 'love should grow' and 'more slow'; 'always hear' and 'hurrying near'; 'turn to dust' and 'all my lust'; 'rough strife' and 'iron gates of life'. So again we find that the contextual function (man addresses woman) is qualified by the poetic–metalingual function in which the substance of the message becomes a condition of its self-evidently metrical structure. But Marvell also plays the cognitive element of the double pattern against its conventional element. In each of the three sections there is at least one instance of a main verb of a sentence placed in the position of the opening rhyme of a couplet: 'to praise/Thine eyes'; 'always hear/Times'; 'shall try/that'; 'Transpires/At every'. There is a similar, but without the rhyme-correspondence less prominent, delayed positioning of the main verb at the beginning of lines. The effect of this deliberate interfusion of the active components of syntax with the arbitrary conventions of form is to give the impression that Marvell (or his vicarious representative within the text) is struggling as much with the conventions of poetic discourse as he is with the referential code of mortal existence and its limited tenure. The voice (the cognitive element of the double pattern) is in a continuously shifting relation with the conditions of the utterance (the conventional element), and by foregrounding the tension between the voice within and the projected voice beyond the text Marvell places himself firmly within the tradition of Donne and Herbert.

I stated earlier that his verse signals the redisposition of the codes of poetic discourse. In this instance and in poems such as 'The Definition of Love' and 'The Garden' we find that the argument of the text shifts away from the complex contrapuntal patterns of the early-seventeenth-century stanzaic forms toward more consecutive, syntagmatic formulae. This, as we shall see, was to become the keynote of the Augustan deployment of the couplet. The principal difference between Marvell and his Augustan successors is in the latter's attempts to marginalise the tension between the arbitrary nature of poetic writing and its counterparts in philosophic, political and social discourses. In the Augustan period the use of the double pattern would be offered as a productive alternative to rather than an aberration from the referential and contextual functions of prose.

Having come to some conclusions about how a number of lyric poems from the early-seventeenth-century work, can we devise a general formula which identifies their common denominator?

Let us return to the model introduced in Chapter 1, the sliding scale. We could argue that Donne, Herbert and Marvell produce poems that belong at the conventional rather than the cognitive end of the scale, where the balance between the two elements of the double pattern is shifted away from those features that poems might share with other linguistic discourses toward elements that are intrinsically and definitively poetic. We might also consider a related binary distinction between the functional and the structural, the context and the text. The functional and the contextual elements of language refer, respectively, to what a statement is meant to achieve and to the circumstances which prompt, and for the reader/ addressee substantiate, this objective. The structural and the textual elements refer, respectively, to the technique employed within a particular statement or utterance and to salient features that allow us to identify each text, in this case each poem, as distinct from yet related to other texts within the same genre or code, in this case early-seventeenth-century English poetry.

Herbert's poems belong at the conventional end of the sliding scale because they exhibit a persistent self awareness of their own formal strategies and limitations. In consequence it is extremely difficult for the reader to make a clear distinction between text and context, structure and function. In an ordinary, non-literary, statement the use of the pronoun 'I' will effectively govern and allow us to distinguish between the structural–textual and the functional–contextual dimensions (it combines both with our knowledge of the internal structure of the statement and with our broader knowledge or assumption about who the 'I' is and why this person is making the statement), but in all of the poems of Herbert's *The Temple* the speaking presence shifts the interpretive focus continuously and uneasily between text and context, structure and function. We might claim that the 'I' of the text is addressing God with the objective of resolving a complex of emotional and theological problems, and that these texts share a similar objective with such non-literary discourses as prayers, sermons or theological tracts. But we must also be aware that the 'I' of these poems is drawn away from this broader contextual–functional condition to become what is effectively a device operative only within the framework comprising other structural devices such as the stanzaic pattern, and the graphic and phonic material of the language. Thus the procedures and objectives of naturalisation become confused: to interpret the speaking presence as the literary counterpart to George Herbert, cleric and theologian, means that we have also to deal with the 'other' presence that literally inhabits the textual structure and whose function can be just as readily explained not in its relation to George Herbert but as an intertextual phenomenon which has close counterparts in the texts of Donne and Marvell.

With the poems of Donne and Marvell we encounter a similar, though less extreme, process of interpretive dislocation. The collective sub-genre of the 'amatory' poem invites us to position each text within the broader social and linguistic context of seduction and gender distinction, but the validity of such an assumption is compromised in 'The Flea' and 'To His Coy Mistress' by the fact that the functional validity of the speaker's techniques is explicitly and self-evidently a consequence of strategies peculiar to the poetic artefact, strategies that it would stretch plausibility to imagine occurring in non-poetic discourses or circumstances.

Let us now propose a common denominator: the lyric poem of the early seventeenth century can be said to place as much emphasis upon explicit textuality as it does upon its functional and purposive relation to other linguistic discourses. The attendant question is much more complex: why?

We do not have the space here to conduct a comparative analysis of the poetic and non-poetic texts of the period, but a number of generalisations are possible. The English 'literary Renaissance' of the sixteenth and seventeenth centuries drew its own generic and broader contextual identity largely from classical precedent. I would argue that the relation between structure and function, text and context, was more uncertain for poetry than it was for such non-literary discourses as the political/philosophic tract or the sermon. The major prose writers of the period, Hooker, Bacon, Hobbes, Browne and Andrewes, all drew upon the stylistic techniques and philosophic propositions of Greek and Roman writing, but they also, by various means, adapted these to the conditions and circumstances of sixteenth–seventeenth-century Europe. Thus the functional and contextual elements of Hooker's *Laws of Ecclesiastical Polity* or Bacon's essays 'Of Truth', 'Of Death', 'Of Love' are positioned on a stable axis between what the author wanted to tell his contemporaries about new interpretations of scripture or codes of behaviour and perception and such textual strategies as syntax and rhetoric that can be seen to migrate between different texts and between the modern and classical periods. The functional purpose of prose discourse in relation to its immediate contextual circumstances was well established, a situation assisted by the proliferation of the printing press as a means of extending the relation between addresser and addressee to broader and definitively modern experience of author, text and addressee. But if we consult the new phenomenon of 'literary criticism' in the works of Sidney, Gascoigne, Wyatt or Puttenham we will find an enormous amount of advice on how English poets should adapt the stylistic precendents of the classics (quantitative versus accentual metre, the naming and classification of rhetorical devices, etc.) but hardly anything on what the poet and the poem were supposed to be and do within the social, philosophic and political circumstances of the composition and the reception of texts. English poetry existed as a discourse, a genre, that was aware both of its own structural framework and of the relation between this and its classical antecedents, but the question of its function, beyond a form of whimsical entertainment, remained unanswered and largely unaddressed. It would be wrong to claim that all the poems of this period adhere to the model of intertextuality that emerges from the texts studied: Donne's *satyres* or Jonson's 'At Penhurst', maintain a relation between textual strategies and a broader contextual situation of real and verifiable events and people. But they also maintain an uneasy condition of awareness that what lies beyond the poetic artefact might well be distorted and transformed by its presence within it.

Let us consider these issues within the broader disciplinary sphere of linguistics and literary interpretation. Jakobson's diagrams of the communicative circuit have provided us with a useful framework for documenting textual features and their cooperation in the production of meaning, but a problem arises when we find that the contact–context, addresser–addressee functions become so closely integrated with the textual components of the message that the process of naturalisation is continuously disrupted. In short the textual–structural and the contextual–functional dimensions of the text seem to operate at two levels. First, we have the one-sided dialogic functions, so prominent in poems of the period, in which contact and context, and the poetic components of the message occupy a realm of signification which is largely enclosed and from which the reader is often excluded. Second, we have the functional relation between text and reader, and here the context is expanded to include the reader's a priori expectations of what poetry is and how it should relate to other discourses; and of how the enclosed context of the poem – man's relation with God or the man addressing the woman – connects with the broader linguistic and non-linguistic context of social-behavioural convention, faith and theology. Between the 1960s and the 1980s linguists attempted to account for this troubling disjunction. Michael Riffaterre's celebrated challenge to Jakobson will be considered in the following chapter, but for our present purposes a more relevant development occurred in the 1970s when M. A. K. Halliday began to supplement his earlier emphases upon the pure mechanics of the text with considerations of its received and intended functions, functions that would be affected if not fully determined by the practices and expectations of the society in which it was written and read (see Halliday, 1978). Roger Fowler in a number of essays in the 1960s and 1970s and in *Literature as Social Discourse* (1981) took this approach a stage further and argued that the patterns of preference shown by a writer in his selection of linguistic and stylistic resources are a function of the particular practices of communities in particular historical periods. What neither writer attempted to do was to chart the causal relation between the movement of the double pattern along the sliding scale and the social, political and aesthetic circumstances of the poem in question. This, as I have stated previously, is the objective of this study. In the following chapter it will become apparent that, in the poetry written during the Restoration and the eighteenth century, structure becomes closely related with a much more certain awareness of social, political and aesthetic function than was evident in the early seventeenth century.

Exercises

When criticising English lyric poems of the late sixteenth–early seventeenth century use the following formula.

First, identify the situation of the utterance. The key factors in this process of speaker–reader orientation are deictics:

(i)   Is the text a record of one person addressing another? Tense, and the use of personal pronouns will provide you with a basic grasp of the situation ('I', 'you' rather than 'he', 'she' for example).

(ii)   Perhaps the text identifies two human subjects but does not specify the presence of the addressee at the moment of speaking. It is possible to encounter the pronoun 'you' while remaining uncertain of whether the subject and the situation are addressed directly, hypothetically or retrospectively.

(iii)   In relation to (ii) further evidence will be supplied by the speaker's deployment of concrete objects and images. These will often provide the vehicle for metaphoric excursions (the fleabite for instance). There will usually be a distinction between images drawn from the memory and experience of the speaker prior to the utterance and those that occupy the perceptual experience of the addresser at the time of the speech act; and the relation between these sources will usually substantiate the spatio-temporal relation between addresser and addressee (compare the images used in Donne's address to the woman in 'The Flea' with those in his address to God in the 'Holy Sonnet').

Second, examine whether the addresser–addressee relationship is enclosed by dense textual patterns or whether the text appears to respond to the pressures of pre-linguistic circumstances.

(iv)   The double pattern is useful in addressing this question. The complexity of the metrical pattern, the stanzaic formula and the rhyme scheme will foreground the dominance of textuality over the situation of the utterance (the most obvious instance is the sonnet), while a more flexible formula suggests a shift in balance from the text toward the pre-linguistic situation.

(v)   The relationship between the syntagmatic and paradigmatic chains (signalling the creation of metaphor) will often correspond with metrical complexity – the more complex the pattern the more violent the disturbance of the syntagm by paradigmatic shifts. The principal question raised by this formula is whether the poet wishes to disclose these figurative uses as planned or whether immediacy and spontaneity is the intended effect.

TEXTS

(a)   Read Donne's 'The Extasie' and pay particular attention to points (i), (ii) and (iii). Addresser and addressee are the subjects of the text but are they both present in the situation of the utterance? Examine the use of tense and pronoun in the closing stanzas.

> To our bodies turn we then, that so
>   Weak men on love revealed may look;
> Love's mysteries in souls do grow,
>   But yet the body is his book.
>
> And if some lover, such as we,
>   Have heard this dialogue of one,
> Let him still mark us, he shall see
>   Small change, when we are to bodies gone.

(b)   Consider Thomas Carew's 'A Rapture' in relation to the same questions. Celia is addressed directly, but the discourse concentrates on images and narratives drawn exclusively from the speaker's imagination and reading. Consider the way in which the dominant syntactic units (the pronouns and the commending verb phrases) suggest immediacy and spontaneity while the referential images continually shift the text away from the present toward the sphere of metaphor, myth and classical learning. In short, does the text create a deliberate tension between the situation of the utterance and the mental world of the speaker? Compare with Donne's 'The Flea' and Marvell's 'To His Coy Mistress'. Does the effect of the enjambed couplet in all three poems foreground the uneasy relation between the poetic (text, structure, artifice) and the imagined situation (see (iv))? The following is the opening verse paragraph:

> I will enjoy thee now, my Celia, come,
> And fly with me to Love's Elysium.
> The giant, Honour, that keeps cowards out,
> Is but a masquer, and the servile rout
> Of baser subjects only bend in vain
> To the vast idol; whilst the nobler train
> Of valiant lovers daily sail between
> The huge Colossus' legs, and pass unseen
> Unto the blissful shore. Be bold and wise,
> And we shall enter: the grim Swiss denies
> Only to tame fools a passage, that not know
> He is but form, and only frights in show

The duller eyes that look from far; draw near,
And thou shalt scorn what we were wont to fear.
We shall see how the stalking pageant goes
With borrowed legs, a heavy load to those
That made and bear him: not, as we once thought,
The seed of gods, but a weak model wrought
By greedy men, that seek to enclose the common,
And within private arms impale free woman.

(c)   Consider Donne's 'The Canonization'. This is arguably the most disorientating of all metaphysical poems. The presence of the addressee seems to be validated by the addresser's urgent questions and declarations, but who is this person? The deictic features suggest that he/she has some influence upon the speaker's relationship with his lover, but is this direct (the addresser's friend, relative, employer even) or imagined (perhaps the speaker addresses his own problems and doubts or confronts God with them) (see (i) and (ii))? Our enquiries are not helped by the poem's shifts between broader contextual images (kings, soldiers, wars, etc.) and self-referential invocations of the poetic (see (iii)). The following are the first and third stanzas:

For God's sake hold your tongue, and let me love,
　Or chide my palsy, or my gout,
My five grey hairs, or ruined fortune flout,
　With wealth your state, your mind with arts improve,
　　Take you a course, get you a place,
　　Observe his Honour, or his Grace,
Or the King's real, or his stamped face
　Contemplate; what you will, approve,
　So you will let me love.

We can die by it, if not live by love,
　And if unfit for tombs and hearse
Our legend be, it will be fit for verse;
　And if no piece of chronicle we prove,
　　We'll build in sonnets pretty rooms;
　　As well a well-wrought urn becomes
The greatest ashes, as half-acre tombs,
　And by these hymns, all shall approve
　Us canonized for love:

(d)   Lastly, Herbert's 'A Wreath'. Consider how Herbert combines the textual and referential functions of poetic language. Is the repetition of words and phrases merely a complex pun on the image of a wreath (the interweaving of components)? Or does this, combined with the thematic–semantic foregrounding of the rhyme scheme (give, live; straight, deceit), produce a form of metasyntax, a secondary pattern of meanings, common to all forms of poetic writing (see (iv) and (v))? Compare the poem with a similar pattern of interactions between the referential and material elements of language in Herbert's 'Paradise'. In your opinion is Herbert's work an exaggeration or an honest disclosure of a dependency between the referential–functional purpose of language and its enclosed poetic–textual structures?

A wreathèd garland of deservèd praise,
Of praise deservèd, unto thee I give,
I give to thee, who knowest all my ways,
My crooked winding ways, wherein I live,
Wherein I die, not live: for live is straight,
Straight as a line, and ever tends to thee,
To thee, who art more far above deceit,
Than deceit seems above simplicity.
Give me simplicity, that I may live,
So live and like, that I may know thy ways,
Know them and practise them: then shall I give
For this poor wreath, give thee a crown of praise.

3 The Restoration and the eighteenth century

The period to be covered in this chapter ranges from the 1660s to the 1780s, and priority will be given to three issues: (i) the development of what in effect was a dominant verse idiom with specified rules for variation – the most significant feature of this being the widespread use of the heroic couplet; (ii) the relationship between poetic writing and a new critical tradition which supplemented advice on how to make poems with directions on how to read them; (iii) the single-handed 'invention' by John Milton of a metrical and stylistic framework for non-dramatic blank verse.

None of these issues can remain immune from the influence of the others and in identifying the correspondences and tensions between them we will provide ourselves with a means of charting the intersections between the formal and referential functions of poetry and the broader cultural/historical conditions of literary history. First, some facts.

CONTEXT

The seventeenth century is divided into three principal historical periods; the pre-civil war/post-Elizabethan period of the Stuarts; the civil war and the Cromwellian Protectorate; the Restoration of the monarchy and the beginning of the recognisably modern social/political structure of government through factional infighting. There are never any direct and predictable causal relationships between history and literary history, but in the period from the beginning of the seventeenth to the beginning of the eighteenth century a number of correspondences become solidly apparent.

From the 1660s to the 1740s poetic writing was dominated by the generic and functional notion of the public poem. This type could range from the direct engagement with contemporary political issues (the so-called 'poem on affairs of state') to the more discursive 'georgic' mode in which matters such as architecture, dress sense, the sanitary conditions of the streets or the practice of sheep husbandry would function as the subject of all or part of the poetic discourse. Poems about real people and events were of course written before the civil war, but in the post-civil war period poems themselves and writings about poetry began to focus more upon the stylistic and formal conditions that would establish poetry as the literary counterpart to the political or philosophic essay. The events and circumstances that prompted and sustained this change in emphasis were political, social and intellectual. The 1688 bloodless coup, also known as the 'glorious revolution', the 1694 triennial act and the 1716 septenial act ensuring parliamentary elections respectively at three and seven year intervals, the lapse of the licensing act in 1695, creating the opportunity for relative press freedom and the proliferation of pamphleteering; all of these and many other factors, not least being the increase in commercial printers and publishers, established the conditions for the emergence of the new social and cultural phenomenon of the professional writer – often disparagingly referred to as the hack. The hack would not necessarily earn his money from sales of published material. As elections became more frequent the ambition to control parliament became stronger; the party lines hardened and the arena of conflict shifted from private mansions into the open street. Ideas had to be transmitted quickly and persuasively and the poem was just as important a medium for such purposes as the essay. It would be wrong to assume that all of the best known poets of the period (Dryden, Swift and Pope for example) were political puppets and hirelings, but it is certainly the case that their objective of using poetry as an instrument for reflecting and influencing public opinion was partly fuelled by these broader changes in status of the poet and the poem.

The intellectual mood of the period was closely related to its turbulent politics. The Royal Society was founded during the Cromwellian Protectorate and in the succeeding decades established itself as a kind of barometric guide to developments in the key areas of thinking and writing. Its best known and most widely quoted statement of purpose occurs in Thomas Sprat's 1667 *History of the Royal Society* (and for history we might read manifesto):

> The resolution of the Royal Society has been . . . to reject all amplifications, digressions, and swellings of style; to return back to the primitive purity and shortness, when men, deliver'd so

many *things* almost in an equal number of words. They have extracted from all their members a close, naked, natural way of speaking, positive expressions, clear senses, a native easiness, bringing all things as near the Mathematical plainess as they can, and preferring the language of Artizans, Countrymen, and Merchants, before that of Wits or Scholars (117–18)

Sprat respects the status of language as an arbitrary self-determined medium of representation (words are not things), but his promotion of the language of 'Artizans, Countrymen and Merchants' over that of 'Wits and Scholars' emphasises the need for a matching or unitary correspondence between our chief representative medium and the concrete and verifiable continuum of events and conditions that determine our condition.

Poetry, in establishing itself as a medium for public debate was readily responsive to such terms and objectives, and Dryden in 1677 restates Sprat's proposition as a manifesto for the poetic deployment of wit: 'the definition of wit . . . is only this: that it is propriety of thoughts and words; or, in other terms, thoughts and words elegantly adapted to the subject'. Or, as Pope later put it,

True wit is nature to advantage dressed
What oft were thought, but ne're so well expressed.

Here we come across the principal distinction between the poetry of this period and the style of the metaphysicals. For the Augustans, the imaginative instinct, that which creates metaphors, is essentially a sorting and cataloguing process by which things and ideas that are already regarded as discrete and separate can be assembled in a manner that reflects their pre-linguistic condition. Thus we find, almost a century later, Johnson objecting to the metaphysical tendency to create correspondences and parallels within language that would change or distort the broadly accepted relations between language and reality: language, including poetic language, was held in the eighteenth century to be a means of clarifying and validating the relation between language and verifiable fact, not as a means of disturbing this balance and shifting the linguistic continuum toward new and unsubstantiated fields of speculation.

We should now move from the general to the particular and the first question to be considered is why the heroic couplet was thought to be the most appropriate vehicle for such ideals and objectives.

THE COUPLET

The heroic couplet (heroic designating it as an appropriate vehicle for the epic) consists of two iambic, decasyllabic lines rhyming aa, bb, cc, etc. It was widely used before the Restoration, but in its post-1660 manifestation it became subject to specific prescriptions and formal regulations. For example, Pope effectively rewrote a number of Donne's *satyres* with the primary objective of reconciling a perceived imbalance between the two dimensions of the double pattern.

> *Donne*: I more amaz'd than Circe's prisoners, when
> They felt themselves turn beasts, felt myself then
> Becoming Traytor, and methought I saw
> One of our Giant Statutes ope his jaw
>
> *Pope*: Not more Amazement seiz'd on *Circe's* Guests,
> To see themselves fall endlong into Beasts,
> Than mine, to find a Subject staid and wise,
> Already half turned Traytor by surprize.
>
> (Pope, Vol. IV, 38–41)

What Pope does is to bring syntax more closely into line with the abstract structure of the couplet. The syntactic constructions that effectively dominate Donne's passage (pronouns, relative pronouns and verbs, 'when/They felt', 'felt myself then/Becoming', 'I saw/One') are in a constant state of tension with the metrical and rhyming framework of the couplets, and as a consequence the speaking presence appears to be in uncertain command of both the subject mediated and of the process of mediation. Pope is careful to ensure that the dominant verb phrase 'Not more Amazement . . . Than mine' and its subordinate clauses accommodate, and are accommodated by, the structure of the couplets: speaking presence and text appear to be united.

To fully address the question of how the stabilising of the double pattern functions in extended poetic sequences we should consider one element of linguistic structure that is fundamental to our perception of how texts are organised, and this is cohesion (see Halliday and Hasan, 1976). Our understanding of textual cohesion is governed by the relation between the basic units of linguistic organisation, sentences. Each sentence of a text, following the first, is linked to the content of one or more preceding sentences by at least one 'tie'. A tie is made by some constituent that resumes, restates or reminds us of something designated by a predicate or a referring expression in a preceding sentence. Consider the following: 'I like dogs. My whole family likes them. At least, most of them do. We used to have six.' None of these sentences can be fully understood without the others. The 'them' of the second sentence ties into the 'dogs' of the first; 'most of them do' (third) ties into 'my family' (second); 'we' and 'six' tie in, respectively, to 'family' (second and third) and 'dogs' (first and second), and the placing of 'used' creates an intriguing temporal distinction between the fourth sentence and the first three. Textual cohesion provides us with a broader textual framework (a 'super sentence'; see Birch, 1989, 145 and Hendricks, 1967) in which we can establish a relation between the deictic and locative pointers and the projected spatio-temporal condition of the speaker or writer.

Practically all work on the literary and linguistic relevance of cohesion has concentrated on its operational function in prose, and very little emphasis has been given to how cohesion is compromised or disrupted when a sequence of syntactic units is supplemented by metrical structure and rhyme. For example the four primary metrical components of the sonnet might bear only an oblique resemblance to its syntactic structure: we might find correspondences between rhyme words or metrical foregroundings that in some way influence our perception of the cohesive structure of the text but which cannot be identified as purely syntactic transferences or ties. The heroic couplet provided the poetic writers of the eighteenth century with a means by which they could effectively control the relation between these two elements of cohesion.

Consider the following verse paragraph from Pope's 'Essay on Criticism',

> But you who seek to give and merit fame,
> And justly bear a critic's noble name,
> Be sure yourself and your own reach to know
> How far your genius, taste and learning go;
> Launch not beyond your depth, but be discreet,
> And mark that point where sense and dulness meet (46–51).

The introduction of the subject, 'you', and the post-modifying phrase identifying 'you' as the critic and attributing specific social/ cultural objectives to critical writing, are neatly enclosed within the opening couplet. The second couplet contains the main verb phrase of the sentence and details of how the critic should, ideally, operate, and the third couplet, beginning again with a verb, contains a subordinate clause with further advice on critical writing. The difference between this sequence and our prose example is that it consists not of four but of one very complex sentence. But in a curious way the progressive pattern of ties and correspondences that allows us to contextualise each prose sentence operates in a similar way for each couplet. 'You . . . the critic' → 'Be sure' → 'Launch not' create a type of progressive metasyntagm very similar to the sequence of expansions and clarifications of 'I' → 'My Family' → 'dogs' → 'them'. The couplet, without necessarily completing a syntactic unit, begins to operate like a sentence: each couplet in this sequence contains a discrete unit of information but the total message cannot be fully understood without our transferring something designated in one unit and transposing it with the constituents of units that succeed it.

A consistent feature of Pope's and Dryden's major couplet poems is their ability to sustain two patterns of signification throughout a single text. The best known manifestation of this has been categorised as the mock heroic, in which individuals and objects are established as phenomena that inhabit a real, contemporary, continuum outside the text while their presence within the text is distorted and transformed by images and patterns of association drawn mainly from classical literature, the bible or myth. The juxtaposition or reconciliation of images drawn from the immediate context of the utterance with those from distant historical, religious or cultural contexts is a common feature of most poems (it corresponds with Jakobson's distinction between the syntagmatic–paradigmatic axes); Donne's transposition of the flea with the marriage bed and the church is an obvious example. But in the Augustan couplet poem the effect of narrative cohesion effectively controls and disciplines the tendency for metaphoric, associative play to disrupt the reader's command of the relation between text, context and signification. Consider the following well-known sequence from Pope's *The Rape of the Lock*.

And now, unveiled, the toilet stands displayed,
Each silver vase in mystic order laid.
First, robed in white, the nymph intent adores,
With head uncovered, the cosmetic powers.
A heavenly image in the glass appears,
To that she bends, to that her eyes she rears;
The inferior priestess, at her altar's side,
Trembling, begins the sacred rites of pride.
Unnumbered treasures ope at once, and here

The various offerings of the world appear;
From each she nicely culls with curious toil,
And decks the goddess with the glittering spoil.
This casket India's glowing gems unlocks,
And all Arabia breathes from yonder box.
The tortoise here and elephant unite,
Transformed to combs, the speckled and the white.
Here files of pins extend their shining rows,
Puffs, powder, patches, bibles, billet-doux.
Now awful beauty puts on all its arms;
The fair each moment rises in her charms,
Repairs her smiles, awakens every grace,
And calls forth all the wonders of her face;
Sees by degrees a purer blush arise,
And keener lightnings quicken in her eyes.
The busy Sylphs surround their darling care;
These set the head, and those divide the hair,
Some fold the sleeve, whilst others plait the gown;
And Betty's praised for labours not her own.

(Canto I, 121–48)

It is possible to divide this sequence into three separate referential patterns, each drawing upon a different extra-textual context. Two of these belong to the cultural code: there is the combination of Christian symbols and images drawn from the more occult and fantastic sphere of Rosicrucian mythology – Belinda and Betty are presented as priestess and inferior priestess attended by sylphs, and the dressing table is described as an altar; this pattern is transposed with a less dominant context of martial combat – her 'pins' are in 'files' and 'shining rows', and her application of the cosmetics is compared with the 'awful' image of the epic hero who 'arms' himself. The third pattern relates specifically to the functional purpose of the poem (Belinda is a thinly disguised version of the real Arabella Fermor, both figures elsewhere conflated as the 'Belle'). This literal pattern (in terms of metaphor, the tenor) provides the consistent undertow against which the figurative patterns of religious ritual and the epic (the vehicle(s)) are foregrounded – the former registering as 'the toilet', 'the glass', 'the combs', 'the files', 'puffs, powder, patches', 'the blush', 'the hair', 'the sleeve', 'the gown'.

To use Johnson's formula it might seem that Pope's 'ideas' of martial combat, religious ritual and domestic detail are just as 'heterogeneous' as Donne's conflation of God, sexuality and war in his 'Holy Sonnet'. So how is it that Johnson could regard such juxtapositions in Pope as consistent with the Augustan objectives of clarification and order, yet condemn the Donne technique as a 'violent yoking', a 'discordia concors'? Pope's achievement of apparent order within the text is due primarily to his use of the heroic couplet as the keystone of textual cohesion.

The relation between the three referential patterns is already well established in the mind of the reader prior to our encounter with this particular sequence. As an isolated unit the opening couplet involves a peculiar juxtaposition of different codes – we hardly expect a 'toilet' or dressing table to be 'unveiled' or to disclose a 'mystic order'. But just as we interpret 'We used to have six' as an extension of the already predicated notion of an individual, a family and a preference for dogs, so we similarly draw upon the by now familiar relation between Belinda as an ordinary, early eighteenth-century female, and images of a priestess attended by sylphs. The part played by the rhetorical and syntactic mechanism of the couplet in this process of cumulative awareness is crucial.

I have already stated that most work on textual cohesion has focused upon the relation between prose sentences (for an accessible survey see Enkvist, 1973, ch. 7), but it becomes evident that Pope's use of the closed couplet represents a significant and as yet undocumented departure from these patterns. Two terms are useful here: theme and rheme. These might be transposed with the more familiar terms, topic and comment, given and new. In syntactic theory the simplest account of the relation between these two elements is as a linear progression in which the established theme of one sentence is taken up by the reader to clarify the rheme of the next, and each successive rheme is contextualised as an addition to or deviation from the established network of relations. The couplet supplements the relation between separate sentences by becoming an independent unit of signification in which the theme–rheme relation can be both restated and extended. Consider the opening couplet of the poem:

> What dire offence from amorous causes springs,
> What mighty contests rise from trivial things

Here two of the dominant referential patterns of the poem are introduced, and indeed the parallelism of the couplet form (dividing the syntax into four metrical units separated by caesura – line ending and rhyme – caesura – line ending and rhyme) succeeds in binding the otherwise disparate concepts of 'dire offence', 'mighty contests' (martial combat, the epic code) and 'amorous causes', 'trivial things' (the familiar, functional code relating the poem to eighteenth–century society) into a purposive structure, suggesting correspondences and causal relations. As the poem proceeds this same structural framework operates as the point of organisation and synthesis in which the three referential patterns are restated and their correspondences clarified. For example in the fourth verse paragraph in which Belinda is addressed by her 'guardian sylph' we find the following sequence,

> Know, then, unnumbered spirits round thee fly,
> The light militia of the lower sky
> These, though unseen, are ever on the wing,
> Hang o'er the box, and hover round the Ring.
> Think what an equipage thou hast in air,
> And view with scorn two pages and a chair.
> As now your own, our beings were of old,
> And once enclosed in woman's beauteous mould;
> Thence, by a soft transition, we repair
> From earthly vehicles to these of air.

(Canto I, 41–50)

The familiar extra-textual pattern of 'the box' (the theatre), 'the Ring' (Hyde Park), 'an equipage' (a carriage) and 'a chair' (a sedan chair) is invoked and drawn into an apparently causal and verifiable relation to the minor sylphs, who 'hang o'er the box' and 'hover round the Ring'. Here we find what might be termed the microlinguistic structure of the individual couplet drawing upon and recontextualising the separate referential patterns. As such the couplet becomes the axis between these microlinguistic correspondences and the broader macrolinguistic structure of the text. For example, the rather vague reference to 'the light militia of the lower sky' is an unsubstantiated rheme that we will carry forward and recontextualise as an element of the martial–epic theme that becomes more fully substantiated in the card game of Canto III.

So when we encounter the sequence describing the toilet–altar we find ourselves locating each couplet as a point of synthesis in which each theme, each given topic, will be recontextualised and related to a new rheme. It should be stressed that the couplet serves a number of interrelated purposes as an instrument of textual cohesion. Often it will maintain the foregrounding of a single referential pattern. Lines 127–32 of the toilet–altar sequence maintain the fantastic image of Betty as the inferior priestess disposing the materials of the ritual, but the four lines, two couplets, following this sequence, reinstate her activities within the more immediate context of where Belinda's cosmetics come from (India and Arabia) and their practical functions (elephant tusks, combs).

We should now broaden the context of our readings and consider the issue of how the poet corresponds with the text. Very few of the archetypal Augustan texts seek to identify the speaking presence as a participant in the events or experiences that brought the poem into existence. Even with Pope's 'Epistles' the notion of the addresser–addressee relation is qualified by the foregrounding of the text as a medium in which the writer/addresser has the opportunity to recuperate cultural and broader contextual codes as elements of immediate functional intentions. The Augustan poem becomes the forum in which the immediate, the contextual and the cultural/intertextual codes can be disposed, juxtaposed and reconciled by the controlling presence of the poet – a presence that determines, rather than in the metaphysical context responds to, the spatio-temporal circumstances of the utterance. The closed couplet operates as the fundamental unit in the realisation of this objective. It coordinates the relation between the codes within the text; and, consequently, stabilises the relation between the text and the speaking presence.

A vast number of critics have commented on the ordering function of the Augustan couplet. They generally agree on the workings of its structural and formal features and they also, generally by implication, offer further evidence of its functional and ideological status. Matthew Arnold classified Dryden and Pope as 'classics of our prose' and in Jakobson's terms it could indeed be argued that their use of the couplet foregrounds the syntagmatic/metonymic element of language at the expense of its paradigmatic/metaphoric counterpart. Donald Davie in *Articulate Energy* (1955) divided poetic syntax into five types (subjective, dramatic, objective, like music, like mathematics). The Augustan couplet is objective (for which we might substitute Benveniste's '*histoire*'): 'it follows a form of action, a movement not through any mind but in the world at large' (79). Its success in impeding the interference of the poet or the text in 'the world at large' is perhaps a means of imparting to the functional role of poetry the much broader eighteenth-century ideals and imperatives of 'order' in politics, society, architecture and philosophic thought. Laura Brown (1985): 'Pope's art is at once a mode of representation and an act of adjudication through which an elaborate and sophisticated linguistic structure, emulative of the imperial age of Roman culture, shapes a "world" where rhetoric, belief and morality perfectly intersect' (7; see also Easthope, 1983, Fussell, 1965 and Price, 1964). Hence, the closed couplet was the perfect vehicle for the so-called 'public poem' whose functional purpose was closely allied to that of the discursive prose essay. But what of those poems that sought to centralise the subjective and perhaps deviant relationship between the speaking presence, language and the world? In the later eighteenth century those writers often regarded as pre-Romantic (particularly Gray and Collins) favoured the complex and unpredictable interweavings of the double pattern in the stanza and the ode, and as we shall see the ode became the archetype of the Romantic interface between text and speaking presence. But a century earlier, John Milton had chosen to use poetry as a means of addressing not merely the verifiable patterns of the pre-linguistic world, but the unverifiable nature of our origins as the human species.

PARADISE LOST

Milton's *Paradise Lost* had an effect upon the compositional and interpretive conventions of the eighteenth century that is comparable with the effect of free verse upon our own. In the sixteenth century there had been a number of attempts, notably by Surrey, to establish blank verse as an acceptable medium for the non-dramatic poem, but by 1667 it was agreed, by general consensus, that its role was limited to drama. There are a number of reasons for this demarcation between formal and generic types, and these are most clearly summarised by Dryden in his *Essay of Dramatic Poesy*, published, with ironic timing, barely a year after Milton's poem. Correct blank verse observes the conventions of the iambic pentameter, but it does not rhyme, and, as Dryden and the vast majority of his contemporaries believed, rhyme was the only device by which accentual, rather than quantitative verse, could signal the presence of the double pattern. Dryden called blank verse *prose mesurée*, and he regarded the measuring of syntax into iambic, decasyllabic units as insufficient to guarantee, for the hearer, the definitive component of poetic discourse, the line. Milton, in his note on 'The Verse' of *Paradise Lost*, disagreed. He claimed that in his poem the 'sense' would be 'variously drawn out from one verse into another', and by establishing a flexible relation between the two elements of the double pattern, he also claimed – *contra* Dryden and practically everyone else – that the unrhymed pentameter possessed a sufficient degree of formal palpability to register as the point of regularity and stability against which syntactic movements could be counterpointed.

This summary is a gross simplication of the creative and interpretative problems that have attended Milton's revolutionary gesture. These problems resonate through the history of English poetry and its criticism, and a number remain unresolved. To consider what they are let us examine the formal unit that, far more powerfully than the stanza, was to present itself as the alternative to the eighteenth-century closed couplet.

> now conscience wakes despair
> That slumbered, wakes the bitter memory
> Of what he was, what is, and what must be
> Worse
>
> (IV, 23–6)

John Hollander (1975) has commented on how the double pattern is here thrown into a state of conflict. Line 25 appears to complete an echo of the prayer-book formula, 'what must be', yet the syntax moves on to connect this with an even more compelling existential state, 'Worse'. There are different ways of naturalising this effect.

We might assume that the poetic function (in this case the line ending) is foregrounded to create the effect of the gradual awakening of Satan to the true nature of his condition. The problem with this is that we know that it is Milton rather than his fictive creation who is speaking here. One solution to this conundrum would be that Milton is attempting to transpose his own first-person account with the projected speech patterns of his characters, and this brings us to an issue that has received little attention in analyses of the history of English blank verse. A great deal of work has gone into comparing and contrasting the metrical and syntactic structures of blank verse texts by Shakespeare, Milton, Wordsworth etc. (see for example Fowler's 'Three Blank Verse Textures', *The Languages of Literature*, 1971), but the crucial issue of how Milton and his successors dealt with adapting this form from the dramatic to the non-dramatic mode has been marginalised. In effect he altered the function of the contact mode and consequently threw the addresser–addressee relation into a state of uncertainty. With dramatic blank verse the physical presence of the speaker and the apparently contingent immediacy of the utterance would promote the contact mode to a level comparable with the poetic function. In short, the addresser–addressee relation would be split between exchanges within the text and between text and listener. *Paradise Lost* partakes of this model to the extent that the structure and narrative movement of the poem is comprised entirely of speaking presences. The most significant difference is that one of these is the author: it is almost as though Shakespeare were to appear on stage in order to comment, in blank verse, on the condition of his characters and advise the listener of the progress of the plot. The reason for this interpolation of the authorial voice is that non-dramatic texts would either be read aloud by a single performer or alone, and probably silently, by someone with a copy of the text. Milton operates as a kind of master of ceremonies, replacing the physical presences of actors and the contextual framework of the stage as a figure who coordinates the progress of the narrative. We know from the basic deictic features when Milton, Satan or Adam is speaking but this effect of individuality is compromised in three ways: first, each of these characters, including their creator, adheres to the same metrical and syntactic patterns that have come to be known as the Miltonic idiom. Second, the contact mode of the single voice, either silent or audible, increases the dominance of collective textuality over separate presences. Most significantly it is the structural function of blank verse that throws the addresser–text–addressee relation into a constant state of flux. Verse without rhyme might well satisfy the abstract criterion of the regular iambic pentameter, but when, as in *Paradise Lost*, this is supplemented by interlineal syntactic promiscuities, inversions, extended parentheses, delayed verbs, it becomes difficult to properly distinguish between verse design and verse instance.

It is this tension between the two elements of the double pattern that allows Hollander to identify an effect he calls 'closure and flow . . . the warp and weft of the verse fabric'. This, he argues, accounts for the polysemous nature of 'must be' and 'must be/ Worse'. It would be wrong, however, to regard the tension between verse design (the metrical structure of the line) and verse instance (the interlineal movements of syntax) simply as an addition to the signifying procedures of the more regular rhymed poems we have already encountered, because with *Paradise Lost* it could be argued that this element of the poetic function depends as much upon the disposition and interpretive faculties of the reader as it does upon the intrinsic structure of the text.

Christopher Ricks (1963) has commented on the following lines,

Thus saying, from her husband's hand her hand
Soft she withdrew.

(IX, 385–6)

Ricks points out that an initial reading of 'Soft' as an adverb 'softly'
or 'yielding' can be modified by the more straightforward literal,
adjectival usage of her 'soft hand'. This produces, 'a delicate fusion
of two points of view, since the adverb has the neutrality of an
onlooker, while the adjective puts us in the place of Adam as he
feels Eve's hand' (p. 90). This would be consistent with Milton's
double function both as 'onlooker' and creator of the events that
he observes, but we will find disturbingly similar effects discharged
by Eve's own speeches. Hollander considers her account to Adam
of her first experiences of existence.

and from that time I see
How beauty is excelled by manly grace.
(IV, 489–90)

She is comparing her narcissistic admiration of her own reflection
in the lake with her vision of Adam, and Hollander comments on
how 'the literal sense of "see" dissolves into a figurative one ("see
how" as "understand that") with a lingering hedging of her commitment' (98). Hollander has identified the same effect in Eve's speech
that Ricks uncovered in Milton's account of her physical actions.
Indeed Eve's entire speech in Book IV is sewn with uneasy tensions
between verse design and verse instance, each of which could be
naturalised as textual clues to her intrinsic unreliability (see Bradford, 1988).

Let us now pause to consider how we have reached these conclusions. First of all we might wonder how it is that we and Hollander can discern a degree of unreliability in Eve's discourse while
this does not become apparent to the person to which this is originally, and orally, addressed, i.e. Adam. We could resolve this
problem by recognising that the characters of the poem are essentially functions of its overall textual–poetic function. The formal
similarities between Milton's and his character's foregroundings of
the design–instance tension grants the reader a command of the text
that is denied to its spoken inhabitants. From this we might assume
that the exchanges that take place within the text (such as those
between Adam and Eve) give greater register to verse instance (the
more transparent interlineal pattern) while the exchange between
text and reader allows us to consider the full signifying potential of

design in conflict with instance. To clarify this distinction between two separate addresser–addressee relationships we should note that as readers we have more opportunity to pause and reread each exchange than would its participants, whose awareness of meaning is limited to a single vocal utterance. John Hollander offers an intriguing formula for this distinction by suggesting that seeing and hearing poems are separate engagements analogous to the Saussurian division of language into a differential system (*langue*) and specific speech events (*parole*).

> It is on the second of these axes that I would pose the ear, the individual talent, the voice, the *parole*; on the first are ranged the eye, the tradition, the mask through which the voice sounds, and the *langue*. The ear responds to the dimension of natural experience, the eye to that of convention (248).

The binary opposition offered by Hollander relates to Jakobson's distinction between the selective–paradigmatic (*langue*, eye, tradition, mask) and the combinative–syntagmatic (*parole*, ear, individual, voice) axes. This would account for Hollander's and Ricks's balancing of the arbitrary double pattern against the transparent register of meaning. What Hollander, Ricks and we ourselves encounter is a productive conflict between syntagmatic progress ('must be worse', 'hand soft', 'see how') and what Jakobson calls the projection of the axis of selection into the axis of combination: our awareness of design (line ending) in conflict with instance (syntactic movement) does indeed transform, in Hollander's terms, the literal (syntagmatic) into the figurative (paradigmatic).

In short, we have encountered in Milton's poem a far more problematic and innovative relation between the text and the voice(s) within the text than occurs in the poems of Donne, Herbert, Marvell and Pope. Why did Milton do this? It could be argued that in a poem which seeks to address the origins and conditions of humanity he deliberately created a tension between language as granting a transparent access to fact and truth (which seems to occur within the exchanges of the text) and language, in this case poetic language, as capable of creating multi-levels of uncertainty, indecision and ever-increasing distance as a reminder of the primary communicative condition of our fallen state.

By establishing a precedent in which the two elements of the double pattern become unstable Milton set in motion a sub tradition of anti-formalism that would eventually manifest itself in the modernist programme of free verse. We shall return to this issue in our discussion of the Romantics and the modernists, but it is important to note that Milton's flexible deployment of the double pattern caused a debate in the eighteenth century that preempts the more recent controversies over whether certain textual effects are intrinsic to the structure of language or whether they are signals that will activate the reader's interpretive resources (see Chapter 1, pp. 13–17). Samuel Johnson's much quoted judgement of *Paradise Lost* as 'verse only to the eye' (see Bradford, 1988) is a straightforward anticipation of Stanley Fish's reader-centred model of interpretation:

> I appropriate the 'line ending' and treat it as a fact of nature [but] what is noticed is what has been made noticeable, not by a clear and undistorting glass, but by an interpretive strategy.
>
> (1980, 165–6)

Both critics base their claims upon an assumed distinction between sign and substance. In Johnson's view the line on the page should be a visual sign of intrinsic poetic structures (rhyme, syntactic and metrical closure) and when these are absent only the signal will remain. Fish takes up this point and claims that a good deal of what we call interpreting poetic structure is in fact the imposition of interpretive strategies upon a network of textual signals that in themselves possess no intrinsic meaning. Their case could be justified by citing the above sequences from *Paradise Lost* as examples of the reader's choice either to interpret the tension between verse design and instance or give primary emphasis to the verse instance.

Johnson's judgement represents an economic summary of a debate that had lasted a century. Some eighteenth-century critics suggested that the unrhymed pentameter was a meaningless concession to printing habit and that *Paradise Lost*, and by implication other unrhymed poems, should be printed as free verse. Others argued that conventions of writing should be developed to accommodate and effectively diffuse the tension between interlineal syntactic progress and the iambic pentameter (see Bradford, 1992). As will be shown in the following section the latter, at least for the poet, won the case.

BLANK VERSE IN THE EIGHTEENTH CENTURY

Within two decades of the publication of Milton's poem blank verse had become fully established as a vehicle for the non-dramatic poem. Although Johnson and a number of other critics remarked upon Milton's success in creating a particular idiom, a syntactic signature, with which his successors would have to engage, it must also be accepted that in the century following his epic its most challenging and perplexing formal innovations were effectively neutralised. Blank verse was brought into line with the rules and conventions that governed its more widely used counterpart, the closed heroic couplet. Edward Young's *Night Thoughts* (1742–6) is the best known and probably the most extreme case of prescriptive cross-fertilisation. His technique has been described as the use of the 'unrhymed couplet'. Young used the individual pentameter as a unit of cohesion in a very similar way to Pope's use of the couplet. As a replacement for the binding mechanism of rhyme he cautiously deployed the syntagm as a progressive movement whose breaks would be synchronised with the closure of each metrical unit. Blank verse of this type was the exception rather than the rule, and far more intriguing are the methods developed by men such as Thomson, Cowper and Akenside to make use of the more flexible Miltonic pattern yet control its effects upon the reader. The vast majority of eighteenth-century blank verse was of the descriptive, georgic type with a single, third person presence controlling the structure of the text. Consequently its practitioners faced the problem of how to create the effect of a relatively unconfined, discursive movement along the syntagmatic chain which would not, in the Miltonic manner, create tensions and conflicts with the metrical–syntactic formula of the pentameter. The following lines are from Thomson's *Summer*.

> The dripping Rock, the Mountain's misty Top
> Swell on the Sight, and brighten with the Dawn
> Blue thro' the Dusk, the smoking Currents shine;
> And from the bladed Field the fearful Hare
> Limps, awkward: while along the Forest-glade
> The wild Deer trip, and often turning gaze
> At early Passenger. Musick awakes,
> The native voice of undissembled joy;
> And thick around the woodland hymns arise.
> Roused by the cock, the soon-clad shepherd leaves
> His mossy cottage, where with Peace he dwells;
> And from the crowded Fold, in order drives
> His flock to taste the Verdure of the Morn.

(54–66)

The most significant formal effect in this passage is Thomson's use of the two elements of the double pattern, syntax and the pentameter, to create the effect of the addresser gradually responding to the patterns of movement that take place in the perceived images. Up to lines 59–60 the more active and purposive components of the syntactic chain – 'Swell', 'Blue', 'Limps' – are placed in positions of stress-reversal at the beginning of lines. Unlike Milton, he is cautious to effectively diffuse any uncertainty that might be caused by these syntactic–metrical conflicts. The effect is that of stasis: the mountain, the field and the hare are presented as self-contained, apparently discrete representations – the verbal and adjectival clauses that qualify their existence seem secondary to the images themselves. In the second half of the passage it is the verb itself that the syntactic–metrical structure throws into the foreground in its placing before the line ending (60–1, 63–4, 65–6). The effect of this redisposition of the verse instance in relation to verse design is the achievement of a kind of formal mimesis: in the first section the placing of the object within one metrical unit and its colour or action in the following one suggests that, for the perceiver, language supplements and clarifies the initial register of impressions, but in the second the placing of mainly active verbs at the interfaces between metrical unit and syntax creates the impression that the poetic function of the language has become synchronised with the physical movements of, and relations between, the objects perceived. But it is important to note that, unlike the apparently similar Miltonic disposition of 'must be/Worse', Thomson's verse form cautiously avoids causing any real sense of disjunction between the two elements of the double pattern. The syntax of the passage is carefully sown with preemptive clues, warnings even, of what will follow the termination of each metrical unit: it is not surprising that the '*fearful* Hare/Limps', that the '*soon clad* shepherd leaves/His mossy cottage' or that from the '*crowded Fold*' he 'drives/His flock'. It could be claimed that Thomson has adapted the progressive theme–rheme principle of the closed couplet to the less stable relation between the progressive movement of syntax and the unrhymed pentameter. To return to Jakobson's formulaic definition of verse as projecting the axis of selection onto the axis of combination we find that Thomson has succeeded in maintaining the parallelism of verse design, the pentameter, while minimalising its effect upon the orderly, one might claim prosaic, relation between the selective and combinative axes. It is the consecutive relation between elements of the syntagmatic chain that governs the interplay between verse design and verse instance, unlike Milton's use of the design–instance conflict which allows the paradigmatic–selective axis to create disruptions along the syntagmatic chain.

There are a number of reasons for these cautious reworkings of Miltonic technique. Most importantly, the eighteenth century was the first period in literary history in which texts could be judged against an accepted grammar of the double pattern, and the most significant rule of this insisted on the maintenance of a stable balance between verse design and verse instance. The following is from the work of a mid-eighteenth-century elocutionist, John Rice, and his prescriptions can be regarded as the shared axiom of contemporary critics and poets.

> In reading poetry, if the Numbers interfere with the Harmony of the Period, there is a Defect in the Composition: For though the Harmony of Prosaic Periods is different, or will admit a greater Latitude and Variety than those of Poetry; yet the Laws of Diction require that the Sense and Meaning of the Writer should be consistent with both.
>
> (1765, 17)

To best understand the Augustan programme in terms of the modern methodology of literary linguistics we should consider Jakobson's (1971, 133–4) summation of the work of Benveniste and Todorov on the spatio-temporal relations between addresser and addressee. Jakobson divides this interactive process into four constituent elements: the speech event (enunciation); the event narrated (the enounced); the subject of the enunciation (the speaking presence); the subject of the enounced (the listener/reader either within or outside the text). What the Augustans effectively ruled against was the interference of the text in the interplay between these four elements. The principal difference between Milton's and Thomson's use of blank verse is that the latter maintains the reader's awareness of the double pattern – his ingenious use of 'grammatrics' to adjust the relation between the enounced and the subject of the enunciation productively foregrounds its presence – while encouraging an effect of closure between speech event, speaker, event and listener. Milton uses the double pattern to cause deliberate and perplexing disruptions between all four elements of the communicative circuit.

The most important point to emphasise here is the effect upon these two techniques upon the subject of the enounced; us, the readers. The shifting of balance away from the intervention of the text in the communicative circuit, both in eighteenth-century blank verse and the closed couplet, places the reader in a far more passive, receptive role than was the case with the textual foregroundings of Milton and the metaphysicals – and one significant point which we will return to with free verse is Hollander's suggestion that in Milton's verse there is a disjunction between the interpretive faculties of eye and ear, with the consequent obligation that the reader will effectively mediate between text and meaning. But for the moment let us consider how this reader–text relation functions in our encounters with the rhymed couplet.

RHYME, THE SUPERREADER AND THE SUPERPOEM

Dryden's notion of rhyme as the only audible record of the existence of the English line is subtly elaborated in his admission that this new technique includes effects entirely absent from its classical predecessors: 'in the help it brings to memory, which rhyme so knits up, by the affinity of sounds, that, by remembering the last word of one line we often call to mind both verses' (1663, 7). His economic diagnosis is significant for three reasons. First, he argues that this crucial element of English verse form is capable of producing an extra-syntactic pattern of meaning. In doing so he anticipates an entire tradition of modern analysis, beginning with Lanz and reemerging in Jakobson, Wimsatt, Wesling, and countless other close readers and literary linguists. Second, he is the only Restoration/eighteenth-century commentator to acknowledge that a coincidence of sound can have a productive signifying function. Third he presents us with a further clue to why the couplet proved to be the most popular medium in a period so committed to the ideals of clarity and transparency: the 'knitting up' of two consecutive syntactic patterns would be far easier to control and negotiate than would the more complex networks of progress and interference in the stanzaic formula. These three, potentially paradoxical, points hold the key to our understanding of rhyme as the most problematic test case for how different readers and analysts have responded to the effect of the double pattern.

We will start with the peculiar distinction between the modern perspective and the apparently unimaginative readings of our eighteenth-century predecessors. We have already considered Wimsatt's seminal essay on 'One Relation of Rhyme to Reason' (1944) and we should note that it anticipates Jakobson's more widely celebrated formula for the poetic function. Wimsatt gives emphasis to rhyme as the 'wedding of the alogical with the logical'; 'the arrest and precipitation of the logical in sensory form'; and the 'ikon in which the idea is caught' (p. 163). For alogical and sensory we might substitute the paradigmatic–metaphoric axis. Here connections can be made between elements of language that, in the logic of the non-poetic text or the syntagmatic chain, have no rational corresponding function. And with the 'arrest and precipitation of the logical in sensory form' we might recall the, 'projection of the principle of equivalence from the axis of selection into the axis of combination'. The most problematic correspondence between the two critics occurs in, 'the phonic equivalence of rhyming words prompts the question of semantic similarity or contrast' (Jakobson) and 'the ikon in which the idea is caught' (Wimsatt). Neither of them fully addresses the following questions: can we assume that every instance of rhyme will produce a correspondent doubling of the signifying function of language? If so, how will this continuous doubling of semantic interfaces be naturalised by the reader?

Wimsatt, dealing with the Popian couplet, claims that its tight syntactic formula allows rhyme to give emphasis to relations between words in a close or extended semantic range or at parallel or dissimilar parts of speech. The following are from *The Rape of the Lock*:

> One speaks the glory of the British Queen
> And one describes a charming Indian Screen
>
>   . . .
>
> Do thou Crispissa tend her fav'rite Lock
> Ariel himself shall be the guard of Shock

From 'British Queen' to 'Indian Screen' from 'Lock' to 'Shock', here is the same bathos he more often puts into one line – 'when husbands, or when lapdogs breathe their last'.

(1944, 162)

Again we find that Jakobson's formula is closely anticipated. In each instance the reader's expectation of what will follow the main verb in the syntagmatic chain is disrupted by the poet's unusual deployment of the paradigmatic axis, and rhyme foregrounds this process. Wimsatt acknowledges that in most couplets this conflict between the combinative and selective axes will not occur, but he does not explain how the reader would respond to the use of rhyme as a signal to less disruptive uses of language. The problem raised by such intensive analyses is of whether the reader should maintain such a degree of attention to interfaces within the double pattern throughout a single reading of the poem. This issue was addressed in what has become one of the most widely discussed disagreements in literary linguistics. Jakobson collaborated with Claude Lévi-Strauss in a description and explication of Baudelaire's sonnet 'Les Chats', and Michael Riffaterre in his essay 'Describing Poetic Structures: Two Approaches to Baudelaire's "Les Chats" ' (1966) challenged the fundamental assumptions upon which such, by then familiar, interpretations were grounded. Riffaterre's case is as follows: he acknowledged that Jakobson's and Lévi-Strauss's approach (see above pp. 12–13 for Jakobson's similar treatment of a Shakespeare sonnet) was precise and correct and that they had successfully identified the grammar of poetic language, but he claimed that their structural model was an entirely inaccurate account of the reader's experience. He argued that by giving roughly equal attention to how each conventional element of the double pattern, primarily metrical structure and rhyme, interacted with its counterpart in syntax, grammatical deviation or metaphoric play, they had created what he termed a 'superpoem', which exists but which bears no resemblance to the real experience of reading it. In short, he insisted that although textual foregroundings could be identified in practically any part of a poem only a small number of these will register as functions of the reader's understanding of what the poem means. He answered Jakobson's creation of the superpoem with his own invention of the 'superreader'. This individual would stand outside the addresser–addressee relation of the communicative circuit and by various means select and emphasise particular elements of the poetic function. This process of selection would be governed by the superreader's awareness of how contact and context relate to the intrinsic structure of the poem. Riffaterre shifted the emphasis away from the reader/addressee as a functional participant in the communicative circuit toward a more powerful individual who could actually determine the relations between the intrinsic and contextual elements of Jakobson's two models of communication. And we might here recall the decision taken by most readers to naturalise Eve's textual patterns as evidence of their speaker's unreliability. This is due as much to our broader contextual awareness of scripture – Eve eats the fruit first and is consequently regarded as more culpable than Adam – as it is to our response to the intrinsic features of the text.

The relation between modern and eighteenth-century perceptions of rhyme provides us with an intriguing test case for Riffaterre's notion of the uncertain balance between the reader's competence and the textual features of verse.

Wimsatt in a later essay on Pope posed the question of why an ethos so dedicated to order and transparency was so addicted to the use of 'so barbarous and Gothic a device as rhyme'? Translated into the terms and methodology of post-Saussurian linguistics, why is it that a discourse such as the Augustan couplet, committed to the preservation of clarity and transparency and the disclosure of the signified, should depend upon a device that foregrounds the random correspondences within the materiality of language, its signifiers? Wimsatt left the question unanswered, but I shall propose a solution.

With the single exception of Dryden, Restoration and eighteenth-century critics regarded rhyme as a metrical necessity which should not contribute the signifying properties of the poem (see Bradford, 1992, Chapter 6). William Cockin (1775) clarifies this collective opinion. Rhymes, he argues, 'as they are interruptedly perceived, appear accidental blemishes of a different style, arising from an unmeaning recurrence of similar sounds' (139). Joseph Priestley (1777) acknowledges the attraction of 'imagining' a correspondence between sound and sense: 'But since this is wholly the work of the reader's imagination a writer doth not need to give himself trouble about it' (292). Priestley cautions the poet against creating an effect of 'double attention' (far more manifest in rhymed than in unrhymed verse) which would cause 'the mind to be drawn off from an attention to the subject' (268).

One is struck by the precise polarisation between eighteenth- and twentieth-century views. Edward Stankiewicz (1961) regards the 'different style' and its maintenance of a 'double attention' as anything but 'unmeaning'.

> Successful rhyme is illogical and canny, striking and familiar, prominent and subsumed; it provides the condensed formula of poetic language; identity and variation, obligatariness and freedom, sound and meaning, unity and plurality, texture and structure (16).

If we accept that our response to a *parole* is determined and conditioned by our awareness and command of its *langue*, then we must also concede that Stankiewicz's, Jakobson's and Wimsatt's notion of a poetic grammar was far more complex and flexible than it would have been two centuries earlier. In short it is possible that the extension of a particular *langue* is capable of transforming the signifying properties of a *parole* that had been created at an earlier stage in its development, and the twentieth-century superreaders had witnessed textual foregroundings by Romantic and modernist poets that would not have been permitted in the eighteenth century. But as well as our experience of a far more complex *langue* of precedents and divergences, our difference from the eighteenth-century reader manifests itself in one other crucial way. From the sixteenth century to the present day the ideal of the poem as a speech act has, both for critics and poets, held prominence over its status as a static, written, text; but in practice, more specifically in critical practice, reading as attendant upon the spatial, graphic dimensions of the text has superseded performance. This was Riffaterre's point. Jakobson and Lévi-Strauss could give attention to each minute instance of conflict within the double pattern because they had a commanding perspective upon the printed text, a perspective that would be lost to the hearer of an individual performance. For the eighteenth-century reader meanings generated outside the communicative circuit of the speech act were invalid. They were in Cockin's terms 'interruptedly perceived' – in a modern context the Wimsatt/Jakobson readings of rhyme would only become apparent if we stopped the film to analyse the stills. For Cockin, Priestley and their contemporaries, meaning could only be generated in relation to the register of a single performance of the text. Again we come upon reasons for the promotion of the closed couplet above the stanzaic form in this period: the signifying mechanism of the couplet poem is progressive and accumulative; it imparts to the double pattern the element of cohesion of the non-poetic single pattern of syntax. It marginalises the complex effects of progress, interruption, delay and return of the stanzaic form, and it consequently comes closer to bypassing the refractory functions of textuality and unites the addressee/listener with the addresser/speaker.

The speech–writing relationship has over the past two decades functioned as the centre-point for a phenomenon that is variously termed post-Saussurian linguistics, poststructuralism and deconstruction (see Culler, 1982, 88–110 for a fuller explanation), but what has not been considered in any detail are the implications of the reexamination of this relationship for our conventional perceptions of what poetry is and of how it can be interpreted. Derrida was responsible for arguably the most significant developments of post-Saussurian linguistics in his uncovering of the contradictions and paradoxes that underpin Saussure's contention that 'the object of linguistic analysis is not defined by the combination of the written word and the spoken word: the spoken word alone constitutes the object' (1959, 23–4). Derrida, particularly in *Positions* and *Of Grammatology*, sought to show that the accepted opposition between speech and writing is in fact a sub-element of a more powerful condition of representation that he called *archi-écriture* or 'archi-writing'. I do not have the space to examine fully Derrida's methods and their consequences, but it is clear that poetry operates as a test-case for the validity of the concept of archi-writing.

Jakobson's second diagram of the communicative circuit shares with all other abstract definitions of the poem and the poem's effects the Saussurian precondition that 'the spoken word alone constitutes the object'. This seems logical enough since the poetic function involves, in various ways, the foregrounding of the phonic signifier in metre, rhyme, line endings, etc. Riffaterre's challenge implied but did not consider fully the curious dependence of the conventional element of the double pattern upon a system of referrals and differences that is more closely associated with writing. Ingarden's concept of the poetic function as something that 'fools' the reader should be recalled here since it would defy plausibility to claim that the complex interweavings of the system of poetic conventions (the iambic pentameter and the rhyme scheme of the sonnet for example) and the situation of the utterance, the speech act, could come into being at a single moment in response to a particular event, image, memory, or emotional challenge. The fact that is generally accepted but which remains absent from the practices of naturalising poetry is that the complex sound patterns of verse effectively invalidate the ideal of the poem as an aesthetic realisation of words issuing from the speaker as the spontaneous and nearly transparent signs of his present thought.

The problem for the superreader – who we can now safely identify as a combination of twentieth-century reader and critic, in short 'us' – is that we face a paradoxical relationship between the protocols of naturalising poetry and the idealised and still very powerful precondition that poems are speech acts. Hollander's notion of a conflict between the receptive faculties of eye and ear is grounded upon a distinction between the written and the spoken text: 'the ear responds to the dimension of natural experience, the eye to that of convention'. A reading based on a combination of these two perspectives corresponds closely with Riffaterre's concepts of superreader and superpoem. The complex formal totality of the superpoem only becomes apparent to a reader who is able to consult a copy of the printed text. The ability of readers such as Ricks and

Hollander to mediate between the dimension of natural experience (speech, verse instance, transparency) and convention (writing, verse design, textual refraction) is a function of their command of the printed text and their consequent freedom to stand outside the consecutive, vocal register of effects. This model of close-reading is the practical manifestation of a much more complex system of archi-writing. To understand this we should return to Jakobson's two diagrams of the communicative circuit.

Diagram 2 is clearly predicated upon the ideal of the poem as a speech act, while diagram 1 indicates the process through which we recognise the circumstances in which a particular speech act takes place (contact) and its linguistic type or genre (code). These two models betray respective allegiances to speech and writing. But by 'writing' I do not simply refer to the silent, black and white graphics of the text in question. Writing, as Derrida argues and Hollander confirms, is a function of our mental and interpretive *langue*. To explain: when we encounter any linguistic event, spoken or written, we carry with us a complex framework of linguistic, cultural, political, social and situational expectations. For instance we already know about the ideological-gendered paradigm of 'Eve' before we encounter her speech acts in *Paradise Lost*, and it is clear that eighteenth- and twentieth-century critics are, in different ways, conditioned in their expectation of what rhyme should do before they encounter its actual use. So, although we might be able to decode the grammatical–semantic features of a speech act at the moment of utterance or performance, we also fit this apparently instinctive process of explication into a much broader, spatial, framework of predetermined paradigms. The acoustic speech act is ratified and contextualised in its relation to the spatial collage of other texts, stylistic precedents and interpretive expectations that constitute our mental dictionary or index. In short the spoken is in constant tension with the written. As we move further through the development of the English poetic *langue* we will find that this tension between the internal features of the text (spoken) and its broader contextual and situational relations (written) increases.

The only constant feature in this shifting relationship between text, response and interpretation is the presence of the double pattern. The objective of most eighteenth-century critics and poets was to stabilise the relationship between its cognitive and conventional dimensions. This would minimalise the reader's awareness of any potential for division between two separate compositional and interpretive codes and consequently create the impression of a single enunciative act. As such the eighteenth century remains as an aberration in the history of poetic form from the sixteenth to the twentieth century. I will substantiate this claim in three closing points.

1　The metaphysical poets created a continuous disjunction between the poem as speech and its function as a contrived synthesis of devices and effects. The reader is consequently obliged to shift uneasily between Jakobson's two diagrams.

2　The Romantics, as we shall see, reinterpreted the Augustan ideal of poetic transparency but at the same time introduced an even more complex tension between text and context, speech act and artifice, diagram 1 and diagram 2.

3　Milton set the precedent for an uncertain relation between the two elements of the double pattern, verse design and verse instance, writing and speech, text and presence. The Augustans effectively marginalised this threat but it would be drawn upon both by the Romantics and, more significantly, by the modernists.

To summarise, the Augustans represent the single generic/historic school of poets and critics who attempt to marginalise the disruptive function of the double pattern. They sought to situate poetry as a stable annex to the agreed author–text–reader relationship of the particular speech act to and the similarly agreed functional purpose of the prose essay.

Exercises

THE COUPLET

We have seen how in Pope's verse the couplet operates at two levels: it organises and often controls syntax at a localised level – as a kind of mini-stanza – and it determines the broader relationships between theme, narrative and perspective throughout the text. Consider how this relationship works in the three pieces quoted below. Use the following interpretive agenda:

(i)　Consider the relationship between the speaker and the subject. Clearly Dryden's piece engages with a pattern of mock-heroic doubling similar to Pope's *The Rape of the Lock* (Flecknoe and Shadwell, his poetic contemporaries, are transposed with the circumstances of imperial Rome). Swift's short piece is more firmly anchored to the situational deictics of a particular street and its inhabitants, while the extract from Johnson focuses upon general and universal themes and conditions.

(ii)   Consider how each poet's use of the couplet creates a close structural correspondence between the three texts, whose referential and functional purposes are quite different. For example, Johnson invokes few particular locative references or cultural/social codes. Compare the way in which his couplets organise this hypothetical, generalised continuum with Swift's use of the form to document a particular spatio-temporal situation and Dryden's use of it as an axis between the two levels of mock-heroic reference.

(iii)   Re-read the above section on Wimsatt, Jakobson, Riffaterre and the use of rhyme (pp. 85–91), and consider how the internal structure of each couplet (metre, syntax and rhyme) either interferes with or effectively determines textual progression. In short, how does each poet reconcile the potential for tension between the enclosed poetic sphere (semantic interfaces between rhyme words for example) and the discursive, referential pattern of the text?

Lines 1–20 of Dryden's *MacFlecknoe*

All human things are subject to decay,
And when fate summons, monarchs must obey.
This Flecknoe found, who, like Augustus, young
Was called to empire, and had governed long;
In prose and verse, was owned, without dispute,
Through all the realms of *Nonsense*, absolute.
This agèd prince, now flourishing in peace,
And blest with issue of a large increase;
Worn out with business, did at length debate
To settle the succession of the state;
And, pondering which of all his sons was fit
To reign, and wage immortal war with wit,
Cried: ''Tis resolved; for nature pleads, that he
Should only rule, who most resembles me.
Sh—— alone my perfect image bears,
Mature in dulness from his tender years:
Sh—— alone, of all my sons, is he
Who stands confirmed in full stupidity.
The rest to some faint meaning make pretence,
But Sh—— never deviates into sense.

Swift's 'A Description of the Morning'

> Now hardly here and there a hackney-coach
> Appearing, showed the ruddy morn's approach.
> Now Betty from her master's bed had flown,
> And softly stole to discompose her own;
> The slip-shod 'prentice from his master's door
> Had pared the dirt and sprinkled round the floor.
> Now Moll had whirled her mop with dext'rous airs,
> Prepared to scrub the entry and the stairs.
> The youth with broomy stumps began to trace
> The kennel-edge, where wheels had worn the place.
> The small-coal man was heard with cadence deep,
> Till drowned in shriller notes of chimney-sweep:
> Duns at his lordship's gate began to meet;
> And brickdust Moll had screamed through half the street.
> The turnkey now his flock returning sees,
> Duly let our a-nights to steal for fees:
> The watchful bailiffs take their silent stands,
> And schoolboys lag with satchels in their hands.

Lines 1–20 of Johnson's *The Vanity of Human Wishes*

> Let observation with extensive view,
> Survey mankind, from China to Peru;
> Remark each anxious toil, each eager strife,
> And watch the busy scenes of crowded life;
> Then say how hope and fear, desire and hate,
> O'erspread with snares the clouded maze of fate,
> Where wavering man, betrayed by venturous pride,
> To tread the dreary paths without a guide,
> As treacherous phantoms in the mist delude,
> Shuns fancied ills, or chases airy good;
> How rarely reason guides the stubborn choice,
> Rules the bold hand, or prompts the suppliant voice;
> How nations sink, by darling schemes oppressed,
> When vengeance listens to the fool's request.
> Fate wings with every wish the afflictive dart,
> Each gift of nature, and each grace of art,
> With fatal heat impetuous courage glows,
> With fatal sweetness elocution flows,
> Impeachment stops the speaker's powerful breath,
> And restless fire precipitates on death.

BLANK VERSE

Blank verse, and more specifically Milton's use of the form, represents an important test case for our methods of dealing with the relation between poetic and non-poetic language. It does so by unsettling any clear distinction between the two elements of the double pattern, the line and syntax. Read the following short extracts from *Paradise Lost*:

> I thither went
> With unexperienced thought, and laid me down
> On the green bank, to look into the clear
> Smooth lake, that to me seemed another sky.

> (IV, 456–9)

> for so
> I formed them free, and free they must remain,
> Till they enthrall themselves: I else must change
> Their nature

> (III, 123–6)

Consider these questions:

(i) Speaker and text. The two speakers are, respectively, Eve and God. Eve seems to hesitate ('The clear' was a widely used substantive form in the 17th century – like 'the sky' or 'the moonlight'). Is her uncertain negotiation of language's substantive and adjectival forms evidence of her intrinsic unreliability? If so could not the same be said of God's apparent hesitation between 'I else must change' (my mind? my plan?) and 'Their' (Adam and Eve's) 'nature'?

(ii) Speaker and context. We know from the extra-textual context (the Bible) that God should not be regarded, like Eve, as unreliable. How do we resolve this conundrum?

(iii) If we read both passages as prose (forget the line ending and the pentameter) then the uncertainties and hesitations seem to disappear. Should we allow context to interfere with text and read Eve's passage as verse and God's as prose?

(iv) Discourse and meaning. The enclosed tension between line and syntax seems to have transformed itself into a far more complex relation between poetry and prose, text and context. If we choose to ignore textual effects in one case and attend to them in the other do we implicitly acknowledge that the relation between poetry and the real world is more unreliable than with its non-poetic counterpart? Could a similar disjunction between our perception of who the characters are and what they say occur in an impartial prose account or in unversified speech acts?

(v) Poetry and criticism. With the above problems in mind re-read Culler's judgement of how we impose meanings upon refractory poetic effects (pp. 13–17) and consider how similarly uncertain relationships between speaker, text and context can be created in modernist free verse (see Chapter 6, pp. 155–7).

4 Romanticism

The Romantic poets present us with a series of problems that demand the cooperation of literary scholarship and linguistic analysis. W. H. Auden, writing as a somewhat sceptical heir to the legacies of Romanticism and modernism, summarised our difficulties. 'Poetry' he wrote, in memory of Yeats, 'makes nothing happen'. What he meant is that, unlike most other forms of linguistic representation or interpersonal exchange, the poem is confined within the vacuum of its own self-determined formal conditions. It can issue orders, promote one particular moral or ethical position above others, or enable its perpetrator to complain about his own existential condition or that which he shares with the rest of humanity, but it forbids itself from entering the same functional circuit of personal, social or political exchange as the letter, the philosophical thesis or the manifesto for the envisaged rights of man. The problem, from which no poet or reader is immune, is of how to balance the paraphrasable, functional message of the text with its specificity as literary discourse, its self-conscious deployment of linguistic properties and conventions which create patterns of signification that poems do not share with non-poetic discourses. Poetry is never immune from the uncertain relation between textual and extra-textual context, but in the period occupied by the Romantics we encounter a particularly difficult interrelation between functional purpose, aesthetics and poetic form.

It could be argued that Romanticism, at least in its somewhat confined designation as a change in the history of English poetry, was a response to an unprecedented pattern of intellectual, social and political developments. The effects of the Enlightenment were felt in the theoretical underpinnings of both the French and the American revolutions. Writers such as Voltaire, Rousseau, Diderot, Paine and Godwin had begun to challenge and threaten the distinction between the literary and political–social functions of writing in ways that went far beyond the Augustan, neo-classical precondition that the text should be grounded upon the empiricism of what is established, precedented and verifiable. Late-eighteenth-century Britain, a country already shaken by war and anarchic economic cycles, was beginning to experience the social unrest that had overthrown the French social order and, in the United States, established a new one. On top of this was what we now refer to as the industrial revolution: individual social functions and instincts were becoming marginalised by a more powerful system of urbanisation, rural dispossession and labour-intensive means of production. The English government under which Blake, Coleridge and Wordsworth lived was engaged either in continental warfare – mostly with the French – or in suppressing internal dissent (see Woodring, 1970).

What, you might enquire, has all this to do with the arcane, internalised world of poetic form and language? Auden might well be correct in his assertion that poetry cannot make anything happen, but he also infers that it is the only medium in which the uneasy relationship between our register of events and our primary means of mediating them can be properly tested and reexamined. Poetry of any type or generic designation will always address its own means of signification: it will be about things, impressions, experiences, events, but it will never fully detach the paraphraseable ideational process of communication from the self-referential interplay between medium and message, form and content. Crucial to this continuous and unremitting interplay is the poem's adherence to the double pattern, its simultaneous engagement with and detachment from the rules and conventions of other linguistic discourses. The question we have to address is of how a period known as the age of revolution can be regarded as influential in a series of more internalised individual revolutions in the progress of English poetry.

LYRICAL BALLADS: POEMS AS PICTURES

Wordsworth, in the preface to *Lyrical Ballads*, made it clear that his intention was to realise, in poetry, the 'real language of men', 'the spontaneous overflow of powerful feeling'. In short, he wanted poetry to operate as the immediate, subjective and emotional counterpart to the conventions of speech. While the Augustans sought to bring poetry closer to the designated and orderly functions of prose, Wordsworth valorised the spontaneous contingencies of the vocal utterance. How did he institute what was in effect the next stage in the uneasy relationship between poetry and the 'real' world of experience and communication?

In most of the *Lyrical Ballads* he achieved what is, for some (particularly Coleridge), a socio-cultural confidence trick. Many of the speaking presences of the ballads will often be (from our retrospective viewpoint) the illiterate, uncultured denizens of the blighted rural landscape of late-eighteenth-century England. Wordsworth, however, presented them as possessed of an intrinsic wisdom, uncomplicated and undiminished by the intellectual constraints of the educated city dweller, and the poems that caused the most controversy among the early reviewers of the collection (see Jordan, 1976, 107) were those which situated the utterance and the speaker as functions of the uncultured events and circumstances of rural existence – the best-known and most discussed being 'The Idiot Boy', 'The Thorn', 'The Mad Mother' and 'Simon Lee'. To have presented these rural figures as speaking within or as the subjects of the established conventions of poetry – such as the iambic pentameter in its couplet form or in its unrhymed, Miltonic version – would have caused an uneasy and potentially derisory tension between code and context. The conventions of poetic discourse were by 1798 locked into a pattern of socio-cultural expectations – Gray's much admired ploughman, the 'mute, inglorious Milton' would have become a farcical and incongruous figure had he addressed the poet in the still respected and much imitated diction and metre of the Master. Nor could Wordsworth replicate the actual speech patterns of such figures and expect them to be interpreted as poems. What he did was to choose a form, the ballad, whose intrinsic features qualified it for the category of the 'poetic' yet whose invocation of familiar lexical, contextual and cultural codes associated it with popular culture. Robert Mayo's seminal piece on 'The Contemporaneity of the *Lyrical Ballads*' (1954) should here be consulted. Mayo's article is as important for linguistic critics as it is for literary scholars because he shifts our attention away from the intrinsic stylistic or linguistic properties of the texts towards their relation with a broader network of socio-cultural sign systems. The late-eighteenth-century publications such as the *Monthly Magazine*, the *European Magazine* and the *Gentleman's Magazine* regularly included versified short stories which gave unashamed prominence to the bizarre and ghoulishly attractive experiences of the 'ordinary man', particularly of the rural type. Their use of the ballad form provided a further link with the contact code of an oral tradition perpetuated by tales told in markets and in the drinking establishments of the unlettered. There is no intrinsic correspondence between the subject matter of the stories by unmarried mothers, murderers, village idiots or disabled farmhands and their medium, but Wordsworth was aware that by offering his ballads as 'serious' poetic reflections on the nature of existence he would cause a disturbance in the established cultural expectations of how form designates content. What we shall now do is to examine Wordsworth's intention in creating such tensions and consider whether the methods of literary linguistics can assist us in our enterprise.

We will start with 'The Idiot Boy'. The deictic features of the text are reasonably informative. Betty, Susan, the boy Johnny, and the doctor are the principal participants in the narrative and its rural setting is designated by regular references to there being 'not a house within a mile', 'the wood', 'the woodman', 'the lane', 'the vale'. The third person speaker narrows the gap between the tale's status as an imagined or even second-hand account and its sense of immediacy by placing the discourse in the present tense and interposing his/her apparent presence within the narrative – "Tis eight o'clock', 'He's at the guide post' – with the utterances of its participants – ' "If Johnny's near"/Quoth Betty'. The consequent shift of emphasis from text to event is supplemented by the maintenance of the syntagmatic–metonymic rather than the paradigmatic–metaphoric axis as the dominant function. When Betty reaches the doctor's house the speaker describes the situation.

> The town so long, the town so wide,
> Is silent as the skies.

This trope is governed by the immediate circumstances of the event: the speaker is unwilling to shift its locative references outside the situation of the utterance – we have already been told that it is a 'clear March night/The moon is up – the sky is blue'.

We might continue to interrogate the intrinsic properties of the text but in doing so we would ignore Wordsworth's deployment of the cultural code. The intrinsic metrical and syntactic properties of the ballad form are of much less significance than its familiar cultural status. Fowler (1981) and Halliday (1978) have written about the use of what they call 'anti-language', particularly in contemporary fiction. Their studies have focused on the relation between the largely spoken register of grammatical deviation, dialect and perverse semantics in groups and individuals that are usually detached from the mainstream of literary culture, and the use of such patterns in novels. The structure of prose fiction can comfortably accommodate such clashes between cultural and anti-cultural registers because there is no general rule which governs the reported speech of its characters – though the relation between these and the first or third person controlling presence has taxed literary linguists since Bakhtin. But with poetry, more specifically pre-twentieth-century regular poetry, problems emerge in the matching of the intrinsic and culturally determined conventions of the double pattern with 'anti-language', because the former are largely restricted to the terms and conditions of the educated, bourgeois poet and his audience. In 'The Idiot Boy' the speaking presence, without any apparent sense of self-consciousness, uses such locutions as 'mighty fret', 'fiddle faddle', 'the thought torments her sore', 'Fond lovers yet not quite hob nob', 'Old Susan lies a' bed in pain'. It would have been difficult for Wordsworth to fit these colloquial patterns into forms such as the Horatian ode, blank verse or the closed couplet, not because the abstract regulations of these structures could not accommodate them – they maintain a regular iambic pattern – but because they function as indicators of language as detached from its poetic/cultural context. What Wordsworth did was to exploit and play upon the cultural expectations of his readers. The 'rural' ballads of the collection either involve a first person discourse by someone like the peasant or the forsaken Indian Woman or they deliberately close the gap between the event of the narration (the enounced) and the subject of the enunciation (the speaking presence) by making it clear that the language of the reporter of events places him within the same socio-cultural sphere as its participants. It is the socio-cultural status of the ballad form that enables him to do this.

Consider the interaction between the speaking presences of the rural ballads and the two elements of the double pattern. In 'The Idiot Boy' and 'The Thorn' there are at least two speakers. In each instance a large number of structural and deictic resources are employed to give the impression that each figure occupies the same socio-cultural sphere. The reported speech passages (indicated by inverted commas) involve a similar amount of colloquial locutions as the third person presences. In 'The Thorn' the reporter of events splits his discourse between himself, an unidentified questioner/interlocutor and the refrain of his subject, Martha Ray (' "Oh misery! Oh misery! Oh woe is me! Oh misery!" '). His persistent use of obsessively exact deictic references (the height, location and condition of the thorn tree, the precise timing of the alleged events of the child murder) add to the impression that the speaker is attempting to transpose textual mediation with pre-linguistic immediacy.

The speaker in 'The Idiot Boy' similarly attempts to reconcile text and event. The language of the poem is shared by himself, Betty, Susan and Johnny's concluding statement (' "The cocks did crow to-whoo, to-whoo / And the sun did shine so cold" '). Each story is delivered in the present tense and this draws the addressee–reader further into a pattern of textual immediacy and contextual reference. We are listening to a single speaker who seeks to involve his listener and his characters in the reported situation of the utterance. For example, in 'The Idiot Boy' the speaker appears to compromise his control of the a b c c b rhyme scheme by repeating the same word – 'And Betty's in a sad quandary' (178) 'She's in a sad quandary' (181). In a couplet poem or in a text that does not offer itself as a 'ballad' contemporary readers might have cited this repetition as bad poetic writing: an instance of the poet unable to negotiate the complexities of the double pattern. Contemporary reviewers did not comment on this involuntary foregrounding of the tension between speech pattern and poetic function because it was accepted that the ballad form operated as a culturally designated sign system that would situate and predetermine the relatively uncultured status of its speaker. The improvisational and repetitive patterns of ordinary speech were accepted as a textual function (the reported speeches of Betty and Susan involve continuous repetitions of the same clauses). Our awareness of this acceptance itself involves a tension between the historico-cultural affiliations of literary studies and the textual focus of linguistics. For instance, the linguist might draw our attention to how the largely inactive connective 'and' is thrown into the foreground by its placing at the first syllable of approximately 10 per cent of the poem's lines. It is usually followed by the present tense positioning of verb and subject – 'And now she's high upon . . .', 'And now he sits . . .', 'And now to the doctor's door', 'And grumbling, he went . . .', 'And Susan's growing worse . . .'. We might reason from this that the speaker wishes to centre himself within the spatio-temporal shifts of the story. This most widely used connective, by being placed at a significant point in the interaction between syntax and metre, allows the speaking presence to interpose himself between the actual story and his own rendition of it.

The literary historian might move outside the text. For instance, a much cited review by Southey (1798) claims that 'The Idiot Boy' 'resembles a Flemish Picture in the worthlessness of its design and the excellence of its execution', and Dr. Burney in the *Monthly Review* (1799) compares the rural ballads with 'pictures', 'as dark as those of Rembrandt' (*Lyrical Ballads*, 318–23). What both of these reviewers infer is that the language of the ballads constitutes an element of their naturalistic or mimetic purpose, that there is no clear distinction between the means of representation and the events and details represented. Their visual arts analogy is consistent with Wordsworth's own remarks on the imagined socio-cultural status of his narrators: 'it is not supposed to be spoken in the author's own person':

> I had two objects to attain; first, to represent a picture which should not be unimpressive yet consistent with the character that should describe it, secondly, while I adhered to the style in which such persons describe, to take care that words, which in their minds are impregnated with passion, should likewise convey passion to Readers who are not accustomed to sympathize with men feeling in that manner or using such language. It seemed to me that this might be done by calling in the assistance of Lyrical and rapid Metre.
>
> (*Lyrical Ballads*, 288)

This passage is sown with a pattern of socio-cultural references that the contemporary reader would easily decode. 'Lyrical and rapid Metre', 'the style in which such persons describe', 'using such language', all of these indicate the status of the ballad as a form of low culture – not a means of actually replicating the spoken and referential patterns of 'such persons' but rather their cultural correlative. The problem for the linguist/literary critic, as Fowler points out in *Literature as Social Discourse* (1981), is of how to balance such *ex cathedra* contextual evidence against the meanings discharged by the intrinsic metrical, syntactic and lexical structures of the texts. If we focus upon the forms and types of 'common' locution or anti-language and such patterns as persistent clause repetition or a near dependence upon connectives, we then have to deal with why Wordsworth chooses to situate his speech events in a subcultural linguistic and social context. We could begin by reexamining the picture analogy used both by Wordsworth and his reviewers.

The best known semiotic distinction between linguistic and visual sign systems was proposed by C. S. Peirce in his use of the terms iconic (visual) and symbolic (linguistic). Iconic signs usually bear a close physical resemblance (through shape, colour or static juxtaposition) to the objects and events that they seek to mediate. Symbolic signs or words are part of an independent system which depends upon the ability of sender and receiver to decode the interface between linguistic event and pre-linguistic experience.

Interpreters and semioticians from Plato, through Lessing, to Wendy Steiner have debated the relative claims of these two media to immediacy and transparency. Visual representation, particularly in its pre-twentieth-century form, is easy to decode – we do not need to achieve competence in a form of visual grammar to recognise in Constable's *Hay Wain* a cart, a horse, and a river, but the phonetic and graphic signs 'cart', 'horse' and 'river' demand a broader awareness of the complex symbolic system from which they are drawn. What visual representation lacks is the ability to fully communicate the temporal process from which the silent, iconic 'snapshot' is taken: what circumstances have led to the positioning of the cart in the river; where is it going; and why? Wordsworth, in his rural ballads plays both the symbolic and the iconic cards. The speakers of the rural ballads literally inhabit the frame of the artefact. Their linguistic–metrical patterns are the equivalents of the smock, the plough or the cottage from which the painted figure can never be fully detached. But at the same time this same linguistic medium enables them to control the consecutive progress of the narrative.

Consider the generic designation of the ballad as a narrative form – in late-eighteenth-century magazine culture it was the equivalent of the short story. Propp, Greimas and Todorov (see Hawkes, 1977, 87–106) have all been influential in their attempts to formulate a grammar of narrative, a means by which the characters and events of prose fiction can be seen to be governed by a set of abstract rules similar to the grammatical units of syntax. All of their theses have been subjected to rigorous and often sceptical examination, but let us see how Greimas's division of narrative into three basic patterns relates to the story of 'The Idiot Boy'. The *syntagmes contractuels* refer to the establishing or breaking of contracts. It is inferred that there is an agreed contract between Betty Foy and her sick friend Susan (ratified by popular notions of rural harmony) and an even deeper bond between Betty and her son Johnny. The *syntagmes performanciels* involve trials, struggles and the performance of tasks, and the task and struggle imposed upon Johnny is to take his pony and seek help for Susan. *Syntagmes disjunctionnels* involve the physical movement of characters, their arrival and departure, as part of their function in relation to contract and performance. This accounts for the major narrative events of 'The Idiot Boy': Johnny departs, Betty is worried about his and Susan's fate and she follows him. We could select sentences and clauses from the poem and find that these broader narrative patterns find their counterpart in the actual syntagmatic structures.

And he must post without delay
Across the bridge and in the dale.

(52–3)

The affirmative main verb 'must post' and the deictic references to 'bridge' and 'dale' correspond with Johnny's contract, his performance and his movement.

The clock is on the stroke of twelve
And Johnny is not yet in sight.

(162–3)

The spatio-temporal references to the time and to Betty's perspective again foreground the nature of the contract and the performance or movement of its contractee.

So far so good, but what Greimas's formulations do not tell us is why Wordsworth, as he implies, regards his rural tales as in any way different from either their prose counterparts in the novel or their poetic counterparts in the magazines. Mayo compares 'The Idiot Boy' with a very similar ballad (published in the *Sporting Magazine*, October 1798) called 'The Idiot'. In this the speaker is similarly governed by the conventions of the ballad form, but shows a greater command of the narrative structure by making it clear exactly why his idiot is unable to fully understand his mother's death, and he goes on to list the macabre and sordid details of the idiot's preservation of the decomposing corpse. What Wordsworth's first and third person speakers do not do is to rationalise or impose explanations upon their own or the reported behaviour of their characters. Greimas's models of the syntagm are invoked both at the broader and localised levels of the texts, but our expectation of syntax and narrative leading us to some kind of conclusion is continuously and consistently disappointed. We don't really know why Johnny has disappeared or what is going through his mind; we are never sure if Martha Ray has killed her infant child or of why and how the Indian Woman or the Mad Mother have found themselves in their reported circumstances. In effect the rural ballads operate simultaneously at two levels, variously termed the symbolic and the iconic, the linguistic and the visual, *discours* and *histoire*. The narrative is like a picture in the sense that characters, objects, circumstances and the relationships between them are depicted without being fully explained or rationalised, while this element of naturalistic transparency is supplemented by a dense pattern of poetic and cultural codes. The resulting effect depends largely upon the predisposition of the reader. Perhaps Wordsworth has success-fully disrupted the structural and representational conventions of eighteenth-century writing and brought verse closer to the sub-cultural 'real world' of sensation, spontaneity and existential contingency. Alternatively he can be seen as drawing upon, even exploiting, these same conventions: the ballad and its formal and representational mechanisms are just as unreal and refractory as the couplet and blank verse – their difference exists only in their cultural associations.

The enigmatic, one might say 'unfinished', nature of Words-worth's ballads manifests itself in other Romantic uses of the poetic narrative. Coleridge's 'The Ancient Mariner' and 'Christabel', Keats's 'Eve of St. Agnes', even Byron's satirical but similarly inconclusive *Don Juan*, all take us through a series of consecutive events but maintain a reluctance to close this progress with reflec-tions upon what these events actually mean. The opposing binary pole of Romantic poetry involves a shift away from narrative toward immediacy, in which the primary structural determinant is the mental and linguistic resources of the speaker rather than the objec-tive, consecutive nature of the events – the most familiar manifes-tation of this being the Romantic Ode (see below pp. 118–28). What unites these two apparently dissimilar poetic functions within the Romantic programme is their attempt to mediate the subjective register of pre-linguistic phenomena. In *Lyrical Ballads* the poem that represents the most conspicuous shift away from the sub-cul-tural circumstances of the rural tale toward the 'high Romantic' fusion of addresser and poet is 'Tintern Abbey'.

Compare the rural ballads with 'Tintern Abbey', lines 4–8:

> Once again
> Do I behold these steep and lofty cliffs,
> That on a wild secluded scene impress
> Thoughts of more deep seclusion; and connect
> The landscape with the quiet of the sky.

There are several ways of reading this passage: none is entirely invalid but each, if isolated from its alternatives, is incomplete. Isobel Armstrong (1978) and Antony Easthope (1983) note that there are ambiguities generated by the terminal verbs 'impress' and 'connect'. With 'impress' there is an apparent hesitation between the cliffs literally imposing themselves upon the landscape (a typical post-Miltonic inversion) and the revelation that the cliffs 'impress' thoughts of more deep seclusion upon the speaker (repositioning 'wild secluded scene' as a prepositional phrase and the 'I' of the sentence as its most dominant function). Similarly 'connect' could refer either to an unbroken unity of panorama, 'the cliffs connect the landscape with the sky', or to the process of mediation 'I connect the landscape with the quiet of the sky', the latter shifting the emphasis toward the subjective, adjectival function of 'quiet' and away from the physical relation between the nouns. How we interpret these ambiguities and, more significantly, explain Wordsworth's reason for inserting them will depend upon two interrelated issues: first, what is the status of this passage as a speech act, to whom is it addressed and what, from the evidence of the text, can we infer about the contextual situation of the speaker? Second, how does Wordsworth's invocation of a series of cultural and poetic codes affect our interpretation?

There is no evidence of an addressee functioning within the enclosed dramatic circuit of the speech act. The reader/listener is addressed directly. This corresponds with a number of signals – its focus upon natural imagery, its use of blank verse – which invite the reader to compare it with the eighteenth-century tradition of landscape poems by, amongst others, Thomson, Cowper and Akenside. The speakers of the rural ballads also address the reader/listener directly, but the cultural codes invoked in 'Tintern Abbey', supplemented by the fact that the structural function of event and narrative is replaced by the relation between perception, mediation and introspection, locate the broader cultural context and contact codes as the silent contemplation of the text or the drawing-room reading rather than the story told in the inn.

Armstrong and Easthope explain the ambiguities of the poem as contrived slippages, Armstrong proposing the text as typically Romantic syntax, effecting 'transformations in perception and relationship' (263), and Easthope as an example of parataxis, 'the juxtaposed syntax of speech' (127). In short, Wordsworth attempts to give the impression that the 'passion' involved in his own perceptions and recollections has unsettled his command of language. The uncertain syntactic relation between the parts of the landscape and their subjective effects is the high cultural equivalent of 'The Idiot Boy' speaker's continuous return to the connective 'and'. What the two critics do not consider is the extent to which Wordsworth deliberately disrupts the reader's certainty regarding our status as addressee. Here we should recall Donne's 'The Flea' where we find that the plausibility of an imagined addressee is at once validated by the deictics of the utterance and invalidated by the foregrounded contrivance of textuality. What are we reading/listening to with 'Tintern Abbey'? A figure who has, like Donne's speaker, or in a similar technical frame, Milton's blank verse speakers, become textual devices, or a figure whose hesitations and syntactic referrals are a transparent sign of heightened emotion? I believe both. The ambiguities are effectively foregrounded by the tension between verse design and verse instance. Were the passage to be printed and consequently interpreted as rhythmic prose a major pause would occur between 'scene' and 'impress' and the ambiguity would be diffused. Similarly, the placing of 'connect' at the line ending gives greater emphasis to its function as a point of tension in the relation between the parts of the landscape and their effect upon the perceiver. Wordsworth exploits what had become, for the late-eighteenth-century superreader, the metasyntax of poetic form. Such a person would have been aware that a tension between design–instance, text–speaker relations had occurred in Milton and been marginalised in the first person blank verse texts of the eighteenth century, and he/she would also be aware that Wordsworth had created an innovative interaction between these two technical and generic expectations. In 'Tintern Abbey' Wordsworth relies just as much upon the register of established textual and cultural signs as he did in his use of the ballad, and it is important for us, as twentieth-century readers, to be as fully aware of the problematic relation between the Romantic text and its broader cultural–aesthetic context as we are of its intrinsic syntactic and poetic mechanisms.

THE ROMANTIC PROGRAMME: PROBLEMS AND CONTRADICTIONS

Let us now consider the problems raised by *Lyrical Ballads*, the creative and theoretical manifesto for Romanticism, and see how these might contribute to our broader understanding of the Romantic programme.

Wordsworth's objective, as he states in the preface, is to bring poetry closer both to spontaneous, spoken discourse and to pre-linguistic experience. This desire for expressive transparency is both the ideal and the collective paradox which binds together the major Romantic poets.

The Ideal

Coleridge, in the *Biographia Literaria*, writes,

> They [images] become proofs of original genius only as far as they are modified by a predominant passion; or by associated thoughts and images awakened by that passion . . . when a human and intellectual life is transferred to them from the poet's own spirit.

Shelley, in *A Defence of Poetry*, writes: 'Poets are the hierophants of unapprehended inspiration; the mirrors of the gigantic shadows which futurity casts upon the present; the words which express what they understand not'. Keats, in a letter to Richard Woodhouse, describes the poetic character: 'it is not itself – it has no self – it is everything and nothing – it has no character – it enjoys light and shade; it lives in gusto, be it foul or fair, high or low, rich or poor, mean or elevated'. The philosophic and aesthetic origins of these aspirations are well documented in Abrams's *The Mirror and the Lamp* (1953). In the late eighteenth century a largely Anglo-German tradition, usually described as primitivism, held that the intrinsic, rhythmical nature of poetic language predated the 'civilised' conventions of prose: the pre-linguistic registers of physical and mental activity – walking, running, desire, fear, hate – would manifest themselves in patterns of language that were uncontaminated by the arbitrary sophistications of culture and reason – in Shelley's terms 'words which express what they understand not'. The Romantics were undoubtedly inspired by this theoretical model, but their problem was how to transform theory into practice.

The Paradox

Wordsworth in *Lyrical Ballads* juxtaposed the sub-cultural status of the ballad with its high cultural counterpart, blank verse, and although in each instance he disrupted the reader's expectations of how stylistic and cultural paradigms should relate to each other he nevertheless fed upon and remained within the established poetic *langue* of generic and structural precedents. In short he had mediated 'the real language of men' by drawing upon the least transparent and most refractory of all linguistic media. In the preface he concedes that there is an irreconcilable fissure between theory and practice:

> The music of harmonious metrical language, the sense of

difficulty overcome, and the . . . pleasure which has been previously received from works of rhyme or metre of the same or
similar construction, an indistinct perception perpetually renewed
of language closely resembling that of real life, and yet, in the
circumstance of metre, differing from it so widely.

In short, poetic language is an autonomous, self-determined system
of rules and conventions, and its 'close resemblance to real life' is
largely the product of an arbitrary cultural phenomenon now
referred to as literary competence: each convention (such as the
ballad) is a sign which must be decoded by the perceiver before it
can be said to correspond with its predicate. Coleridge, in the
Biographia (written during the later more embittered period of his
relationship with Wordsworth), foregrounds the paradox: '[The best
part of human language] is formed by a voluntary appropriation of
fixed symbols to internal acts, to processes and results of imagination, the greater part of which have no place in the consciousness
of uneducated man'. Roughly translated: poetry is a high cultural
game played only by trained and competent participants.

In terms of the issues raised so far regarding the structural and
functional conditions of poetry, Romanticism is a turning inward.
The conventions and objectives of Augustanism were the reconciliation of the poetic with the prosaic functions of disclosure, exposition, cataloguing, the rational contemplation of thesis and antith-
esis. This, according to the Romantics, falsified the contingent,
spontaneous relation between poetic expression and the pre-linguistic world. Their problem was that this relationship is, in any event,
false and arbitrary. Without the double pattern language is unpoetic
and unpoetic language surrenders either to the institutional imperatives of prose discourse or to the unstructured localised patterns of
speech; with the double pattern language becomes further enclosed
within the systematic complexities of the poetic *langue*. For the
rest of this chapter we will examine extracts and individual poems
and consider the ways in which Wordsworth's precedent, in the
Lyrical Ballads, of reintegrating and juxtaposing the already established codes governing the structural and contextual registers of
poetry, was both maintained and extended by his peers. We will
begin with Blake.

BLAKE AND THE ARBITRARY NATURE OF LANGUAGE

William Blake both embodies yet moves beyond the Romantic archetype of innovation. More than any of his contemporaries he attempted to reconstitute, or more accurately remythologise, an entire Western tradition of poetic, theological and philosophical writing. In terms of the functional status of poetry he sought to break down the stylistic and interpretive distinctions between these three discourses. For Blake the poem was the natural medium within which man would once again unify the conditions of mystical self-awareness, natural justice and external, undimmed truth that had been so cruelly thrown apart by centuries of 'civilised' belief, behaviour and convention. He believed that the functional and referential conditions of all discourses, but particularly poetry, were responsible for distorting and effectively determining man's vision of himself and the world, and in his own poetic writing he sought to draw attention to these falsifications by juxtaposing familiar codes, referential patterns and stylistic conventions in a way that can best be described as a form of linguistic pre-Surrealism – familiar linguistic integers and structures were repositioned in an unprecedented and, according to a number of commentators, inaccessible manner.

His early, twin collections *Songs of Innocence and Experience* (1789–1805) are often regarded as his most accessible work, but the intrinsic peculiarities of these poems hold the key to his broader visionary enterprise. The majority of these lyrics are comprised of short stanzas, often using trisyllabic feet and moving away from the spoken iambic pattern to a form of musical 'sung' metre. As such he draws upon a familiar cultural code – in this case the popular type of poem/hymn published and distributed by dissenting preachers, poets and hymn writers of the eighteenth century for the religious and moral instruction of children. In a similar way to Wordsworth's use of the rural ballad Blake causes a deliberate conflict between formal/cultural expectation and realisation. But the situations of the utterance created by the *Songs* are far more perverse and intangible than those of the *Ballads*. Blake creates a continuous sense of disorientation for the reader, not as a consequence of a particularly obscure programme of syntactic or metrical innovation but by causing continuous and unremitting tension between lexical and sentence semantics and the situation of the utterance. Consider the Introduction to *Songs of Innocence*:

> Piping down the valleys wild
> Piping songs of pleasant glee

On a cloud I saw a child.
And he laughing said to me.

Pipe a song about a Lamb;
So I piped with merry chear,
Piper pipe that song again –
So I piped, he wept to hear.

Drop thy pipe thy happy pipe
Sing thy songs of happy chear,
So I sung the same again
While he wept with joy to hear

Piper sit thee down and write
In a book that all may read –
So he vanish'd from my sight.
And I pluck'd a hollow reed.

And I made a rural pen,
And I stain'd the water clear,
And I wrote my happy songs
Every child may joy to hear.

Superficially, this lyric creates an impression of syntactic and metrical simplicity. Each quatrain consists of regular seven-syllable lines, largely trochaic (indicating song rather than speech) but ending with an emphatic stress reversal for each rhyme word (see the boy's song to Mariana in *Measure for Measure* for a precedent). Each line achieves a large degree of discreteness by the placing of the main verb at a stress position, but the relation between such localised effects and the broader cohesive pattern is deliberately disruptive. The lexical and sentence semantics of each individual line are transparent and undemanding. The speaker sets the scene, the child issues orders and the speaker responds accordingly, but when we examine the interactive relation between these units of cohesion the effect is disorientating. The line/phrase 'On a cloud I saw a child' involves straightforward semantic relations – the speaker 'I' sees the 'child' on the 'cloud'. But we are uncertain whether the speaker also shares this locative position (perhaps they are both on the cloud) or whether the speaker views the child from the ground. The confusion becomes even more intriguing when we look back to the opening line, 'Piping down the valleys wild'. Does this refer to the sound of the pipe in the valleys or to the movement of the piper (perhaps on a cloud)? The child speaks to him so we must either assume that they share the cloud or that the child's voice carries from the sky – an effect consistent with his unreal, fantastic status. The confusing relation between the active verbal movement which creates the narrative and cohesive structure of the poem and its deictic features becomes even more pronounced in the two closing stanzas. The piper/speaker sits down on the ground to 'pluck' a 'reed' and 'stain the water'. Has he descended from the cloud and does the intimacy and immediacy of his exchange with the child mean that they are now both on the ground?

Throughout the poem the curious tension between the localised semantic simplicity and the less stable cohesive and narrative pattern creates, for the reader, a continuous sense of uncertainty. The final two lines,

And I wrote my happy songs
Every child may joy to hear

exhibit an enclosed and unambiguous sense of transparency and completeness. But interpreted in relation to the child's order to write 'in a book that all may read' and the speaker's description of how he 'stained the water clear', these lines become a component of an unresolvable paradox. Writing on water is as impermanent as speech; no-one will later be able to 'read' these songs nor are they records of songs that the conditional/'future' child 'may joy to hear'. Localised semantics depend equally upon the reader's awareness of internal syntactic relations and our broader sense of the situation of the utterance – the latter provided either by an actual context or implied context provided by deictic features (see Traugott and Pratt, 1980, 187–8). In Blake's poem any sense of an implied context is continuously disrupted by the shifting relation between the spatial and active linguistic indicators, and as a consequence the sum of the localised, transparent parts creates a disorientating, incoherent whole. Blake's apparent wish to juxtapose these two elements of localised order and referential disorder depends largely upon his use of the enclosed lyric pattern of the verse form. The regular pattern of short lines and stanzaic repetition provides a relatively stable axis between the two elements, and we should note that the Augustan programme of deploying the double pattern as a sup- plement to the ordering features of syntax and contextual reference is clearly and deliberately disrupted. Here metrical order is juxta- posed with syntactic and referential disruption. Clearly this lyric fits into the generic–stylistic category of texts in which the 'baring of the device', the self-conscious interplay between the referential and the poetic function is their most prominent feature (see discussion of Herbert, pp. 52–5), and it sets the tone for the rest of the collection. In each of the songs we remain uncertain of the true situation of the utterance: the more immediate localising functions of the deictics will allow us to position the speaker as child or adult; the frame of reference might shift from the immediate condition of orphans, chimney sweepers or little black boys to the more abstract philosophical significances of rose trees, tigers or lambs.

Blake's songs differ from Wordsworth's ballads in the sense that they constantly deny the reader any certain encounter with a specific and persistent cultural or poetic code. Religious or mythological patterns of imagery and symbolism might be foregrounded in one poem and in the next be replaced by concrete references to child exploitation or the sordid condition of the London streets. In short any attempt to reconstruct a particular speaker from the linguistic constituents of the text and consequently to balance textual features against implied context is consistently subverted. The first serious attempt to deal with this problem of textual–contextual coordination is in Robert F. Gleckner's 'Point of View and Context in Blake's Songs' (1957). Gleckner advises the reader to read the sequence as a textual whole, carrying themes and contextual references from one poem to the next rather as we do with the individual sentences that make up a prose sequence: 'since each state is made up of many poems, the other poems in that must be consulted to grasp the full significance of any one poem' (92). This might be a valid formula were it not for the fact that each separate poem causes internal disturbances of point of view and context. Consider 'London' from *Songs of Experience*:

> I wander thro' each charter'd street,
> Near where the charter'd Thames does flow.
> And mark in every face I meet
> Marks of weakness, marks of woe.
>
> In every cry of every Man,
> In every Infants cry of fear,
> In every voice: in every ban,
> The mind-forg'd manacles I hear
>
> How the Chimney-sweepers cry
> Every blackning Church appalls,

And the hapless Soldiers sigh,
Runs in blood down Palace walls

But most thro' midnight streets I hear
How the youthful Harlots curse
Blasts the new-born Infants tear
And blights with plagues the Marriage hearse.

The point to note in this poem is the way in which the verbal shifts
between seeing and hearing cause a correspondent uncertainty about
the perceptual and the expressive stability of the experiencer. In
grammatical terms the experiencer is the role of the animate being
inwardly affected by an event or characterised by a state (see
Traugott and Pratt, 193) and in this poem the speaker is very much
the experiencer. In the first stanza the verbal emphasis is visual – he
'marks' the 'marks', or, roughly translated, he visually apprehends
evidence of weakness and woe. In the second stanza the visual is
superseded by the auditory verbal function – he 'hears' 'crys' and
'voices'. In the third and fourth stanzas any stability between these
two grammatical and perceptual conditions is subverted. How can
the speaker 'hear' how every church is appalled by the chimney
sweeper's cry ('appalls' in any event involves both its modern figurative usage and its original spatial designation of draping with a
pall)? And although a sigh can be heard, it is curious to find that
its visual metaphoric transformation into blood on palace walls is
still governed by the auditory verb phrase. Even more confusing is
the harlot's curse which is 'heard' to 'blast' the 'infant's tear' and
'blight' ('with plagues') 'the marriage hearse'.

Scholars and critics have toiled for decades over the strange syntactic and semantic relationships between the deictic features of this
poem. For example 'mark' could simply mean appearance or it
could invite comparison with the biblical 'mark' upon the victimised
and downtrodden inhabitants of Jerusalem (Ezekiel 9:4, a passage
with which Blake was almost obsessively familiar). 'Charter'd' could
mean both the 'charter'd rights of Englishmen', a much used
counterblast to the repressive regime of Pitt, and also refer to
the urban topography, including the Thames, as literally 'charted',
owned, confined, mapped out, designated for commercial use. 'Ban'
could mean an element of contemporary legislation or it could refer
to the agreed prohibitions of the marriage announcement. In each
ambiguous semantic instance the speaker shifts us between the
immediate and specific – people or events that he might encounter
on the streets – and the broader existential condition of humanity.

This effect is supplemented by the speaker's repetitive use of 'every'. Its first usage links it with the condition of the utterance, 'every face I meet', but its attachment to 'every Man', 'every Infant', 'every voice', 'every blackning Church' sets up a tension between a universal, generalised frame of reference and the equally prominent definite article, '*the* Chimney-sweepers', '*the* soldiers', '*the* youthful Harlots', '*the* new-born Infants', '*the* Marriage Hearse'. Are these individual instances of the speaker's reported experience or is 'the' substituted for the generic predeterminer 'all' or 'every'? These uncertain lexical semantics and the spatial and auditory shifts between verbs and objects focus our attention upon the condition of the experiencer and the nature of the speech act. The present tense relations between the first person pronoun and verb, 'I wander', 'I meet', 'I hear' create the impression of immediacy and particularity, yet the semantic and syntactic excursions discussed above isolate the text as a self-determined synthesis of largely disparate linguistic and referential patterns.

The anchor point for any sense of interpretive stability is provided by the double pattern. At the junction between the closing and opening lines of stanzas 2 and 3 we encounter an example of enjambment that John Hollander terms the *contre-rejet*, which, roughly summarised, creates two separate deep structures within the same syntactic unit. The verb phrase 'I hear' is vital both for the syntactic structure of stanza 2 and for that of stanza 3 (punctuation differs from edition to edition, but in the original the full stop is absent). Technically this is an instance of grammatical deviation, but within the specific context of metrical–syntactic structure it creates a double effect of parataxis (structure is determined by the impassioned nature of the speech act) and textual foregrounding (the overlaying of two syntactic patterns upon a single syntagmatic sequence is neatly accommodated by its division between two stanzas). But it is more than simply a technical device, because it draws the reader's attention to a more complex thematic shift from the largely metonymic pattern of the first two stanzas to the extravagantly metaphoric elaborations of the third and fourth. In the former the dominant trope of 'mind forg'd manacles' is cautiously preempted by the accumulation of physical and figurative semantics denoting imprisonment and subservience – particularly 'charter'd' and 'mark'. The experiencer and his language are tied closely to the immediate circumstances of the speech act. But in the second half of the poem the imagined inhabitants of the streets become more the constituents of a detached textual field, in which the surreal spatio-acoustic relation between objects and actions unsettles any particular semantic chain.

It is significant that this vast thematic and contextual shift should be signalled, perhaps initiated, by a point of interaction between speech act and textuality, because the only feature of all of the songs that can be said to be persistent and predictable is their enclosure within a regular metrical–stanzaic pattern. It is almost as though Blake in the *Songs* set himself a task similar to Herbert's in *The Temple*: both recognised that the arbitrary conventions of language are capable of inhibiting and distorting the mediation of truth, and both, perhaps perversely, chose the most self-consciously arbitrary linguistic medium to explore such issues. But there the resemblance ends. Blake in many of his earlier poems displays an unease with the inherited *langue* of metrical structures. In the blank verse pieces of *Poetical Sketches* (1783) he experiments regularly with the tension between verse design (text) and verse instance (speech pattern) in a manner that recalls Milton and predates 'Tintern Abbey' by almost two decades. The sense of self-referential unease, evident both in the *Sketches* and the *Songs*, eventually resulted in the only real textual manifestation of the pre-Romantic theories of primitivism (see Abrams, 78–84 and Bradford, 1992, 103–32) and during the 1790s Blake began to write in a form of early free verse. His programme was based upon the rejection of any predetermined structural tension between the line and syntax. An early example of this practice can be found in 'The Argument' to *The Marriage of Heaven and Hell* (1790–3). A roughly iambic sequence is maintained but the length of each line is determined only by the unpredictable occurrence of major rhetorical or syntactic pauses (see also *The First Book of Urizen*, *The Book of Ahania* and *The Song of Los*). In his later long poems such as *Milton* and *Jerusalem*, Blake abandoned all concessions to metrical regularity and the only feature which distinguishes these texts from prose is their use of the unmetrical line. He states his case in the introduction to *Jerusalem*.

When this Verse was first dictated to me, I considered a Monotonous Cadence, like that used by Milton and Shakespeare and all writers of English Blank Verse, derived from the Modern bondage of Rhyming, to be a necessary and indispensible part of Verse. But I soon found that in the mouth of a true Orator such monotony was not only awkward, but as much a bondage as rhyme itself. I therefore have produced a variety in every line both of cadences and of number of syllables. Every word and every letter is studied and put into its fit place; the terrific numbers are reserved for the terrific parts, the mild and gentle for the mild and gentle parts, and the prosaic for inferior parts; all are necessary to each other. Poetry Fetter'd Fetters the Human Race (Blake, 1966, 434).

He raises issues here that lie at the heart of the innovative programme of Romanticism and which would be returned to by the modernists. Metre even in its freer, unrhymed forms is unnatural, and thus we encounter an uncomfortable paradox, largely ignored by the theorists of primitivism and effectively marginalised by the Romantics. If, as was widely believed, the rhythmic structure of poetry was a palpable token of its link with pre-linguistic experience, how could a metrical style be devised which did not confine itself within the conventional patterns of form yet which exhibited structural and signifying functions which differed from other linguistic discourses? Wordsworth and the other major poets of the period submitted to convention. Wordsworth: 'the tendency of metre is to divest language in a certain degree of its reality . . . an indistinct perception perpetually renewed of language closely resembling that of real life, and yet, in the circumstances of metre, differing from it so widely'. There were other contemporary attempts to break the 'fetters' of conventional metrical forms, the best known being Coleridge's method of 'counting in each line the accents, not the syllables' in *Christabel*, but there remains a strange inconsistency between their shared objective of revolutionising the functional purpose of poetry and their maintenance of an eclectic conservatism in matters of poetic form. With the exception of Blake's later poetry, the Romantics engage in an uncomfortable and largely indecisive struggle with precedent.

THE ODE AND DECONSTRUCTION

There is often a predictable correspondence between the genres or types of the Romantic poem and its deployment of poetic form. The narrative poem will generally involve the use of the ballad, the stanza or blank verse. The accumulative, consecutive nature of these forms can accommodate and stabilise the relationship between the speaking presence and the pre-linguistic spatio-temporal nature of the reported events. The individual line or the stanzaic unit will not necessarily parallel the progress of syntax, but their predictable, repetitive function will at least establish a shared emphasis upon the forward movement of the syntagm through both dimensions of the double pattern. With the poem which does not foreground a series of events and causal circumstances, and which addresses issues whose relation to one another are determined more by their emotional or intellectual impression upon the speaker, we are more likely to encounter the ode. There are of course exceptions to this generalisation: Wordsworth used blank verse both for his more contemplative, introspective pieces such as 'Tintern Abbey' and *The Prelude* and in rural narratives such as 'The Brothers' and 'Michael', but one should note that in the latter he maintains the eighteenth-century tradition of coordinating syntax with verse design and consequently diffuses any tension between text, speaker and event. Coleridge, in *Christabel*, uses an accentual rather than an accentual–syllabic form and largely succeeds in drawing attention to the spoken immediacy of the story rather than its textual enclosure (we should also note that *Christabel* bears an ironic resemblance to the ode in that it is a deliberately unfinished narrative). But it is the ode that prevails as the most discussed and widely celebrated vehicle for the Romantic programme of recording and reconciling individual experience, perception and mediation. The reason for this is that the ode, at least in its post-classical form, was the only alternative to blank verse in its allowance of flexibility for both elements of the double pattern. It at once encodes, and often promotes, the foregrounding of linguistic materiality in metre, rhyme and sound pattern, yet permits a far broader and less predictable range of interactions between syntactic and poetic structures than would blank verse, the couplet or the stanza. The largely predictable form of the classical Pindaric or Horatian ode had, since the sixteenth century, been overridden by deviations that were largely a consequence of the greater prominence of accentual and sound-correspondence patterns in English verse, so that by the time Wordsworth wrote the 'Immortality Ode' it was acceptable to alternate line length and rhyme scheme almost at random (see Shuster, 1940). As a consequence the sliding scale between the cognitive and the conventional elements of the double pattern becomes invalid as a means of analysing the poem as a whole: the relation between the two elements will change at unpredictable, localised points throughout the entire structure. In short, the ode, particularly the irregular ode, is able to promote the illusion of the speaking presence as both in command of the subject matter and as responsive to the vagaries of pre-linguistic experience and perception.

Consider the opening strophe of Wordsworth's 'Immortality Ode'.

There was a time when meadow, grove, and stream,
The earth, and every common sight,
            To me did seem
        Apparelled in celestial light,
The glory and the freshness of a dream.
It is not now as it hath been of yore;
            Turn wheresoe'er I may,
                By night or day,
The things which I have seen I now can see no more.

The utterance at one level appears to be improvised and uncon-
strained by predetermined structures. The verb phrase 'to me did
seem' is pitched between the itemised description of natural objects
and the more introspective, subjective semantics of 'celestial light',
'glory', 'freshness', 'dream'. But at the same time the entire syntactic
unit operates within a symmetrical rhyme scheme (a b a b a). We
are never certain whether the shortening and opening of line lengths
delimits or responds to the irregular and apparently improvised
syntactic structure. One consequence of such uncertain relations
between the two elements of the double pattern is an unsettling of
the readers' cognitive and interpretive faculties. The much debated
problem of whether a poem's syntactic or formal features should
dominate the process of naturalisation is here thrown into an even
more chaotic cycle of response and interpretation. When, in an
ode, we encounter such textual foregroundings as stress reversal or
enjambment our response is limited by the fact that there is no
regular and predictable pattern of form and syntax against which
such 'deviations' can be counterpointed. The Romantic taste for the
ode encompasses the uneasy relationship between their *ex cathedra*
statements on language and pre-linguistic experience and the manifestation of this polarity in verse, because in freeing syntax from
the repetitive formulae of line length and stanzaic rhyme scheme
the ode sets up a continuous and unpredictable tension between the
referential function of language and its materiality. Consider the
opening strophe of Keats's 'Ode to Psyche'.

O Goddess! hear these tuneless numbers, wrung
    By sweet enforcement and remembrance dear,
And pardon that thy secrets should be sung
    Even into thine own soft-conchèd ear:
Surely I dreamt today, or did I see

The wingèd Psyche with awakened eyes?
I wandered in a forest thoughtlessly,
  And, on the sudden, fainting with surprise,
Saw two fair creatures, couchèd side by side
  In deepest grass, beneath the whispering roof
  Of leaves and trembled blossoms, where there ran
    A brooklet, scarce espied:

The deictics of this passage are entirely self-referential. The situation of the utterance is the speaker's consciousness: he moves from an address to the goddess Psyche through an uncertain recollection of his dream to a rural setting that resembles Eden and which may or may not be connected with the dream. We are not prompted to ask where or even who the speaker is at this particular moment of mediation. In an important sense this, like many other Romantic odes, resembles the modernist technique of interior monologue or stream of consciousness. Language and consciousness, rather than any spatio-temporal relation between language and events, control the syntactic and semantic pattern. Its most obvious difference from the interior monologue is its adherence to the conventions of poetic syntax, metre and sound pattern. As a consequence the addresser–addressee relationship is focused less upon the imagined situation of the speech act and far more upon the internalised patterns of cultural and referential codes and poetic devices. Indeed, in this instance the poetic function effectively governs and marginalises its referential and contextual counterparts. Any attempt to follow the ideational pattern of the Goddess invoked, the dream and the Edenic images is countered by a persistent interweaving of the material functions of language. The relation between the irregular accentual–syllabic pattern, the rhyme scheme and the syntax is further complicated by continuous foregrounding of aspirates and fricatives, all founded upon the consonant 's' (at least two in each line). This moves the text away from an adherence to formal pattern for its own sake and toward a suggested relation between the material and referential functions of its language. In effect the opening consonant of 'Psyche' occurs continuously within the opening strophe and is maintained, with not quite such persistent emphasis, throughout the poem. It would be wrong here to invoke Jakobson and Wimsatt's formula for the semantic–phonemic correspondence of rhyme words because there is no particular semantic or syntactic relationship between *s*ecret*s*, *s*ee, *s*oft, creature*s*, leave*s*, e*s*pied. Hearing the poem we are left with the impression that it gives as much attention to echoes of the signifier 'Psyche' within the enclosed sphere of linguistic materiality as it does to the function of the signified goddess in the mind and the cultural experience of the speaker.

We should now turn to an issue that has been widely discussed in recent debates on language and literature: why do the so-called poststructuralist/deconstructionist critics find Romantic poetry so fruitful in their interpretive encounters? A number of summaries should precede our discussion. Poststructuralism and deconstruction are notoriously resistant to abstract summation, but it is generally agreed that they draw upon Saussure's model of language as an enclosed differential sign system and extend the implications of this thesis in ways that had not been fully considered in literary criticism and linguistics before the mid-1960s. If, as Saussure argued, it is the difference between linguistic signs themselves that enables us to posit and stabilise the relation between constituents of the pre-linguistic continuum of existence, then it could be argued that language does not reflect or mediate reality (*contra* the premise upon which both Romanticism and traditional linguistics and philosophy is grounded); rather that language constitutes and determines reality both for individuals and for collective ideological–societal groups. Christopher Norris in *The Deconstructive Turn* (1983) offers an economic summary of the Romantic–poststructuralist relationship:

> Once the critic despairs – as despair he must – of attaining the 'unmediated vision', the unimpeded merging of mind and nature held out by the Romantic metaphor, he is then set free to explore the endless complexities of textual meaning and configuration (31).

So, the sense of doubt that has attended academic literary criticism regarding its apparent inability to define a method that brings about some form of closure between the textual play of literature, particularly poetry, and its specific meaning is, in its encounters with the Romantics, comfortably accommodated by the latter's similarly unsuccessful attempts to fuse,

> language and reality, mind and object, such that all extraneous detail falls away in the moment of achieved communion . . . Where the Romantics typically overreach themselves – in aiming for a pure unmediated vision, a perfect correspondence between idea, language and reality – their failure is a heightened and dramatized version of the problems which beset all thought.
>
> (Norris, 129–31)

The eminent US deconstructionists – de Man, Hartman, Hillis-Miller, Bloom – found in the Romantics a means of justifying the notoriously uncertain role and function of literary studies. Literature consciously engages with and foregrounds the illusion that there is or can be any natural or unitary relation between sign and referent, language and reality. Therefore literature, more than any other discourse, involves us in the honest, if somewhat tragic, awareness that language can only ever address or mediate language. The validity of this claim is still open to question, but one issue that has been consistently marginalised in the ongoing debate is Romanticism's tendency in its use of poetic form to foreground the materiality, the non-signifying palpability, of language.

Norris's essay focuses upon a text that represents the archetype of Romantic overreaching, Coleridge's 'Kubla Khan'. For a number of reasons this poem (in the ode form) is regarded as a self-deconstructing text. It is largely impossible to encounter a published version of the poem without also encountering Coleridge's prose description of its sources and its compositional genesis: he claims that it is the record of a probably opium-induced dream, 'in which all the images rose up before him as *things* with a parallel production of the correspondent expressions, without any sensation or consciousness of effort'. On awakening he wrote these down. This statement is significant, firstly, because it economically summarises the entire Romantic programme: his ratiocinative and linguistic resources have been transformed into a vehicle for communicative transparency. Secondly it engages with the post-Saussurian concepts of sign and referent, signifier and signified. Derrida claims that the differential system of arbitrary signs involves 'syntheses and referrals that prevent there from being at any moment or in any way a simple element that is present in and of itself and refers only to itself' (*Positions*, 26). Coleridge claims to have achieved exactly this transparent unity of sign, presence and reference. The most famous attempt to resolve this conundrum occurred, half a century before deconstruction had been heard of, in John Livingstone Lowes's *The Road to Xanadu* (1927). This masterpiece of scholarly source-hunting attempts to trace each of the poem's references to mysticism and middle-Eastern culture back through Coleridge's own reading and experience. As such it acknowledges that, as in Keats's 'Ode to Psyche', our attempts to relate the deictics of the text to a particular situation of the utterance confront us with two alternatives. We can, like Lowes, effectively relocate the text as a function of a much broader survey of its biographical, historical and cultural contexts (and this, as we have seen, is an option that also confronts superreaders of Wordsworth's ballads and Blake's songs). Or we can consider the extent to which the text, again like Keats's ode, replaces deictics with poetics. Once more we find ourselves with a potential for conflict between the literary scholar and the linguist, and in the case of 'Kubla Khan' the latter will hold the centre ground.

The poem makes use of a number of proper names from classical and middle-Eastern mythology (Kubla Khan, Alph, Xanadu, Mount Abora) and immediate locative references to unnamed rivers, chasms, fountains, a pleasure dome, an Abyssinian maid, all witnessed by the poet himself ('In a vision once I saw'). But any attempt to coordinate these as functions of a particular contextually determined speech act would have to rely upon Lowes's programme of biographical source hunting. If we focus upon the poem itself our attention is drawn away from the cultural, semantic or circumstantial designation of each sign and deictic signal and toward their relation to one another as functions of an enclosed, self-referential pattern of sound, syntax and semantics.

> In Xanadu did Kubla Khan
> A stately pleasure-dome decree:
> Where Alph, the sacred river, ran
> Through caverns measureless to man
>   Down to a sunless sea.

It is virtually impossible to isolate a single word or syllable that is not linked phonetically with at least two others: *X*ana*d*u, *d*i*d*, *d*ome, *d*ecree, *D*own; *s*tately, *s*acred, *s*unless, *s*ea; *K*ubla *K*han, de*c*ree, sa*c*red, *c*averns. Such a listing could be extended and supplemented by an almost infinite series of permutations in which alliteration connects with stress pattern, semantic foregrounding, syntactic structure and rhyme scheme. The effect of this complex interrelation between the material and the signifying dimensions of language creates two problems for the reader. Firstly it is largely impossible to justify the selection of a particular series of formal, semantic or syntactic correspondences as the basis for a naturalisation of the poem. Our choice to foreground or to exclude certain elements can never be founded upon any reliable invocation of the context of this speech act. And a reading that attempted to take every element of the double pattern into account would move us beyond Riffaterre's human superreader to the computer printout. Secondly we find that there is a self-deconstructive relation between Coleridge's claim to have produced a transparent record of his dream experience and the undeniable fact that the text does, in Derrida's words, 'prevent there from being at any moment or in any way a simple element that is present in and of itself and refers only to itself'. Derrida refers chiefly to the differential nature of syntactic and semantic designation, but here this self-contained system is supplemented by an equally complex fabric of relations between material signs. It is impossible to fully detach the intense correspondences between the sound patterns from what should be the more stable undertow of 'normal' syntactic and semantic correspondences.

Hence we either attempt to naturalise the poem by effectively forgetting its intrinsic signifying function (Lowes), or we acknowledge that any attempt to demystify this function and translate it into the metalanguage of paraphrase and closure will be continuously thwarted. For modern criticism the most notorious examples of Romantic textual foregrounding occur in the work of Shelley. His reputation as a poetic dilettante was established in dismissive judgements by Lamb, Carlyle and Arnold and was sustained with merciless precision by the textual analysts of the New Criticism (T. S. Eliot, F. R. Leavis, Donald Davie and Allen Tate included). The most common complaint is that his poems lack textual cohesion. Tate and Leavis draw attention to how a pattern of images or a metaphoric chain might begin with a specific noun or verb phrase but be followed by such a proliferation of wild and often discordant paradigms drawn from an apparently limitless frame of reference that any certain awareness of who is talking about what is effectively disrupted. And in an important sense Shelley could be regarded as the heir to the textual surrealism of Blake's *Songs*. Leavis (1949) comments on the following stanzas from the 'Ode to the West Wind',

> Thou on whose stream, mid the steep sky's commotion,
> Loose clouds like earth's decaying leaves are shed,
> Shook from the tangled boughs of Heaven and Ocean,
>
> Angels of rain and lightning: there are spread
> On the blue surface of thine aëry surge,
> Like the bright hair uplifted from the head
>
> Of some fierce Maenad, even from the dim verge
> Of the horizon to the zenith's height,
> The locks of the approaching storm.

In what way, asks Leavis, are the 'Loose clouds' like 'decaying leaves' and how can the 'Heaven and Ocean' be comprised of 'tangled boughs'? How can 'clouds' be 'shed' and how can the 'blue surface' of the sky 'surge' (346)? Leavis concludes that Shelley suffered from a 'weak grasp upon the actual', which, roughly translated, means that his shifts between the paradigmatic and syntagmatic elements have detached his language from any regular or reliable correspondence with perceived reality.

In the context of normative and functional linguistics Leavis has a valid case, but throughout his reading (and in Allen Tate's similar analyses) he conveniently forgets that the double pattern, as Jakobson was later to argue, removes language from its normal structural and functional mode. What Shelley does is effectively to transfer the cohesive, consecutive function of the text from the syntactic to the poetic sphere – and we will find similar shifts in the poetry of Hopkins, Eliot, and Dylan Thomas. The phonetic correspondences between who*s*e, *s*tream, *s*ky'*s*, loo*s*e cloud*s*, earth'*s*, leave*s*, *s*hed, *s*hook, bough*s* and O*c*ean effectively demolish Levin's demarcation between the syntactic–semantic function as cognitive and the poetic as conventional (see Chapter 1 pp. 15–16). Our cognitive resources are drawn as much to the material relation between these linguistic units as they are to their syntactic–semantic correspondences. Leavis partially acknowledges this by stating that the 'sweeping movement' and the 'plangency' of the verse are so 'potent' that we do not ask 'the obvious questions' (346). By 'obvious questions' he means the type of analytic uncertainties that might attend our reading of a non-literary text, but he did not consider the attendant question of how, when naturalising the text, we might balance the 'potency' of the verse (its poetic function) against our 'obvious questions' (its referential function). He did not do so because criticism and textual analysis did not (and probably still do not) possess sufficient resources to enable the reader to stabilise the tension between poetry's foregrounding of the material constituents of language and our normative, ratiocinative isolation of specific meanings.

To deal with this problem we should begin with a comparison between Shelley's and Coleridge's deployment of textual cohesion on the one hand, and Pope's on the other. The former effectively disrupt the Augustan programme of a balanced and parallel relation between the syntactic–semantic and the purely poetic dimension of the text and cause a continuous, and from the reader's perspective disorientating, pattern of interactions. Syntactic–semantic cohesion is not entirely disrupted but we find ourselves unable to move from the process of documenting the patterns created by alliteration, rhyme scheme and metrical foregrounding to any certain and productive model of signification. Consider how this shift of emphasis relates to the conventional programme of linguistic analysis. The poetic element of the double pattern is generally categorised within the broader study of phonetics. 'Phonetics is the branch of linguistics concerned with the physiological and acoustic bases of speech, and with such questions of how speech sounds are produced and perceived' (Traugott and Pratt, 51). Phonetics is essentially the study of linguistic material, and as such it gives as much attention to the physical origins of these phenomena as it does to their relationship with the lexical, semantic and syntactic production of meaning. The concept of phonetics as in some way isolated from the systematic complexities through which language generates meaning is important in our understanding of why the Romantics were drawn so regularly to the construction of self-contained patterns of sound. As we have seen, such patterns effectively work against the protocols of naturalisation and this may well have been an important element of the poet's intention. To naturalise a poetic text is to strip it of those features that constitute the poetic, and to effectively construct a metatext involving the addressee in the imagined situation of the utterance and its broader cultural, stylistic and social contexts (see Chapter 1, pp. 17–21). With poems such as Coleridge's 'Kubla Khan', Keats's 'Ode to Psyche' and Shelley's 'Ode to the West Wind', the dense fabric of sound patterns ensures that the text is largely detached from inferred or direct correspondences with pre-linguistic reality. To understand why the Romantics, whose programme was founded upon the mediation of pre-linguistic continua, might betray themselves into such gestures, we should return to the deconstructive analyses of speech and writing. Derrida:

> The privilege of the *phonè* does not depend upon a choice that might have been avoided. It corresponds to a moment of the system (let us say, of the "life" or "history" or of "being-as-self-relationship"). The system of "hearing/understanding-oneself-speak" [*s'entendre parler*] through the phonic substance – which *presents itself* as a non-exterior, non-worldly and therefore non-empirical or non-contingent signifier – has necessarily dominated the history of the world during an entire epoch, and has even produced the idea of the world, the idea of world-origin, arising from the difference between the worldly and the non-worldly,

the outside and the inside, ideality and non-ideality, universal and non-universal, transcendental and empirical, etc.

(*Of Grammatology*, 1977, 7–8)

By foregrounding the '*phonè*' these poets present their texts as pure moments of speech where the phonic substance seems to have isolated itself from the parasitic contingencies of other texts and extra-textual circumstances. It becomes impossible to detach the paraphrasable, referential meaning of each poem from its sound patterns – and sound patterns to be properly appreciated demand speech and presence. Hence we encounter manifestations of Derrida's disclosure of 's'entendre parler' as a self-deceiving illusion: speech and hearing guarantee presence and presence guarantees sincerity, truth and meaning. The deconstructive paradox exists in the fact that in order to transcend the deterministic function of the linguistic and interpretive system each poem has become in itself an isolated self-referential construct of language. In shifting the balance of the double pattern away from the intelligible toward the sensible dimension of language these poets effectively subvert their shared objective of preserving a pre-linguistic experience: the speaker effectively surrenders to the spoken text.

THE ROMANTIC PARADOX: A SUMMARY

The Romantics foregrounded a perennial and so far unresolved linguistic problem: they sought to close the gap between what occurs outside language and the means by which we address, mediate and communicate these phenomena. But to do so they drew almost entirely upon the linguistic genre which both intensifies and encloses language's function as a differential, self-determining sign system: poetry. For the reader, particularly the critic/superreader, they caused a fissure between the two frames of reference shared by linguistics and literary studies: text and context. Each of the texts examined, from Wordsworth, Coleridge, Blake, Shelley and Keats, shares a tendency to create an uncertain relation between our awareness of its intrinsic features and its consequent designation as a speech act and our broader awareness of the cultural, stylistic, biographic and socio-political codes upon which it draws. The primary cause of this interpretive disjunction is their continuous and unremitting interfusion of the referential and the material dimensions of the linguistic sign. It becomes virtually impossible to base a naturalisation upon a clear distinction between the internal, interconnected sign systems of each poem and the points at which the semantic, contextual and cultural designation of each dominant thematic sign (Psyche, Innocence, Experience, The Idiot, Tintern Abbey, Immortality, Kubla Khan, The West Wind) connects with its counterparts in the world outside the text.

The problems engaged with by the Romantics would be largely marginalised by the poets of the later nineteenth century and returned to, with a vengeance, by the modernists. They are embodied in the distinction between the later poems of Blake and the notoriously self-referential sound-texts of Shelley. Both poets shared the objective of capturing in a single text the complex relation between the spatio-temporal nature of events and experiences and their effect upon the speaker. Their diametrically opposed practices offer us an intriguing insight into the perplexing choices that confront all poets. To move, as Blake did, toward the end of the sliding scale that reduces the poetic function to the use of the unmetrical line will involve the reader in an interpretive bind. If the poetic function is not palpably and self-evidently present how do we judge the signifying processes of the text against other discourses that are not intended to engage with issues that our cultural programming obliges us to associate with poetry? If, on the other hand, we encounter texts such as Shelley's in which the poetic function supersedes both the internal syntactic–semantic and the related contextual functions, how can we claim that poetry is anything other than an enclosed self-perpetuating game, without any relevance for 'real' interfaces between language and the world? As we shall see this problem becomes even more complex for the reader of twentieth-century poetry, but for the moment consider the following conundrum. Poetry inscribes and effectively validates the specificity of literature. Unlike other forms of discourse it encloses, animates, and sometimes creates the situation of the utterance. Yet poets, particularly the Romantics, argue that it is the only form of language that can disclose the purity of pre-linguistic experience. The question of why this peculiar paradox has endured and persists will be considered more fully in Chapter 6.

Exercises

Use the following poems and extracts to test my thesis that Romantic poetry opens a fissure between the poetic function, the elements that combine to produce complex textual patterns, and its referential counterpart, the inferred pre-linguistic situation or the intention of the utterance. The best way to conduct such an exercise is to monitor your own processes of naturalisation. Ask what Leavis refers to as the 'obvious questions'. Who is speaking to whom? What do the syntactic and deictic features tell us about the situation of the utterance? How does the conventional element of the double pattern (metre, rhyme, etc.) relate to its cognitive counterpart (the paraphrasible message)? Use these questions as anchor points in your decoding of each text, and then consider two crucial problems: have you marginalised or perhaps corrected internal patterns of signification in order to 'make sense' of the text? Does the metrical or rhyming pattern of each passage operate as a substitute for continuities of syntax and points of reference?

(i)   The opening paragraph of Coleridge's 'The Eolian Harp'. Is the speaker addressing Sara directly, or are the events and feelings recollected and mediated at some later point? Do the deictic references and the shifts in tense allow us to properly answer this question?

> My pensive Sara! thy soft cheek reclined
> Thus on mine arm, most soothing sweet it is
> To sit beside our Cot, our Cot o'ergrown
> With white-flowered Jasmin, and the broad-leaved Myrtle,
> (Meet emblems they of Innocence and Love!)
> And watch the clouds, that late were rich with light,
> Slow saddening round, and mark the star of eve
> Serenely brilliant (such should Wisdom be)
> Shine opposite! How exquisite the scents
> Snatched from yon bean-field! and the world so hushed!
> The stilly murmur of the distant Sea
> Tells us of silence.

(ii)   Lines 11–30 of Coleridge's 'Limbo'. What exactly is 'Limbo'? A mental state? An imagined but indescribable condition? A place? Does the complex pattern of metaphoric excursions distort or clarify the situation that Coleridge attempts to describe?

> 'Tis a strange place, this Limbo! – not a Place,
> Yet name it so; – where Time and weary Space
> Fettered from flight, with night-mare sense of fleeing,
> Strive for their last crepuscular half-being; –
> Lank Space, and scytheless Time with branny hands

Barren and soundless as the measuring sands,
Not marked by flit of Shades, – unmeaning they
As moonlight on the dial of the day!
But that is lovely – looks like Human Time,
An Old Man with a steady look sublime,
That stops his earthly task to watch the skies;
But he is blind – a Statue hath such eyes; –
Yet having moonward turned his face by chance,
Gazes the orb with moon-like countenance,
With scant white hairs, with foretop bald and high,
He gazes still, – his eyeless face all eye; –
As 'twere an organ full of silent sight,
His whole face seemeth to rejoice in light!
Lip touching lip, all moveless, bust and limb –
He seems to gaze at that which seems to gaze on him!

(iii)   Introduction to Blake's 'Songs of Experience'. Compare this
with the above discussion of the Introduction to 'Songs of Innocence'. Who 'walked among the ancient trees' – 'The Holy Word'
or 'The Bard'? Are stanzas 3 and 4 the words of the Bard or the
words of the speaker addressing the Bard? Who is asked to 'Turn
away no more' – The addressee (us), the Bard, someone else?

Hear the voice of the Bard!
Who Present, Past, & Future sees
Whose ears have heard,
The Holy Word,
That walk'd among the ancient trees.

Calling the lapsed Soul
And weeping in the evening dew;
That might controll,
The starry pole
And fallen fallen light renew!

O Earth O Earth return!
Arise from out the dewy grass;
Night is worn,
And the morn
Rises from the slumberous mass.

Turn away no more:
Why wilt thou turn away

The starry floor
The watry shore
Is giv'n thee till the break of day.

(iv)   Lines 46–54, Book I, of Wordsworth's *The Prelude*. If, as Wordsworth states, this is the memory of a moment of poetic inspiration (note the tense of the passage), are the 'measured strains', 'here/Recorded' an admission that the original experience is irretrievable?

Thus far, O Friend! did I, not used to make
A present joy the matter of a song,
Pour forth that day my soul in measured strains
That would not be forgotten, and are here
Recorded: to the open fields I told
A prophecy: poetic numbers came
Spontaneously to clothe in priestly robe
A renovated spirit singled out,
Such hope was mine, for holy services.

(v)   Lines 1–17 of Shelley's *Alastor*. Try to paraphrase this passage. Do the repeated conditional phrases ('If') make sense in themselves? Why does the speaker ask for forgiveness? What exactly is 'this boast'?

Earth, ocean, air, belovèd brotherhood!
If our great Mother has imbued my soul
With aught of natural piety to feel
Your love, and recompense the boon with mine;
If dewy morn, and odorous noon, and even,
With sunset and its gorgeous ministers,
And solemn midnight's tingling silentness;
If autumn's hollow sighs in the sere wood,
And winter robing with pure snow and crowns
Of starry ice the grey grass and bare boughs;
If spring's voluptuous pantings when she breathes
Her first sweet kisses, have been dear to me;
If no bright bird, insect, or gentle beast
I consciously have injured, but still loved
And cherished these my kindred; then forgive
This boast, belovèd brethren, and withdraw
No portion of your wonted favour now!

5 Victorian poetry

This will be the shortest section of the book; more an interchapter than a chapter. The Victorian poets, by which I mean those whose reputations were made and sustained between the 1830s and the 1890s, are often celebrated as the most skilled and meticulous stylists of post-Renaissance English verse, and it is for this reason that their work will be treated more economically than that of their predecessors and successors. The stylistic and formal paradigms that the Victorians inherited from three centuries of writing would be perfected, extended, even challenged, but they would not in any significant way be altered. The term Victorian poetry is a rather vague methodological convenience. Tennyson and Browning (born between 1809–12) and Arnold, Swinburne, Hardy and Hopkins (born 1822–44), are effectively the second and third generations of Romanticism. But they are also, in a less tangible way, the anxious and uneasy final stage in what is variously termed traditionalism or pre-modernism. These two elements – the Romantic affiliation to poetry as the supremely subjective medium for expression and poetry as a particular system of prescribed devices – are the unifying features of Victorian verse.

In terms of prosody and metrical patterning this period is one of eclecticism, bordering on but never fully entering the realm of experiment. Tennyson was the master of stanzaic and rhythmic precision; Browning adapted the more permissive elements of the poetic *langue*, particularly blank verse, to the contingencies of the speech act and circumstance; Patmore and Swinburne pressed the conventional line–syntax relation of the double pattern to its pre-modernist limit; and Hopkins, though occasionally celebrated as the precurser of modernist experiment, should more accurately be regarded as the final inheritor of Shelley's addiction to the fore-grounding of acoustic material.

In what follows we will consider texts and extracts that embody this tension between enclosure within tradition, post-Romantic exuberance and pre-modernist innovation. Tension will be our key-note, because the Victorians, more than any other historical or generic school, exhibit a tangible consciousness of being prisoners of the double pattern, sometimes rebellious, sometimes stoical. We will begin with Tennyson, arguably the most stoical of them all.

TENNYSON

In Memoriam A.H.H. is both in structural and functional terms a vast network of tensions. It is a long poem, addressing itself to the death of Tennyson's friend Hallam and maintaining this single event as the correlative for lyrical explorations of the meaning of life, death, love, art and all manner of permutations on the relationship between subjective existence and the events that control and determine this condition. Its consistent thematic and structural motif is that of unrealised possibility. It is about Tennyson and Hallam, but the latter no longer exists; it is an attempt to mediate in language the true essence of their lives, but it returns continuously to the speaker's awareness that such a task is beyond the powers of language. We have already considered the inherent paradoxes of the Romantic programme – essentially the more a poet attempts to transcend the refractory nature of the medium the more its arbitrary impersonal density becomes the subject of the discourse – and *In Memoriam* is the archetypal post-Romantic poem. It is as much about poetry as it is about Tennyson and Hallam.

David Lodge (1977) has pondered Jakobson's thesis that the dichotomy between the syntagmatic–metonymic and the paradigmatic–metaphoric poles of language is 'of primal significance and consequence for all verbal behaviour and for human behaviour in general' (80–1): in short, the long-sought methodological link between the communicative and behavioural elements of human life. Lodge drew up two columns of communicative and existential categories beginning with the monoliths of metaphor and metonymy, and the following is a revision of this diagram. It is also the key to our understanding of *In Memoriam* and other manifestations of nineteenth-century post-Romanticism.

Metaphor	Metonymy
Paradigm	Syntagm
Selection	Combination

Poetic Function	Referential Function
Romanticism	Realism
Lyric	Epic
Poetry	Prose
Text	Context

In Memoriam engages with each of these oppositions, and more significantly it foregrounds their distinction of being at the heart of the tragic nature of human existence.

The poem returns continuously to specific and deictic references to Tennyson's and Hallam's lives: see, for example, section VII on the 'Dark house', 'the long unlovely street', 'the door', 'the drizzling rain'; section IX on the 'fair ship', 'the Italian shore', 'Arthur's loved remains'. These references to an extra-textual series of events and experiences anchor the poem to the syntactic–realist–epic–contextual pole, and we should be aware that during the period of the poem's composition (1830s–1850s), the novel had gained acceptance as a respectable literary genre whose structure was determined more by the events outside the narrative than by any intrinsic textual formula. But, perhaps as an implicit disengagement from this cultural circumstance, Tennyson foregrounds the localising effect of the lyric, the most intense and self-consciously poetic genre. Milton's *Paradise Lost* and Wordsworth's *The Prelude* had trod an uncertain path between the extra-textual demands of narrative and autobiography and the ability of poetry to draw events into isolated moments and processes of linguistic mediation. Both had deployed blank verse, the most prominent pre-modernist means of reconciling local intensity with narrative, but Tennyson's poem is comprised of stanzas (iambic octosyllables, rhyming a bb a). Each of these causes an uneasy tension between any broader pattern of narrative or cohesive structure and single units of lyrical intensity. A number of critics (A. C. Bradley in particular) have attempted to impose a structural pattern upon the poem's 131 sections (each consisting of a variable number of stanzas) but it is possible to enter the poem at any point, read a section at random and not sense that an injustice has been done to any broader pattern of narrative cohesion. Again we should note that the tension between syntagm and paradigm, progress and focus, epic and lyric is invoked but not reconciled.

Within each section of the poem there is a persistent and meticulous distinction between contiguity–combination and similarity–selection. In the prologue the opening lines of each stanza preserve the deictic circuit of human being addressing both God and the

reader: the first four foreground the addresser–addressee relationship with attributive adjectives, 'Thine are . . .', 'Thou wilt . . .',
'Thou seemest . . .', and the section closes with direct transitive
verb phrases, 'Forgive what . . .', 'Forgive my . . .', 'Forgive
these . . .'. But within each stanza this pattern of extra-textual
continuity is counterpointed against more personal, metaphoric
patterns.

> Thine are these orbs of light and shade;
>> Thou madest Life in man and brute;
>> Thou madest Death; and lo, thy foot
> Is on the skull which thou hast made.

The opening lines maintain a continuous point of contact between
text and context – the speaker invokes conventional perceptions of
God – while the internal structure of each stanza allows the speaking
presence to integrate extra-linguistic projection with subjective
intensity – 'Thine' (i.e. God's) 'orbs of light and shade' (the planets)
is literal, while 'thy foot . . . on the skull' is figurative. This pattern
of opening lines as referential and stanzas as intensively poetic,
textual registers, operates throughout the poem. It is almost as
though Tennyson is torn between the discursive referential structure
of prose (each section as a means of positioning writer, reader and
subject in the manner of a journal or diary) and the ability of poetry
(the stanza) to both enclose this referential functional and shift the
register of images away from the combinative, verifiable continuum
toward the more speculative, metaphoric realm.

Section V is in effect the metatextual manifesto for the poem's
uneasy sense of division. In stanzas 1 and 4 Tennyson foregrounds
in the opening lines the personal pronoun 'I' but his subject is
poetry, and each stanza gradually encloses the specific referential
image of a speaker within the poetic function.

> In words, like weeds, I'll wrap me o'er,
>> Like coarsest clothes against the cold:
>> But that large grief which these enfold
> Is given in outline and no more.

The first line positions the poet as the controlling presense – words
are like clothes (weeds), superficial – but this sense of control drifts
into a far more speculative, uncertain pattern: clothes/words both
protect the user against the cold (pre-linguistic facts, death?), but
they also 'enfold' this same feeling of pain. This paradox is given a

self-consciously mimetic edge: in the first two lines the referential function is literally 'enfolded' in an alliterative pattern.

In the preceding stanza Tennyson writes:

> But, for the unquiet heart and brain,
>   A use in measured language lies;
>   The sad mechanic exercise,
> Like dull narcotics, numbing pain.

This is a candid summary of the post-Romantic condition. The speaker is fully aware of the heroic failure of the first generation of Romanticism: measured language, the poetic function, is an enclosed self-referential state detached, in this case mercifully detached, from the 'pain' of unmediated existence. In section XXI he addresses the same theme; the opening line of the first stanza foregrounds the paradox: 'I sing to him that rests below'. His addressee is, in every sense, non-existent. And he invents three sceptical interlocuters to tax him 'harshly' with the question of poetic relevance: what use is a continuous return to 'sorrow's barren song' in an age when 'the people', 'the civil power', 'Science' should hold the attention of anyone concerned with the condition and future of humanity? (Tennyson was no doubt aware of phenomena such as the Chartist Movement, the Reform Bill, the European Revolutions of the 1840s, the Crimean War, the socio-political effects of the industrial revolution.)

In Memoriam is important. It could be interpreted as an elegy upon the death of poetry, not as an art form but as a discourse whose relationship with non-poetic and pre-linguistic continua could be direct and influential. The two columns of structural and functional conditions that Jakobson and Lodge offer as an analytical tool were for the Victorian poet a dismaying and unresolvable separation between the poetic and the non-poetic. The enclosed, self-referential world had been offered by the metaphysicals as an alternative to the harsh, contingent realities of non-poetic discourse and the pre-linguistic continuum – the right-hand column was confidently subordinated to the left. For the Victorians the two were continually at odds with one another. T. S. Eliot has charged the post-metaphysical tradition of English poetry with a 'dissociation of sensibility', an inability or unwillingness to synthesise in poetic language the disparate, and in rational terms, unrelated elements of our linguistic and pre-linguistic experience. His point, as Tennyson demonstrates, is valid. The addresser of *In Memoriam* is both the self-consciously ineffectual poet lamenting the very real departure of his friend, and the linguistic craftsman able to construct worlds of metrical and metaphoric self-reference safely detached from this 'other' reality.

Three centuries of writing had created an uneasy collection of structural and functional conditions: the metaphysicals had created purely poetic worlds cohabited by addresser and addressee (left-hand column); the Augustans had subdued poetic self-reference to a structured idiom which the addresser would command and manipulate (a shift to the right); the Romantics had attempted to transcend the structural and functional conditions of self-reference and transparency (a merger of left and right).

ARNOLD

The problem faced by the Victorians is captured in Matthew Arnold's classic essay 'The Study of Poetry' (1880). The essay addresses the relationship between the structural and the functional identity of poetry and it contains what would appear to be a fundamental contradiction. Arnold implies that the post-Shakespearean *langue* of forms and stylistic devices is effectively complete; the question is what its nineteenth-century inheritors should do with it: 'poetry is at bottom a criticism of life; . . . the greatness of a poet lies in his powerful and beautiful application of ideas to life, – to the question: How to live' (p. 376). This sounds like a plea for a return to the relevance and accessibility of the Augustan public poem, but elsewhere in the essay he dismisses Dryden and Pope as 'classics of our prose'. His argument, roughly summarised, is this: poetry is able to address moral, philosophical and even political themes and disclose absolute conditions of knowledge and truth that would be contaminated and distorted by the prose treatise or, by implication, the novel. He wanted poetry to replace religion and science as an instrument of personal and social harmony, but he maintained that it could only achieve this by retaining its structural difference from prose: Non-poetic discourses – speech, fictional and non-fictional prose – were limited by their structural dependency upon pre-linguistic circumstances and the only discourse that could be relevant to these uncertain conditions was that which removed itself from them. How did this seemingly contradictory thesis translate into practice? The double pattern is the element from which the speaking presence, whether textual, imagined or verifiably real, can never fully detach itself. The common feature of all Victorian poems is their self-conscious awareness of the double pattern which the speaker must inhabit (without it the text would not be poetic) but which exists uneasily as a legacy, something which cannot be discarded but whose relevance to the non-poetic social, intellectual and emotional condition is uncertain.

Arnold's 'The Scholar Gypsy' (1853) is a curious and often misinterpreted instance of this conflict. The most recent misinterpretation occurs in Belsey's *Critical Practice* (1980). Belsey regards it as a culmination of the tradition of the Romantic ode (Wordsworth, Shelley and Keats in particular) in which there is a decentring, 'a formal absence at the centre of the poem'. This most certainly is not the case. It is true that Arnold invokes various elements of the Romantic programme – the eponymous scholar gypsy personifies the Romantic ideal, consciously and deliberately detaching himself from conventional systems and institutions of learning, thinking and behaviour. But unlike its counterparts in Keats's or Shelley's odes the speaking presence of this poem establishes his condition as a non-participating observer of the aesthetic and existential ideal. The poem's deictic pointers, again unlike those of its Romantic predecessors, are clear, specific and unambiguous. He is in a field near Oxford with a copy of Glanvil's book open on the grass (stanzas 3–4) and throughout the poem he balances the imagined situation of Glanvil's subject (the eponymous seventeenth-century ex-scholar turned to simple rural existence) against a very specific pattern of images drawn from the immediate circumstances of the speech act: 'the Stripling Thames', 'Godstow Bridge', 'the Cumner Hills', 'Bagley Wood', 'Hinksey', 'Christ-Church'. You will search in vain for a high Romantic ode which situates the speech act within such specific spatio-temporal conditions. Again we find that the text invokes but does not reconcile crucial elements of the metaphor–metonym columns. Belsey claims that the erratic shifts in tense (stanzas 15–16, principally 'Hast' and 'Had'st') contribute to the decentred illogic of the text, but the opposite is the case. The distinction between the scholar's absence (past tense, since he is dead) and presence (present tense, since his story occupies the mind of the speaker) effectively guarantees the speaker's control of the text and its ideational pattern: 'I' (speaker) contemplate the past in relation to the present. The poem is post-Romantic in that it is both about Romanticism (left-hand column) and structurally unromantic (right-hand column). Compare it with the odes of Coleridge, Keats and Shelley discussed in the previous chapter and you will find that its syntactic and deictic features concentrate the reader's attention upon a stable speaking presence subtly interposing his own controlled imaginative resources with a creative and existential ideal that is touching but in practical terms unrealistic. The high Romantic ode draws the speaker into the shifting images and patterns of the text (left-hand column); this poem foregrounds the extra-textual presence of a particular speaker inspired by a particular book in a particular time and place (right-hand column). It is the equivalent of interposing the prose description of 'Kubla Khan' with the textual substance of the poem.

In Memoriam and 'The Scholar Gypsy' submit readily, perhaps too readily, to the protocols of naturalisation. Their deictic features are sufficiently detailed to subdue any serious imbalance between poetic intention and the situation of the speech act – a stable relationship between addresser–poet and addressee–reader is maintained. The relationships between the metonymic-realist and the metaphoric–Romantic dimensions are dutifully poetic but at the same time coordinated so that the reader remains clearly aware of distinctions between contact, message, context and code. The stabilising axis between these potentially disruptive elements is the regular double pattern. In both poems the stanzaic formulae are complex enough to allow the type of textual–contextual disorientations of metaphysical verse, but the nineteenth-century inheritors of the poetic *langue* display a control of the double pattern that is comparable to a contemporary prose writer's control of the sentence. In this respect the nineteenth-century poets were the most confidently yet cautiously literate generation of the pre-modernist canon. The *langue* of iambic, trochaic patterns, stanzaic formulae and complex rhyme schemes was their grammar; and grammar is the science or at least the competence that enables the linguistic addresser to achieve a transparent agreement with the addressee.

EXPERIMENT

The Victorian poets certainly experimented with the accepted coordinates of the double pattern, but there is a clear distinction between their excursions and the twentieth-century free verse/modernist tradition, and it is this: the nineteenth-century innovators never allowed their use of the material density of poetry, the double pattern, to dislocate text from speaker and referent. The modernists, as we shall see, did.

The obvious test case for this claim is the verse of Gerard Manley Hopkins. Hopkins's reputation as a 'modernist-before-his-time' is due partly to the fact that his poems were not published until 1918, in the midst of the first decade of modernist experiment. In fact his poetry is firmly rooted in the tradition of the Romantic ode: he is the most extreme personification of the Romantic paradox. His *ex cathedra* statements on form and imagination are original only in the oddness of their vocabulary. 'Inscape' and 'instress' are renamed elements of the late-eighteenth-century Romantic school of primitivism, a desire to isolate a transparent and unitary correlation between experience, feeling and linguistic expression. Phenomena such as 'sprung rhythm' and 'outrides' are said to originate in Old English verse and questions of what they are and how they work have provided a minor growth industry for twentieth-century prosodists. To simplify matters, sprung rhythm is the maintenance of a regular pattern of major stresses in each line with a variable number of lesser unstress–stress patterns or outrides – a formula not too distant from Coleridge's accentualist experiment in 'Christabel'. It would be difficult and I believe pointless to attempt to summarise or judge the vast amount of work on Hopkins's syntax, sound patterns, etymology, metre, diction (see Milroy, 1977 for an accessible guide). Instead we will attempt to identify a common stylistic feature which draws together these cognitive and conventional elements of the double pattern.

In Hopkins's sonnet 'The Windhover' we encounter a somewhat eccentric form of syntactic compression or sentence embedding. In ordinary language an embedded syntactic structure is the equivalent of making two statements at the same time: for example the sentence 'James, who is Irish, eats mushrooms' involves two propositions, 'James is Irish', 'James eats mushrooms'. In Hopkins's poem the embedding is far more dense and grammatically deviant.

> I caught this morning morning's minion king–
> dom of daylight's dauphin, dapple-dawn-drawn Falcon. . .

The subject of the sentence, the falcon, is the beloved (the 'minion') of the morning and also 'dauphin' (heir) to the kingdom of daylight, not to mention being 'drawn' (silhouetted? or drawn out?) by the 'dapple dawn'. The concentrated, elliptical structure of the syntax is matched by a similarly localised pattern of stress groupings and alliterative–assonantal clusters. Consult any study of Hopkins's technique and you will find that critics concentrate upon dense, localised structures while paying much less attention to broader patterns of coherence. The reason for this is that Hopkins balances intense and disorientating moments of formal and referential synthesis against very conventional anchor points. In 'The Windhover' these involve the persistent use of the personal pronoun – 'I caught', 'my heart', 'my chevalier', 'my dear' – and the slightly irregular but undeniably insistent presence of that structural archetype, the sonnet. The effect, in this and many of his other much discussed poems, is of a specific presence struggling with the arbitrary conventions of poetic and non poetic language. It is this tension within the double pattern, between the poetic and the non-poetic functions of language, that enables us to locate the true historic and aesthetic affiliations of Hopkins's verse. Milton and Blake had practised a moderate form of grammatical deviation, but Hopkins is the first poet in English to write consistently in a way that is by all normal standards ungrammatical.

We have already encountered a form of syntactic compression, and in poems such as 'The Wreck of the Deutschland' we will find syntactic expansion: verbless or subjectless sentences, incomplete clauses, interruptions and exclamations by non-designated speakers, colloquial insertions and repetitions. This is stanza 28 from 'The Deutschland',

> But how shall I . . . make me room there:
> Reach me a . . . Fancy come faster –
> Strike you the sight of it? look at the loom there,
> Thing that she . . . there then! the Master,
> *Ipse*, the only one, Christ, King, Head:

The poem is an attempt to capture the physical, emotional and spiritual experience of imminent death, and it differs from his first person lyrics in that Hopkins interposes the perceptual and verbal presences of the shipwreck victims with his own. In lyrical pieces such as 'The Windhover' syntactic concentration is deployed as a register of immediacy and spontaneity and in 'The Deutschland' this same sense of the immediate context of the utterance distorting its linguistic register is supplemented by the chaotic multiplicity of voices. In both instances Hopkins attempts to bring the text as close as possible to the pre-ratiocinative function of the speech act. And again we encounter the Romantic paradox. In all of his poems we make sense of the various forms of syntactic deviation and incoherence by imposing the order of deep structure upon the disorder of surface structure, but as we do so we are aware of a pattern that is persistent, if not entirely regular, and intrinsic to the structure of the text. In 'The Windhover' we encounter the sonnet; in 'The Deutschland' the potentially chaotic synthesis of voices is enclosed and to a degree stabilised by sound patterns: the continuities of rhyme scheme and assonantal–alliterative pattern are counter-pointed against syntactic discontinuities.

I stated earlier that the Victorians are the grammarians of poetic form, the inheritors of a complex meta-*langue* of patterns and devices. Hopkins has been praised for his attempts to bring poetry closer to the immediacies of ordinary language, but such praise should be qualified by our awareness that the more he unshackled his words from the impersonal determinants of non-poetic syntax, the more he foregrounded the equally impersonal structures of the purely poetic *langue*. One early reviewer of his posthumous collection (1918) commented on how the 'strangeness' of his grammatical constructions is at odds with the 'traps for the attention' offered by the persistent sound patterns (Milroy, 2).

Much attention has been paid to Hopkins's experiments with conventional notions of semantics and etymology (in 'The Wind-hover' we find 'wimpling', 'Buckle', 'sheer plod', 'sillion'). Words are drawn from contexts not normally associated with the situation of the utterance: contemporary dialect and referential arcana, roots pulled from Latin, Welsh, German and Old English. As we attempt to isolate and recontextualise these semantic oddities we will find that they also function within the text as links in a phonemic chain (billion, sillion, shine, vermillion; riding, striding, wimpling, wing, swing). Once more we find that abnormalities in the cognitive register of the double pattern (the words signify outside their normal or expected context) are stabilised by its conventional register (they are fitted into a sound pattern that is vital to the structure of the text).

The relationship between Hopkins's verse and modernist experiment is and will remain uncertain. He sustains the Romantic ideal of transparency and immediacy which would be readdressed by the early modernists, but his almost obsessive reliance upon the material elements of metre and sound pattern were the very elements that the modernists rejected. His closest link is with the eclecticism of the postmodern (see Chapter 6, pp. 173–89). Dylan Thomas and T. S. Eliot juxtaposed discontinuities of narrative, syntax and deictic reference with textual patterns of metre and rhyme. Hopkins, Thomas and Eliot are traditionalists in the sense that each concedes that poetic individuality and immediacy can only become valid if the voice of the poet is an element of the intrinsically poetic structure of the text.

CONJECTURES

One of the more unsettling elements of the vast network of modern interpretive disciplines – structural linguistics, structuralism, post-structuralism – is the idea that language is not something that we as human beings use as a medium, a register of our perceptions, beliefs and experiences, but a continuum that we inhabit, a system through which we construct patterns of faith, order and perceptual stability. Poetry, particularly regular poetry, further complicates the relationship between language and identity. If we accept that language is an autonomous system, then to supplement existing rules and conventions with an even more arbitrary set of structural regulations would seem to deny the speaking subject and the originator yet another dimension of individuality and expressive freedom. But it could also be argued that the separation of the intrinsically poetic text from all other linguistic types and functions actually guarantees a form of independence. I would cite this second argument as the key to our understanding of why the Victorian poets, even in their most innovative moments, refused to dissolve the interdependent relationship between the manifest tradition of the poetic (its metrical and phonemic devices), and its ability to mediate particular situations of experience, perception and reflection. Think about Arnold's thesis that poetry would compensate for the gradual but incessant fragmentation of systems of belief and social organisation. By the mid-nineteenth century most other linguistic genres had in various ways been adapted to the new and uncertain conditions of existence and thought. Marx and Engels, amongst others, were collapsing pre-nineteenth-century distinctions between philosophical, historical and political discourses. Huxley and Darwin were combining the disturbing empiricism of science with subjects and discourses that had once been comfortably protected by theological absolutes. The novels of Dickens, Thackeray and the Brontës were structured as much by the unpredictable contingencies of life as by any corresponding duty to the orders of art. In 1889 Walter Pater (see 'Style', in *Appreciations*) argued that the 'chaotic variety and complexity of the modern world' could not be properly mediated by 'the restraint proper to verse form', that the 'special art of the modern world' was imaginative prose. This is both a diagnosis and a misrepresentation. The double pattern, the essence of Pater's concept of 'restraint', was the poet's final point of resistance. If the forms and functions of other discourses had been shaped and conditioned by circumstances then at least the tangible presence of metre would maintain a sense of continuity with the (imagined) order of the past, against the unpredictable contingencies of the present – and in the following chapter we will find a similar desire for continuity in the work of Eliot.

It might seem rather presumptuous to base such a sweeping generalisation on the work of three poets but my thesis can be tested against the following texts and issues.

BROWNING

Browning's most celebrated contribution to the poetic *langue* is the dramatic monologue, and his development of this form constitutes a literary sub-genre in its own right. It implicitly acknowledges the uneasy relation between the two competing discourses of the novel and the poem. Each first person account differs from the metaphysical or Romantic lyric in its meticulous foregrounding of deictic references, and it would be useful to compare the effects created by these versified short stories with those of a contemporary first person prose narrative – Dickens's *Great Expectations*, for example.

In 'My Last Duchess' and 'The Bishop Orders His Tomb' the speakers are figures from the Italian Renaissance, and in each the reader is drawn into the spatio-temporal conditions of the speech act. Compare these poems with those of Donne and Marvell (Chapter 2). In Browning's pieces the poet cautiously avoids any conflict between the poetic–textual function and the imagined situation of the utterance. 'My Last Duchess' consists of enjambed couplets, and there is certainly a tension between the metrical pattern of each pentameter (verse design), the interlineal syntax and rhythm (verse instance) and rhyme, but it is a controlled and orchestrated tension.

> Oh sir, she smiled, no doubt,
> Whene'er I past her; but who passed without
> Much the same smile? This grew; I gave commands;
> Then all smiles stopped together. There she stands
> As if alive.

(43–7)

The syntax reproduces a pattern of unforced, coordinated speech: his point of reference is the painting of the duchess and the entire grammatical structure of shifts in tense, pronouns and verbal inflections is anchored in the situation of the utterance. In one sense the pattern resembles the so-called free indirect style of the modern novel (see Traugott and Pratt, 301–2), except that the entire poem is cautiously sown with cohesive deictic references that allow us to identify a real extra-textual relationship between the 'she' and the 'I'. At another level the contrapuntal tension between syntax, line structure and rhyme is brilliantly balanced so that the poetic devices (such as run-on lines and rhymes occurring within grammatical clauses) cooperate rather than interfere with the speech pattern. In the closed couplets of Pope the referential function is effectively determined by its poetic counterpart; here the double pattern becomes far more flexible and responsive to context. We are aware that the rhyme scheme and the pentameter distances the text from non-poetic forms of speech and writing but this distancing does not create conflicts between the textual and referential functions.

'The Bishop Orders His Tomb' is in blank verse, and again there is not the same sense of interference between the materiality and the signifying function of the text that we have encountered in the blank verse of Milton and Wordsworth.

Browning's monologues are attempts to rescue the poetic function from the distancing effects of high Romantic form, to maintain the devices of poetry while reconciling these to the naturalistic contexture of prose, both fictional and non-fictional. Consider again the metaphor–metonym columns and you will find in Browning a continuous pattern of checks and balances: Romanticism and Realism, Paradigm and Syntagm, Text and Context. In monologues such as 'Johannes Agricola in Meditation' and 'Soliloquy of the Spanish Cloister' he tests this balancing procedure against very complex stanzaic and metrical patterns, and it is as though he is, perhaps like George Herbert, continuously exploring the relationship between the functional and structural conditions of poetry. If this is his programme we might be prompted to ask why none of these meticulously detailed situations are set in the mid-nineteenth century. Ruskin said of 'The Bishop' (*Modern Painters*, 1856, IV, 380) that 'I know of no other piece of modern English, prose or poetry, in which there is so much told, as in these lines, of the Renaissance spirit', and he generously praised it as a social, cultural and historical study more penetrative than his own *The Stones of Venice*. Why then did Browning not employ these resources to 'tell as much' about, in Pater's phrase, 'the chaotic variety and complexity of the modern world'?

In 1880 William Morris delivered a lecture called 'The Beauty of Life' (in *Collected Works*, 1966) in which he compared contemporary social and cultural conditions with those of earlier periods, descending to such particulars as the public parks and suburban developments of Birmingham. He begins, 'I stand before you this evening weighted with a disadvantage that I did not feel last year – I have little fresh to tell you'. Could not such a direct address to the immediate concerns of the audience be versified in the manner of Browning's monologues? The picture of the duchess or the Bishop's tomb, with all their social, emotional and aesthetic associations could be substituted by Morris's 'the huge chimney there [in Bradford] which serves the acres of weaving and spinning sheds of Sir Titus Salt and his brothers'. Consider the result of changing a few of the nouns and adverbs at the beginning of Browning's 'My Last Duchess' (original in brackets).

>   [my last duchess]   [wall]
> That's the huge chimney painted on the sky
>   [she]   [call]
> Looking as if it were alive. I cry
>   [Fra Pandolf's]
> That piece a wonder now, Sir Titus's hand's
>   [she]
> Worked busily a day, and there it stands
>   [her]
> Will't please you sit and look at it?

This seems to work well enough, but you will search in vain for an example of the Victorian poet anchoring deictic and referential patterns to those subjects, such as the Smoke Act and industrial development, that occupied the attention of prose essayists. To address the question 'why not?' we should return to Arnold's essay. Poetry is 'a criticism of life', but it must address itself to the atemporal ahistoric conditions of life that mid-nineteenth-century man shares with figures from myth, classical literature and the past. Browning's monologues are 'realistic' in the sense that they subdue the textual function to the immediate and conditional circumstances of the speech act, but to have allowed these circumstances some interface with the minutiae and complexity of contemporary existence would have reduced the mysterious nature of the poetic (signalled by the double pattern) to the status of an incongruously decorative means of addressing practical issues.

The adaptation of the dramatic monologue to the terms and conditions of contemporary experience would have to wait until Eliot's 'The Love Song of J. Alfred Prufrock' (discussed in Chapter 6). You will need to judge for yourself whether modernist formal innovation significantly altered the nineteenth-century perception and practice of poetry as enclosed within a universalised–ahistoric function.

CONCLUSION

Victorian poetic style is at once eclectic and regressive. Between the 1830s and the 1890s every established form of the regular double pattern was revived and sometimes reworked. The period is the terminus of the traditional poetic *langue* and as such it played a significant part in causing the free verse revolution: poetic form had nowhere else to go. For the Victorians the relationship between the conventional and the cognitive elements of the double pattern was comparable to the public relationship between men and women. The marriage was necessary. It ensured that poetry could maintain a stable aloofness from the rapidly changing and potentially chaotic relationship between non-poetic discourse and the pre-linguistic world. At the same time, convention ruled against the discernable, procreative coupling of the two elements: the poetic and the referential (respectively, the elements that made poetry mysterious and accessible) would cohabit but they would not interweave in the disturbing manner of the metaphysicals or the Romantics and they would not, in the manner of Swift or Pope, become the vehicle for the disclosure of the disturbing actualities of existence.

Exercises

It is difficult to isolate a single stylistic or thematic thread which unites Victorian poetry as a genre. As I have already stated, the term is a historical and, from the literary historian's point of view, methodological convenience. The most fruitful approach is to compare texts from the 1830s–1890s with their immediate Romantic predecessors. The most obvious example of post-Romantic difference is discernable in the Victorian poem's maintenance of a far more stable relationship between the poetic and the functional elements than will be found in its Romantic counterpart. Find an anthology of Victorian verse – the Oxford Anthology volume edited by Trilling and Bloom, and Ricks's *New Oxford Book of Victorian Verse* are the best (see Bibliography). Choose poems at random and conduct the same experiment in naturalisation suggested in the Exercise section of the previous chapter. Begin with the following texts and interpretive questions.

(i) **Textual density** Jakobson's formula of similarity (metaphor) superinduced upon contiguity (metonymy) is certainly relevant to Victorian texts, but the relationship between these two linguistic poles is far more controlled than in Romantic or metaphysical verse. The double pattern is generally stabilised so that it is rare to find interweavings of the material and signifying functions of language that are so dense and refractory as those of the Romantic Ode.

Read Arnold's 'Dover Beach', and pay particular attention to the following structural issues: how does Arnold deal with the syntax–metre interplay? Line length and rhyme scheme are irregular and the balance seems to shift toward to cognitive (referential) element of the double pattern. This concession to the discursive nature of prose creates fewer localised, multi-dimensional effects than in the Romantic ode. The first two strophes are essentially metonymic. Concrete objects and their perceptual effects are itemised. Self-conscious metaphor is introduced in strophe 3, and only fully integrated with textual deictics (the sea, the wind, the coast) in strophe 4. Compare the effects created by this use of controlled, progressive interweaving of textual patterns with Coleridge's 'Limbo' (see above, pp. 130–1). The following are strophes 1 and 4. Consider how each respectively isolates the metonymic and metaphoric functions.

> The sea is calm tonight.
> The tide is full, the moon lies fair
> Upon the straits; – on the French coast the light
> Gleams and is gone; the cliffs of England stand,
> Glimmering and vast, out in the tranquil bay.
> Come to the window, sweet is the night-air!
>
> The Sea of Faith
> Was once, too, at the full, and round earth's shore
> Lay like the folds of a bright girdle furled.
> But now I only hear
> Its melancholy, long, withdrawing roar,
> Retreating, to the breath
> Of the night-wind, down the vast edges drear
> And naked shingles of the world.

Now read Arnold's 'Stanzas from the Grand Chartreuse'. Compare Arnold's use of the stanza with the Augustan poets' use of the couplet (see Exercise section of Chapter 3). Each stanza operates as a metasyntactic unit. In lines 1–66 each unit is governed by a specific deictic point of reference ('the Alpine meadows', 'the silent courts', 'the garden', etc.) and like 'Dover Beach', metonymic item- isation dominates the opening of the poem. Between lines 67 and 169 consider how the points of reference become far more intern- alised and metaphoric, and how names and references unrelated to the situation of the utterance are drawn into the text ('Gods', 'A Greek', 'Achilles', 'Byron', 'Shelley', etc.). The concluding section (lines 169–210) returns us to the locative deictics of the monastery, but interfuses these with the now established pattern of metaphor and extra-contextual reference. Again we find that the definitive elements of poetic structure, metre (the stanza), metonymy– cognitive, metaphor–associative are brought together in a con- trolled, almost cautious manner. The following stanzas indicate the changes that occur through the three sections of the poem. Compare them with blank verse sequences from Wordsworth's *The Prelude* (see the Exercise section of Chapter 4).

> Approach, for what we seek is here!
> Alight, and sparely sup, and wait
> For rest in this outbuilding near;
> Then cross the sward and reach that gate.
> Knock; pass the wicket! Thou art come
> To the Carthusians' world-famed home.   (25–30)

> Our fathers watered with their tears
> This sea of time whereon we sail,
> Their voices were in all men's ears
> Who passed within their puissant hail.
> Still the same ocean round us raves,
> But we stand mute, and watch the waves.   (121–6)

> We are like children reared in shade
> Beneath some old-world abbey wall,
> Forgotten in a forest-glade,
> And secret from the eyes of all.
> Deep, deep the greenwood round them waves,
> Their abbey, and its close of graves!   (169–74)

(ii)   **Metrical Eclecticism** Consult your anthology of Victorian verse and consider the following question: is there any predictable, causal relationship between the verse form of the poem, the issues addressed by it, its predicated situation, and its dominant thematic motif? Relate this to your experience of Augustan and Romantic verse. In the eighteenth century blank verse was thought more appropriate than the couplet to the flexible discursive pattern of the landscape poem, and the ability of the couplet to isolate a specific issue or physical element made it the ideal vehicle for the public or satirical poem. For the Romantics the broader cultural status of the ballad corresponded with the generic subdivision of the rural or gothic tale, while blank verse and the ode seemed more suitable for introspective 'high Romantic' discourse. It is difficult to find similar generic–stylistic correspondences in Victorian verse, and this apparently unrestricted mixing of stylistic and functional frameworks returns us to the issues raised in the above section on textual density: if metre, metaphor, reference and deictics are allowed to cooperate but restricted in their ability to create disorientating, interwoven complexes of effects, then it should be possible to mix and match stylistic features at will. It would have been seen as a violation of the accepted poetic *langue* for Wordsworth to have written *The Prelude* in Popian couplets, or the 'Immortality Ode' in ballad form. Why is it that these implicit regulations had become far more flexible for the Victorians? For example, both Tennyson's 'Merlin and the Gleam' and Swinburne's 'Hertha' are ruminations upon the relation between the existential and the creative condition. The former is comprised of a type of disciplined free verse with irregular unrhymed lines rarely extending beyond five syllables, and the latter consists of the complex stanza of a six syllable quatrain followed by a thirteen syllable coda. Compare the processes of naturalising or paraphrasing these two poems and you will find that their very different verse forms are similarly unrestrictive in allowing us to separate the message from the medium. It is possible to do this because the Victorians (with the exception of Hopkins) rarely allowed the two elements of the double pattern to interfere with each other. The two dimensions of convention (metre) and cognition (reference) belong together but there is no particular rule governing exactly which type (narrative, introspective ode, the couplet, the stanza, blank verse) belongs with which.

The best way to test this thesis is to compare extracts from Browning's dramatic monologues. Refer to the two columns of genres and stylistic forms listed beneath metonymy and metaphor (see above pp. 134–5). Read each of the following extracts from the beginnings of Browning's monologues and draw up a hierarchy of categories which corresponds with your experience of reading and understanding. For example if your attention is drawn first to the deictic features of the speaker's discourse (the specifics of the situation of the utterance), then context features more prominently than text. As a consequence you will pay much more attention to the referential function of the verse (what it is actually about) than you will to its poetic counterpart (whether it is in blank verse, stanzas, etc.). In short, does the fact that all three extracts are written in very different verse forms play any significant part in our recognition of them as different texts, addressing different issues? Does Browning subdue the signifying function of the poetic to the extent that it becomes a decorative accessory to the more powerful referential function?

Stanzas 1 and 2 from 'A Toccata of Gallupi's':

> Oh Galuppi, Baldassaro, this is very sad to find!
> I can hardly misconceive you; it would prove me deaf and blind;
> But although I take your meaning, 'tis with such a heavy mind!
>
> Here you come with your old music, and here's all the good it
>   brings.
> What, they lived once thus at Venice where the merchants were
>   the kings,
> Where Saint Mark's is, where the Doges used to wed the sea
>   with rings?

Stanzas 1 and 2 of 'Master Hugues of Saxe Gotha':

> Hist, but a word, fair and soft!
>   Forth and be judged, Master Hugues!
> Answer the question I've put you so oft: –
>   What do you mean by your mountainous fugues?
> See, we're alone in the loft, –
>
> I, the poor organist here,
>   Hugues, the composer of note,
> Dead though, and done with, this many a year:
>   Let's have a colloquy, something to quote,
> Make the world prick up its ear!

Lines 1–9 of 'Andrea del Sarto':

> But do not let us quarrel any more,
> No, my Lucrezia; bear with me for once:
> Sit down and all shall happen as you wish.
> You turn your face, but does it bring your heart?

I'll work then for your friend's friend, never fear,
Treat his own subject after his own way,
Fix his own time, accept too his own price,
And shut the money into this small hand
When next it takes mine. Will it? tenderly?

6 Modernism and criticism

WHAT IS FREE VERSE?

This will be the most important and exploratory chapter of the book. The above question has taxed the interpretive resources of critics and poets since the first decade of this century and has resulted in a rich variety of solutions. None of these can claim to be a comprehensive, abstract definition of what free verse is or of how it works and many remain as angry attempts to dismiss the validity of their competitors. Free verse is the most significant contribution by poetry to the formal aesthetics of modernism, and in the following pages I shall attempt to provide a thorough account of how it began, why it persists and of its structural and functional identity. In the process we will be forced to reconsider the standard, conventional perceptions of how language works and more significantly of how poetic language can claim to be different from its non-poetic counterparts.

TO DEFINE THE INDEFINABLE

Consider the following task. Choose a poem and then define the metrical–prosodic form in which it is written. Most people will be able to identify *The Rape of the Lock* as a sequence of heroic couplets, *Paradise Lost* as blank verse and Shakespeare's sonnets as indeed sonnets. At the irregular end of the sliding scale, the Romantic ode, Hopkins's sprung rhythm or Coleridge's accentualist experiment in 'Christabel' will make concessions to identifiable patterns of syntax, alliteration, rhythm or rhyme scheme – their irregularity is validated by their invocation of regular precedent. But with Williams's 'The Red Wheelbarrow', Pound's 'In a Station of the Metro' or Eliot's 'Ash Wednesday' we can agree to designate all three as free verse only because they persistently evade the abstract patterns of regular verse. We know what they are because of what they are not. It might be possible to draw up a diagram of stress patterns and line lengths, but this would not represent an abstract formula for free verse, only a plan of the particular free verse poem that we happen to be reading.

The only unifying element in the free verse canon is the use of the poetic line – the so-called prose poem can be dismissed as an intriguing aberration. But what is a poetic line? If it does not establish its formal identity in deploying a regular or irregular pattern of sound (metre, rhythm, rhyme, assonance, alliteration) it cannot, at least in the abstract, be said to exist. We might shift our perceptual focus from the conventional to the cognitive end of the double pattern and still be disappointed: there is no rule or convention that obliges the free verse poet to construct his line according to any particular syntactic formula. The free verse line might consist of a complete sentence or of a single word (adjective, noun, verb, connective) whose relation to the syntactic structure of preceding and succeeding lines is infinitely flexible. By establishing this peculiar precedent the free versifiers have caused a number of problems for readers, critics and other poets. At the root of these problems is the relation between the tangible presence of the free verse line – it exists on the page and if we cannot hear it the speaker must have chosen to marginalise its graphic status – and its signifying function.

It is not too difficult to identify incompetent writing in regular verse in the sense that an aspiring poet's inability to properly reconcile the twin demands of the double pattern will become painfully evident. But with free verse there are no particular syntactic or metrical rules that the reader might invoke to judge the quality of a poem. As we have already seen (Chapter I, pp. 13–14), Jonathan Culler can turn a prose discourse into a free verse poem by visually foregrounding parts of its syntactic framework, and Stanley Fish claims to have distilled impressive naturalisations from his students in response to a poetically 'shaped' list of surnames on the blackboard ('How to Recognise a Poem When You See One', 1980). At the less serious end of the aesthetic paradigm *Private Eye*'s resident free versifier, E. J. Thribb ('a poet, 17', though by now probably 47) has produced absurd and amusing examples of 'occasional' free verse.

Erratum
In my last poem
'Lines on the
100th Anniversary
Of the Birth of
W. Somerset
Maugham'

The word 'Yorkshire'
Appeared as
'Workshire'.

Keith's mum
Spotted it
Immediately though
I confess I did
Not when I read
The proofs.

I regret the
Inconvenience this
May have caused to readers.

One mispelt word
Like this can
Completely destroy
A poem.

                                        8 February 1974

Thribb has established himself as a comic institution (four of his works feature in D. J. Enright's *Penguin Book of Light Verse*, 1980) because we, his amused readers, are still uncertain about what the writing and interpretation of free verse actually involve. The cognitive pattern of the above poem makes its context clear enough: an erratum by an unselfconsciously adolescent poet ('Keith's mum spotted it immediately'). As a prose note this text would function as an engaging, even charming, example of ingenuousness, but it becomes comic because its division into lines projects it into the 'serious' sphere of the poetic. But why do we not find William Carlos Williams's 'This Is Just To Say' (1934) equally laughable?

This Is Just To Say
I have eaten
the plums

that were in
the icebox

and which
you were probably
saving
for breakfast

Forgive me
they were delicious
so sweet
and so cold.

Jonathan Culler (1975), amongst others, offers an admirably straightfaced naturalisation of this poem. It is, he points out, 'a mediating force', it engages the reader in the semantics of 'forgiveness', 'the sensuous experience' of eating fruit, and it foregrounds a situation of domestic intimacy ('I', 'you', 'me') (175). It would not be quite so easy to remain serious about the projected situation of a teenage poet confessing his incompetence as a proofreader and invoking the sagacious vigilance of 'Keith's mum'. The qualitative distinction between these two texts is grounded entirely upon the pre-poetic, cognitive dimension of the double pattern (its syntactic–semantic structure and its imagined context). The poetic function (division into unmetrical lines) plays very little part in the process of naturalisation; rather, it simply recontextualises the original statement, urges us to shift our interpretive focus from the practical and utilitarian to the aesthetic context. A visual arts analogy might be found in the 'framing' of a lavatory seat or Andy Warhol's famous 'picture' of a soup tin. In short it would seem that free verse is the final realisation of Johnson's fears regarding blank verse: it is a cultural–aesthetic sign without substance. Our judgemental resources are based only upon how we grade the appropriateness of recontextualisation: Williams's line divisions foreground the enclosed pleasures of domestic intimacy, Thribb's foreground the farcical dimwittedness of the teenage poet.

Not all free verse poems involve the same structural framework as Thribb's and Williams's and in what follows we will encounter two basic distinctions: poems that draw upon conventional patterns of sound and metre, and poems that demand a redefinition of the line as neither a subsidiary element of syntax nor a measurement of metrical patterning.

BEGINNINGS

The three writers whose postulations on the structure and purpose of free verse encouraged the most vociferous debates were Ezra Pound, Amy Lowell and Harriet Monroe. Monroe founded the Chicago-based journal *Poetry: A Magazine of Verse* which from 1912 provided an outlet for innovative US poets and London-based Imagist groupings whose most prominent early members were Ezra Pound, Richard Aldington, F. S. Flint and T. E. Hulme – soon to be joined by T. S. Eliot and William Carlos Williams. Lowell moved from Boston to London in 1914 and went on to edit and write prefaces to three annual anthologies of *Some Imagist Poets* (1915–17) – though scholars are still uncertain about the relative contributions of Lowell and Pound to the ground-breaking assertions of these prefaces. The poets published in these volumes are often divided by conflicting personal and aesthetic affiliations, but it is possible to identify a number of recurrent questions and issues raised both by the poems themselves and in the critical debates that attended them.

In the *ex cathedra* writings of Pound, Lowell and Monroe the most consistent, unifying maxim is that the double pattern of regular verse operates as pure artifice and that it should be the objective of their generation to develop a method of writing which fuses both dimensions of the pattern into a single unitary sequence. Pound:

> *Rhythm*. – I believe in an 'absolute rhythm', a rhythm, that is, in poetry which corresponds exactly to the emotion or shade of emotion to be expressed. A man's rhythm must be interpretative, it will be, therefore, in the end, his own, uncounterfeiting, uncounterfeitable (in Faulkner, 1986, 64).

In short, the poetic function (particularly rhythm, metre and sound pattern) should be determined not by concessions to precedent but by a natural correspondence between pre-linguistic feeling and impression and poetic form. This recalls the Romantic programme, but the modernists translated theory into practice by rejecting the rules and precedents of metrical convention. Amy Lowell proposed that the primary unit of measurement for free verse should not be the foot or the line but the 'cadence' comprised of no particular number of syllables and comforming to no particular metrical rule. Instead this unit would reflect the natural pre-linguistic rhythm of physical and mental experience: 'a rhythmic curve . . . corresponding roughly to the necessity of breathing' (Lowell, 1920). Again we find echoes of the Romantic (and Hopkins's) ideal of spontaneity and transparency, but the modernists actually did with verse form what the Romantics, with the exception of Blake, found themselves unable or unwilling to attempt. But what did the former actually achieve?

We will begin with a much quoted and discussed poem that is often regarded as the archetype both for the Imagist movement and for Pound's later experiments in *The Cantos*: Ezra Pound's 'In a Station of the Metro':

> The apparition of these faces in the crowd;
> Petals on a wet, black bough.
>
> (in Poetry, April 1913)

It is known that when this and a number of similarly clipped and enigmatic pieces were written Pound was deeply interested in the Chinese and Japanese ideogram (see Kenner, 1972, pp. 195–7). In 1913 Mary Fenollosa sent Pound the unpublished manuscript of her late husband Ernest's essay on the relation between Chinese and Western poetry, which Pound eventually edited and published in 1919 as *The Chinese Written Character as a Medium for Poetry*. Hugh Kenner has called this document 'the *Ars Poetica* of our time' and Donald Davie has compared its influence with that of Wordworth's Preface to *Lyrical Ballads* and Shelley's *Defence of Poetry*. Why? Fenollosa claims that the Chinese written sign, the ideogram, is capable of representing single images and relations between them in a way which by-passes the systematic, successive rules of Western language. For example, the three ideogrammic signs, roughly translated as 'man sees horse', consist of three visual figures, and in each of these the pictorial image of legs is represented: man is a thing with two legs, the movement of his eyes is (metaphorically) represented by moving legs and the horse is denoted as a figure with four legs. The attraction for Pound and others of this method of representation lay in its apparent ability to transcend the refractory nature of language (a persistent post-Romantic ideal). In the English version, 'man sees horse', the matrix of subject, verb and object is deterministic. We could transform the sentence into 'Horse is seen by man' but we will never be able to escape from the dominant function of the verb 'to see' in the relation between the two syntactic functionaries, man and horse. In the Chinese version the verbal structure of seeing actually blends into the existential condition of these functionaries. One element of the shared experiential continuum (legs) is shared by all three signs:

thus the processes of witnessing (seeing) and existing (man on two legs, horse on four) become interdependent elements of a single multi-dimensional figure. Pound's problem (not unlike Wordsworth's) was of how to make this ideal of transparency and immediacy correspond with the conditions of Western language. He could hardly abandon linguistic signifiers in favour of purely visual images. What he did was to transform the poetic line from its conventional function as a foregrounding of sound patterns into a unit whose means of signification could be accounted for neither in purely syntactic nor purely prosodic–poetic terms.

Consider 'In a Station of the Metro' with these extra-textual issues in mind. It is a sentence without a main verb or preposition. The two parts of the text (indicated by its division into lines) operate as the western linguistic counterparts to ideogrammic visual images, but how do we go about documenting and describing the effect of their juxtaposition? Harvey Gross (1964), in a respected study of modernist verse form, gives us an example of how to naturalise this poem, and in doing so provides an unsettling counterpoint to what we know or assume about Pound's intention.

> No harm comes if we want to see this as vaguely analogous to Chinese writing; the two images have spatial and emotional relationships. Grammar, however, is not missing; it is automatically supplied by the reader (162).

Gross claims that the cupola and relational word 'are like' are 'implied' by the syntactic and semantic constituents of the two lines. The problem, which Gross does not address, is that by 'automatically supplying' the missing grammatical components the reader is negating the effect that Pound was attempting to achieve. Gross's reading imposes a grammatical structure upon a juxtaposition of images which attempts to transcend such structures. For example it would be equally plausible to claim that Pound perceived the faces in the urban crowd as sadly and tragically 'unlike' the life-enhancing images of the petals on the bough. Perhaps we should not attempt to establish the 'correct' interpretation because Pound's intention was not to offer us a rational (i.e. grammatical) link between the two images but to recreate the original process by which these images register *prior* to the imposition of a single post-experiential analysis. Pound's enthusiasm for the multi-dimensional immediacy of the ideogram is echoed in the *ex cathedra* writings of his contemporaries.

T. E. Hulme called Imagist poetry 'the new visual art' consisting of 'the succession of visual images'. 'It builds up a plastic image which it hands over to the reader, whereas the old art endeavoured to influence him physically by the hypnotic effect of rhyme'. In practical terms the poetic line should be constructed as a 'method of recording visual images in distinct lines'. We will later examine a creative manifestation of this thesis in Hulme's poem 'Autumn'. There is a constant tension between the creative and interpretive thesis offered by Pound, Fenollosa and Hulme, and the condition of the competent reader: what the former envisage as a snapshot of pre-linguistic experience, uncontaminated by the complexities of conventional linguistic and literary rules, is relocated and normalised by the reader for whom the prerogatives of syntactic cohesion (see Chapter 3, 69–70) are attendant upon our encounters with any pattern of linguistic integers. This problematic relation between literary modernism and the practices and expectations of naturalis-ation reaches beyond free verse: for example by 'making sense' of Joyce's or Woolf's use of stream of consciousness are we doing an injustice to their aesthetic intention?

The best anthology of early modernist poetic techniques is Jones's *Imagist Poetry* (Penguin, 1972). Dip into this and bear the following in mind. Can it be argued that the majority of poems in this anthology attempt to realise the *ex cathedra* Imagist objectives by deploying the poetic line as an alternative rather than a supplement to the traditional rules and conventions of language and literature? More significantly, do the line–syntax relationships in these poems create an intrinsic structure or do they demand the normative inter-vention of the reader?

One of the most widely discussed manifestations of Imagism was H. D.'s 'Oread':

Whirl up, sea –
Whirl your pointed pines,
Splash your great pines
On our rocks,
Hurl your green over us,
Cover us with your pools of fir.

Conrad Aiken, in reviewing *Some Imagist Poets 1915* in which 'Oread' appeared, observed that 'of organic *movement* there is prac-tically none'. In short, the rules of extra-syntactic cohesion which normally govern texts seem to have been rejected. Apart from the opening line, which establishes the sea as a subject, it would be possible to rearrange the lineal order of the poem without doing much damage to its already tenuous framework of cohesion and continuity.

Not all early free verse poems deploy the line as a discrete discontinuous element. Consider the similarities between 'In A Station of the Metro', 'Oread' and T. E. Hulme's more complex syntactic continuities in 'Autumn'.

> A touch of cold in the Autumn night –
> I walked abroad,
> And saw the ruddy moon lean over a hedge
> Like a red-faced farmer.
> I did not stop to speak, but nodded,
> And round about were the wistful stars
> With white faces like town children.

The question we should ask is how this text might be defended against the anti free-verse charge of lacking organic form. Do the lines operate as anything more than a support mechanism for prose punctuation? On the surface the interlineal pattern of active and perceptual verb phrases seems far more significant than the line divisions – 'I walked', 'saw', 'did not stop', 'nodded'. But in fact the line structure operates as a form of metasyntax, tracing out the progress from impression to self-conscious metaphor. In line 3 the syntagm–paradigm relation is exploratory and tentative – human attributes and activities (ruddy and lean) are interposed with an image of the moon, but in the following line ('*Like* a red-faced farmer') this uncertain interplay between language and perception has become far more controlled. In lines 5 and 6 we are returned to a pattern of unselfconscious impressionism: the human moon becomes a condition of the speaker's verbal self-possession ('stop to speak', 'nod') and the 'wistful stars' are similarly embued with emotional life. Line 7 repeats the earlier progress from impression to contrived metaphoric enclosure: the human adjective 'wistful' is transformed into a self-conscious comparison, '*With* white faces *like* town children'.

Hulme uses the free verse line as a means of recording the subtle shifts in balance between the visual, mental and linguistic registers of impression. As he states in his prose discussion, the 'hynotic' and progressive 'effect of rhythm' (the traditional double pattern) has been replaced by a 'building up' and 'handing over' of 'plastic images' in various states of construction.

The poems dealt with so far allow us to construct three separate models of free verse structure.

1 In the poems by Williams, Thribb and in the critical example by Culler, the syntagmatic patterns of prose construction maintain a hold over the textual structure. The line divisions function as a secondary pattern which foregrounds elements of the pre-existent structure that might appear insignificant in the normal typographic layout of non-poetic language. The poetic function is not, as in regular verse, intrinsic to the text; rather it serves to direct the interpretive faculties of the reader. The classic test case for this form of text–reader interplay was originally provided by Chomsky and was reexamined in a poetic/literary context by John Hollander (1975). The sentence, 'They don't know how good meat tastes', can be visually divided in six different ways and in each instance the thematic centre of its surface structure changes. The words remain the same but as our centre of interpretive attention is redirected their relation to one another is altered.

2 In Pound's 'In a Station of the Metro' and H. D.'s 'Oread' emphasis shifts towards the line as a discrete linguistic and signifying structure. In these texts the reader is allowed much more freedom in supplying the broader syntagmatic connections between the units of the text. We play out this role by choosing to foreground and trace correspondences between elements of the text (in Gross's analysis 'faces'–'crowd' *are like* 'petals'–'bough'), and in doing so we draw upon the examples of textual cohesion provided in regular verse (the progressive and transformational use of 'ties') and impose these upon the fragmentary, juxtaposed units of this particular free verse type.

3 Hulme's 'Autumn' offers the most intriguing example of how free verse might involve a new form of interplay between line and syntax that is intrinsic to the structure of the text. His line divisions constitute a metasyntax which at once reflects and controls the speaker's disposition of the syntagmatic and paradigmatic chains. Here the reader genuinely responds to, rather than provides, a valid poetic structure. In the following section we will examine how a number of other free verse poets have developed methods of deploying the line as a unit that discards prosodic regularity yet functions as a purposive formal and signifying element of the text.

WILLIAMS AND VISUALISM

In the years following the Imagist anthologies, and particularly in the 1920s and 30s, modernism and the free verse revolution became fraught with functional and formal divisions. The principal distinction was between those who perpetuated the drive towards innovation and experiment and those who sought to reconcile these instincts with the precedents of tradition and regularity. In the former category the more familiar names are William Carlos Williams and Ezra Pound and, in the latter, T. S. Eliot and W. H. Auden. Pound extended the method of 'In a Station of the Metro' into the multi-dimensional juxtapositions of linguistic and cultural referents of the *Cantos*, but a more intriguing development of modernist poetic writing occurs in the poems of Williams.

Consider the title poem of Williams's 1923 collection, *Spring and All*.

> By the road to the contagious hospital
> under the surge of the blue
> mottled clouds driven from the
> northeast – a cold wind. Beyond, the
> waste of broad, muddy fields
> brown with dried weeds, standing and fallen
>
> patches of standing water
> the scattering of tall trees
>
> All along the road the reddish
> purplish, forked, upstanding, twiggy
> stuff of bushes and small trees
> with dead, brown leaves under them
> leafless vines –
>
> Lifeless in appearance, sluggish,
> dazed spring approaches –

The consistent formal element of this poem is the tension between the poet's deployment of the poetic line and the progressive forward movement of the syntagm. Williams creates this tension as a means of realising the modernist ideal of poetic language as at once an art form and a register of pre-linguistic events and impressions; and the *contre-rejet*, the splitting of the deep structure by line division, is a persistent feature of the text. The two opening lines could stand as a complete syntactic–poetic unit, but 'blue' is transformed from its static, substantive sense into an adjectival dependence upon the 'mottled clouds' of the next line. The effect recalls Eve's similar perception of the 'clear/Smooth lake' (see the Exercise section Chapter 3). The difference is that the regular iambic–decasyllabic undertow of her speech pattern is now missing. Williams's lines are structured not according to an impersonal, abstract regulation; the governing principle of the line–syntax relation is the poet's desire to record the very uneasy interplay between perceptual experience and its linguistic register. Syntactic patterns are begun, readjusted, reengaged, transformed, and the line provides the metasyntactic instrument for this uncertain impressionistic sequence. Lines 3 and 4, ending with the definite article 'the', attempt to recreate in language the timing of experiencer's receptive faculties: the ungrammatical break at each line is the equivalent of the gap that allows the experiencer to register the northeast as the direction from which the wind is driven (lines 3–4) and the predeterminer 'Beyond' prepares us for gradual shift of focus – again marked by a pause – from the sky to the land (lines 4–5). When the experiencer contemplates

> [the] small trees
> with dead, brown leaves under them
> leafless vines –

the moment is a perfect synthesis of Poundian technique and unreflecting slang. In a continuous syntactic sequence, 'with dead, brown leaves under them leafless vines', 'them leafless vines' echoes the colloquial and ambiguous title of 'Spring and All' (all what?). But the line division preserves this improvisational informality and complements it with a stark visual juxtaposition, recalling 'In a Station of the Metro'.

> with dead, brown leaves under them
> leafless vines –

The break isolates 'leafless vines' as a stark metaphoric counterpoint (recalling perhaps Milton's 'darkness visible') to the more discursive pattern of the previous line.

The point to be made about the structure of this poem is that it is unlike the above categories 1 and 2. There is no sense that the poet has simply reshaped a prose discourse, but nor can each line be fully isolated from the broader progressive pattern. We, the readers, are not arbiters of the relation between form and signification, but we are thrown into a constant state of uncertainty by the shifts between the poetic function (the line) and its referential counterpart (syntax). Williams acknowledges conventional precedent (there are resonances of Milton's blank verse technique) but he reintegrates these echoes with an unprecedented method of deploying the unmetrical line as a register of the tension between experience and linguistic mediation. The degree of his achievement can be judged by comparing this poem with Blake's 'London' and Wordsworth's 'Tintern Abbey' and 'The Idiot Boy' (see Chapter 4). Bear in mind the extent to which the two Romantics depend upon the signifying function and the cultural status of the regular double pattern to achieve their impressions of immediacy while Williams creates an entirely new model for the cognitive and conventional registers of poetry.

Having identified the structural operations of this model in a single text, how should we go about constructing an abstract definition? First, we should reexamine conventional perceptions of what constitutes the poetic. The conventional dimension of the double pattern – rhyme, metre, sound pattern, etc. – depends upon a regular and persistent deployment of the acoustic tension between the purely material and the signifying functions of poetic language only because the former is patterned and repetitive – all spoken language consists of sounds but its deliberate and purposive foregrounding becomes evident only with regularity and repetition (in Jakobson's terms parallelism). If we accept that a tension between the material and signifying functions is essential to our differentiation between poetic and non-poetic discourses, the only material element available to replace acoustic regularity is the graphic, visual dimension – a phenomenon which has been marginalised by linguistics and confined as a sub-genre (concrete and pattern forms) by literary criticism. To understand how visual form can operate as a productive element of the text we should consider the relation between the cultural status of the graphic sign and its ability to create meaning.

Below is 'The Red Wheelbarrow', another poem from Williams's *Spring and All*.

so much depends
upon

a red wheel
barrow

glazed with rain
water

beside the white
chickens

Here the initial signal is visual: this looks like a poem. Moving from recognition to naturalisation we would note that in the absence of any normal form of punctuation its division into four units resembling stanzas will probably tell us something about how the poetic function organises meaning. The next stage of interpretation is problematic: lines and stanzas signal a concession to regularity, and at least two of this poem's many commentators (see Hartman, 1980 and Ramsey, 1968) have gone on to 'scan' the text with the objective of establishing an albeit irregular metrical double pattern as the foundation for further interpretive strategies. But should shape and visual texture always be regarded as merely a signal to acoustic substance (remember Johnson on Milton)? Perhaps shape can in itself produce meaning. Forget scansion and the acoustic double pattern and consider how each stanza operates both as a grammatical–syntactic demand and a delayed payment. John Hollander observes that the lines 'cut . . . into their constituents, without the use of hyphenation to warn that the first noun [or colour] is part of a compound *with the implication that they are phenomenological constituents as well . . .* in the freshness of the light after the rain . . . things seem to lose their compounded qualities' (p. 111). Look more closely at the difference between the opening and subsequent stanzas. The primary distinction is in their relative ideational effects (the ability of words to generate specific mental pictures). 'depends/upon' is a syntactic connective: we know what it means but without nouns we cannot be certain if the dependency is spatial, physical, intellectual, moral or emotional. As such the opening stanza becomes the functional deep structure of the text to be transformed and specified in each subsequent stanza: 'wheel' depends upon 'barrow', 'rain' upon 'water', 'white' upon 'chickens'. Williams has succeeded in creating a visual counterpart to the acoustic double pattern of regular poetry. The poetic function of the text (its line divisions) creates a complex interface between the arbitrary relational structure of the medium and the relations between phenomena in the pre-linguistic world.

It is possible to claim that in the two poems above, Williams generates a multi-dimensional reading experience that would be limited by the dominance of acoustic patterns. In both he obliges the reader to be continually aware that the successive, linear dimension of linguistic structure is in a state of tension with its static, visual juxtapositions; and it could be argued that this disorientating effect is as close as poetic form can come to recreating the dynamics of perceptual and emotive experience – the reason for Pound's enthusiasm for the ideogram. Consider the following poems by Williams and Charles Tomlinson.

Williams: section II of 'Perpetuam Mobile' from *Pictures from Brueghel* (1949)

To all the girls
of all ages
who walk up and down on

the streets of this town
silent or gabbing
putting

their feet down
one before the other
one two

one two they
pause sometimes before
a store window and

reform the line
from here
to China everywhere

back and
forth and back and forth
and back and forth.

Charles Tomlinson: 'Lines' from *Seeing is Believing* (1960)

You have seen a plough
the way it goes breeds
furrows line on line
until they fill a field?

What I admire in this
is less the page complete
and all the insatiable
activity towards it

than when, one furrow
more lies done with
and the tractor hesitates:
another line to be begun

and then it turns and drags
the blade in tow and that
turns too along the new
and growing groove

and each reversal thus
in mitigating mere aggression
prepares for the concerted
on-rush of the operation

and then the dark the cool
the dew corroding the
intent abandoned
mechanism that
contemplates accomplishment

It should be clear to any competent reader that each poet is self-consciously aware of a tension between the ideational function of language (a.k.a. its referential function) and language as a material entity consisting of concrete graphemes, phonemes and the rules that bind these units together. In Williams's poem the subject is 'the girls', but their mediated, non-linguistic activities are interfused with the similarly physical process of linguistic mediation. The movement of 'their feet' encodes an echo of the unit which in regular verse governs the process of poetic writing (the foot). Note how 'one before the other' and 'one two' govern the structural identity of separate lines, and how 'they' (the girls or the language?) 'pause' both before a 'store window' and before the poet shifts from one line to the next. 'They' (governing verb phrase for linguistic units and for the girls) 'reform the line' (Whose line? The poet's or the girls'?). The poem concludes with the triple image of the poet's hand and mind, the reader's eye, and the girls moving 'back and/ forth and back and forth/and back and forth'.

With Tomlinson there is a similarly interactive relation between what language does and what language is. The subject is the tractor pulling the plough, but the lines on the field become inseparable from the poet's negotiation of the lines on the page. The tractor, like the poet, 'hesitates:/another line to be begun'. We should here recall Jakobson's model of the poetic. If we accept that the complexities of the double pattern succeed in foregrounding and intensifying the metonymic–metaphoric capacities of language, is it not the case that this unmetrical, visual foregrounding of linguistic materiality adds an extra level of density to this formula? The verbal constituents of the text – 'complete', 'activity', 'hesitates', 'turns', 'drags', 'along', 'on rush', 'intent', 'contemplates' – are divided between their literal, referential function (the movement of the plough) and their figurative function (the activities of the poet in mediating the movement of the plough). Does the 'abandoned mechanism' and the contemplation of 'accomplishment' refer to the perceived image of the plough and ploughman or to the sense of satisfaction felt by the poet in his successful negotiation of the complexities of the text?

It could be claimed that these texts are self-referential, about the process of writing, but could we not make a similar claim for practically all regular poems? When a poet deploys rhyme and metre he/ she is engaging both with pre-linguistic experience and with the reprocessing of such experiences as texts. Williams's and Tomlinson's double-edged used of terms such as 'feet', 'line', 'hesitation' are examples of what Jakobson calls the metalingual – a self-evident announcement of the text's status as poetic. The fact that both poets, writing almost half a century after the birth of free verse, feel confident enough to proclaim their use of visual form is the equivalent of such traditional metalingual signals as Shakespeare's reference to 'this memorable rhyme' (sonnet 55). Visual poetics has arrived.

Visual form is a complex and elusive phenomenon; it is neither a constituent of conventional linguistic patterns nor merely an alternative method of punctuating these patterns, but it is clearly capable of organising poetic structure and generating meaning. For a more comprehensive account of how it has come to replace sound pattern as an element of the post-free verse double pattern see Bradford's *The Look of It* (1993) and Cushman's *William Carlos Williams and the Meanings of Measure* (1985).

Consider the following from e. e. cummings's *95 Poems*,

```
l (a
le
af
Fa
ll
s)
one
l
iness
```

If we attempt to naturalise this poem we must effectively isolate two linguistic–syntactic units, the word 'loneliness' and the sentence (in brackets) 'a leaf Falls' – in this case the referential sense of falling is paralleled by the literal falling down the page of the linguistic components. We might then suggest a thematic connection between the human condition of being alone and its natural correlative of autumn (decay, the end of summer often being associated with sadness and isolation). In doing so we will have imposed a temporal metatext upon a non-temporal, spatial effect. Jakobson has commented on the difference between visual and linguistic naturalisation.

> When the observer arrives at the simultaneous synthesis of a contemplated painting, the painting as a whole remains before his eyes, it is still present; but when the listener reaches a synthesis of what he has heard, the phonemes have in fact already vanished. They survive as mere afterimages, somewhat abridged reminiscences, and this creates an essential difference between the two types of perception and percepts.
>
> (1964, 472–3)

cummings's poem obliges the reader to participate in both of these processes of interpretation. It disposes the graphic constituents of language in the same way that the painter arranges visual images, while their function as linguistic signs prompts us to interpose a conventional, linear reading with the simultaneous, synthetic effects of visual juxtaposition. It should not be dismissed as a bizarre aberration from the modernist mainstream since it foregrounds elements of composition and interpretation that we have already encountered in the work of Milton, Williams and Tomlinson. A useful method of distinguishing between types of visual form is to invoke Jakobson's opposition between temporal and static signs. If the text involves a persistent tension between the temporal movement of linguistic signs and their static configuration then it can be categorised as a type of visual free verse: cummings's poems are an intriguing test case since they at once invoke and continuously disrupt the expectations of reading from left to right and down the page. With concrete poems we will encounter a number of varied syntactic, semantic, thematic and iconic patterns, but there will be no constant tension between a single enunciative, temporal movement and a visual framework. Consider the following by Eugen Gomringer:

```
            w   w
        d       i
      n     n     n
    i     d     i     d
  w                 w
```

(Solt, 1968, 93)

The word w i n d can be 'read' along separate diagonal, angular or curved planes, and we might surmise that the poem demonstrates that the signifier, like its referent, involves being literally blown around. In naturalising the text we should also acknowledge that, unlike poems within the sliding scale, it makes no concessions to the temporal nature of the syntagm: it has no particular beginning or end.

Visual form is too often regarded as eccentricity, a mildly engaging off-shoot from the broader modernist enterprise. I am convinced of its importance in our understanding of how and why the concept of the 'modern poem' encompasses so many different and often divergent technical and stylistic formulae. Consider Jakobson's description of how the two elements of the double pattern interlock: 'metrical parallelism' and 'phonic equivalence', 'prompt' questions of semantic similarity or contrast, and consequently promote selection and metaphor above contiguity and metonymy. The visual line effectively replaces the foregrounding functions of metrical regularity and rhyme by creating a tension between the static and kinetic dimensions of language. In regular poetry we encounter an interface between syntagm, paradigm and the acoustic materiality of language; in free verse that employs visual structure a similar interface occurs between syntagm, paradigm and the graphic materiality of language.

The following sequence is from section V of T. S. Eliot's *Ash Wednesday*.

> If the lost word is lost, if the spent word is spent
> If the unheard, unspoken
> Word is unspoken unheard;
> Still is the unspoken word, the Word unheard,
> The Word without a word, the word within
> The world and for the world;
> And the light shone in darkness and
> Against the Word the unstilled world still whirled
> About the centre of the silent Word
>
> O my people, what have I done to thee.
>
> Where shall the word be found, where will the word
> Resound? Not here, there is not enough silence

The referential and thematic motif of this passage is the paradoxical relation between language (the 'word') and pre-linguistic truth (the 'lost word', 'the spent word', 'the unspoken/Word', 'the silent Word'). This paradox is foregrounded and intensified by the peculiar and continuous tension between the silent, graphic text and its spoken counterpart. We can see the distinction between the 'unstilled world' and (the) 'still whirled', but the acoustic–semantic distinction is delayed until the verb connects with its object in the following line. The 'unspoken/Word' is literally 'Still' (static, frozen in print), and the printed characters of 'w o r d' are indeed literally 'within' the graphemes of 'w o r l d'. The spatial question of 'Where' the word might 'be found' is granted a mimetic edge by the apparently gratuitous, but conspicuously spatial, placing of the echo 'Resound' at the beginning of the next line.

The unmetrical line could, as we have seen, become merely a sub-component of the general rules of syntax and punctuation (1), or operate as a signal for reader-centred strategies of interpretation (2). Visual form allows the poet an extra dimension of signification and control. It functions as a counterpattern that is at once independent of the conventions of syntax, semantics and acoustic structure yet capable of interfering with their patterns of signification. Hence visual form satisfies the objectives of category 3. It provides a supplementary level of interplay between the referential and the material functions of the poetic.

Eliot's interposing of visual form with the more conventional patterns of sound and rhyme provides a convenient link point for the introduction of a fourth category of free verse, which includes texts that draw upon yet rework the sound patterns of pre-modernist poetry. Eliot and Auden are probably its most eminent practitioners, but, as we shall see, their work is by no means merely a return to the forms and expectations of tradition.

T. S. ELIOT

Eliot is the archetypal middleman between modernist innovation and its traditional antecedents – a role which has earned him the contempt of Williams. His earliest, most discussed piece of experimental conservatism is 'The Love Song of J. Alfred Prufrock' (1917). The poem draws upon the established precedent of Browning's dramatic monologues, but it goes further than Browning in its use of irregular form as an axis, an anchor point for a number of bizarre deployments of deictic referents; these shift the reader between a tentative awareness of the situation of the utterance and moments of individual consciousness detached from any particular pre-linguistic spatial or temporal continuum. The opening verse paragraph:

> Let us go then, you and I,
> When the evening is spread out against the sky
> Like a patient etherised upon a table;
> Let us go, through certain half-deserted streets,
> The muttering retreats
> Of restless nights in one-night cheap hotels
> And sawdust restaurants with oyster-shells:
> Streets that follow like a tedious argument
> Of insidious intent
> To lead you to an overwhelming question . . .
> Oh, do not ask, 'What is it?'
> Let us go and make our visit.

The reader who hopes that attention to textual deictics will provide a link between the enclosed sphere of the poetic and the situation of the utterance will be disappointed. The 'I' is obviously the speaking presence, but who is the 'you'? It might be us, the hearers, who are invited to join him in this peculiar journey. But we cannot be sure. He might be addressing someone else within the imagined situation of the poem; or he might be talking to himself, constructing an alter ego or situating his uneasy sense of mental and emotional division as separate pronouns. Our attempts to solve this puzzle by further examining the details of the text will create more problems. Is the simile of the 'patient etherised' supposed to refer to the sky or to the condition of the travellers (traveller)? Is the question to which they (he) will be led, 'What is it?'? Or is the speaker advising his companion (other half) not to ask what the question is? Are the streets and restaurants that lead to this unasked and unanswerable question literal and real – perhaps the question will become apparent when they/he get to a particular place – or do they represent a figurative journey through fragments of memory and consciousness?

Read on and become even more confused. The particular and locative ('my hair', 'my trousers', 'my head', 'the cups', 'the marmalade', 'the tea') are interposed with a bewildering collage of references to literature, the bible, history, nature, art and all manner of other referents that might drift through the mind, irrespective of the spatial, temporal or social conditions of the utterance.

In the broader aesthetic context we might find links between the disorientating shifts of the poem and the prose techniques of the interior monologue developed by Joyce and Woolf. But there is a difference. The interior monologue (a.k.a. stream of consciousness) attempts to realise in language the multi-dimensional tension between the inner and outer dimensions of consciousness – the condition of our mental and perceptual worlds prior to the ratiocinative processes of thought and conventional linguistic organisation. Eliot, although creating a similar effect, qualifies his concession to impressionistic formlessness with a persistent and self-conscious use of form – poetic form. The metrical pattern and the rhyme scheme are irregular but they are continuously present. In an important sense they replace the orderly disposition of the syntagmatic and paradigmatic axes as the speaker's only, albeit tenuous, link point between consciousness and mediation.

Consider the following metaphor:

The yellow fog that rubs its back upon the window-panes,
The yellow smoke that rubs its muzzle on the window-panes,
Licked its tongue into the corners of the evening,

Lingered upon the pools that stand in drains,
Let fall upon its back the soot that falls from chimneys,
Slipped by the terrace, made a sudden leap,
And seeing that it was a soft October night,
Curled once about the house, and fell asleep (15–22).

Which part is the vehicle and which part the tenor? The animal or the fog? By the end of this verse paragraph the speaker seems to have forgotten the purpose of his comparison. The image of this sinister creature has effectively replaced any conscious grasp upon its use as a point of comparison. The abandonment of the irregular couplets with which the poem begins seems to signal a further loss of control, but in the paragraph following this section we find that a slight but conspicuous sense of continuity is resumed with the repetition of 'panes' in the rhyme position, and off-rhyme echoes of 'leap' and 'asleep' in 'street' and 'meet'. Think again about Jakobson's model of the relation between the regular double pattern and metaphor: Eliot offers a revision of this formula by matching an irregular pattern of metre and rhyme with a correspondly uncertain control of the syntagmatic and paradigmatic chains.

Throughout the poem our only reliable sense of its status as a speech act – something which allows us to reconnect linguistic units, however fragmentary, with a controlling human presence – is found in the speaker's constant return to irregular metrical and rhyming patterns. Eliot has engaged with a tradition of poetic writing – particularly that of the metaphysicals and the Romantics – which foregrounds a tension between the imagined speaking presence and the tangible density of the text, but he has shifted the balance and the readerly focus toward a self-evident dependence upon the poetic function as affecting both the circumstances and the process of mediation. With 'Prufrock' our awareness of any real or imagined speaking presence cannot be fully detached from our sense of that presence as a poet. Eliot's message seems to be that once our grip upon the moral, social, cultural and even the spatio-temporal conditions of existence is loosened, all that is left to connect us with any consoling pattern of continuity and stability is the poetic. In short, the poet has submitted willingly to his status as a function of the text. Eliot's manifesto for modernist form is neatly encapsulated in the following statement from 'Reflections on "Vers Libre" '.

We may therefore formulate as follows: the ghost of some simple metre should lurk behind the arras even in the 'freest' verse; to advance menacingly as we doze, and withdraw as we rouse.

Or freedom is only truly freedom when it appears against the
background of an artificial limitation.

(1917, 101)

He refers specifically to the need for a metrical undertow to anchor
unrhymed verse, but his claim that freedom is only discernible when
counterpoised with tangible form could stand as the model for his
own richly diverse oeuvre.

'Whispers of Immortality' (from *Poems 1920*) is, in metrical terms,
a regular and traditional poem consisting of eight four line stanzas,
rhyming at the second and fourth lines. But in all other respects it
is a bizarre and finally incomprehensible assembly of references and
images. The first four stanzas identify Donne and Webster as the
subjects, and it is only through our broader awareness of the tendency for their work to foreground the tangible and often uneasy
physicality of the human condition that we can make sense of the
syntax. For example, Donne is described as finding 'no substitute
for sense' and at this point we are uncertain of whether 'sense'
refers to physical sensation or linguistic meaning. But when we read
on to clarify this localised semantic problem we encounter only
deeper rifts between semantics and continuity. Beyond what *sort* of
'experience' is Donne 'expert'? Is the 'anguish of the marrow', 'the
ague of the skeleton', a form of morbid anxiety? And if Donne
could find 'no substitute for sense', but 'no contact possible to flesh'
could 'allay the fever of the bone' he would seem to be a rather
sad embodiment of uncertainties and contradictions. At least he
would were he not identified as John Donne, a person whose poetry
is celebrated (by Eliot particularly) for its ability to negotiate such
tensions and ambiguities. In short, to understand the first half of
the poem we need to invoke the cultural code; to displace the
intrinsic peculiarities of the text onto our extra-textual knowledge
of the two writers. In the second half (the poem is divided enigmati-
cally by five dots) the cultural–deictic foci of Donne and Webster
are replaced by the well endowed figure of Grishkin (who may well
be Russian and who occupies a maisonette), a Brazilian jaguar, a
marmoset (origins unknown) and a cat. We know nothing of this
peculiar ensemble beyond what we are told in the poem. The
declarative, insistent pattern of the verb phrases in the second part
is a close copy of the first part, but because the relationship between
the noun phrases of the former is so enclosed, so immune from any
particular contextual frame of reference, we find ourselves unable
to close the gap between what the language does and what it is

actually about. The tangible physicality of Grishkin (she is fat, possibly sensual, and she relates, at least syntactically, to the instinctive determinants of the natural world) might well be a preparation for the unphysical imagery of the closing stanza, and we might, by invoking the concept of syntactic–poetic cohesion, suggest that 'our lot' (the human condition?), 'dry ribs' and 'metaphysics' reconnects part two with part one – Donne was a metaphysical whose anxious contemplation of the human condition involved the 'ague of the skeleton', 'the fever of the bone'. We might, but we would be left with a join-the-dots pattern of fragments and references that depend for coherence more upon the interpretive acumen of the reader than upon a verifiable intrinsic structure. The only persistent textual pattern that links the parts to the whole of the poem is its adherence to a regular metrical form. It is almost as though Eliot, in 'Whispers' and 'Prufrock', is seeking to reverse the traditional relationship between the poem as contextually rooted speech act, particular to a given set of circumstances and inferred feelings, and the poem as a continuation of the *langue* of stylistic conventions and techniques generally regarded as the poetic. The poet and the speaker/persona become united not because of the reader's ability to transcend the poetic and relocate the speech act in relation to other non-poetic discourses and pre-linguistic situations, but because the poet and the speaker achieve unity in their use of poetic technique. In 'Tradition and the Individual Talent' (1919) Eliot declares that:

> The poet has, not a 'personality' to express, but a particular medium, which is only a medium and not a personality, in which impressions and experiences combine in peculiar and unexpected ways . . . The emotion of art is impersonal. And the poet cannot reach this impersonality without surrendering himself wholly to the work to be done.
>
> (1919, 84)

This is a complete overturning of the Imagist manifesto that emotion, experience, expression should cut through the arbitrary barriers of the 'medium', and it is the premise that governs Eliot's entire poetic output. Its closest counterpart in literary linguistics will be found in Jakobson's 1935 lecture (in Czech, recapitulating the insights of his colleague Tynjanov) on the concept of 'the dominant'.

> The dominant may be defined as the focussing component of a work of art: it rules, determines, and transforms the remaining components. It is the dominant which guarantees the integrity of

the structure . . . [Throughout literary history] the elements which were originally the dominant ones become subsidiary and optional . . . a poetic work [is] a structural system, a regularly ordered hierarchical set of artistic devices. Poetic evolution is a shift in this hierarchy.

(Jakobson, 1935, p. 108)

The element of the structured system which dominates all of Eliot's poetry is the formal, conventional dimension of the double pattern.

The Waste Land, that presiding monument to modernism, is a collage of perspectives, voices, snatches of German poetry, Hindu and Christian scripture, allusions to Goldsmith and Marvell, juxtaposed with visions and sounds from 1920s London. 'These fragments have I shored against my ruins' says the speaker at the end of the poem (Tiresias? The Fisher King? Eliot? Everyman?); and the only point of stability for the reader of this ahistorical multicultural assembly is the means by which the fragments have been so desperately 'shored'. The dominant, ever-present element is the poetic line. The famous opening verse paragraph reproduces the Shakespearean/Miltonic device of the blank verse *contra-rejet*. The line structure is governed by the anxious foregrounding and splitting of verb phrases. The 'breeding', 'mixing', 'stirring', 'covering' and 'feeding' shift us uneasily between the literal and the figurative notions of spring and life. Throughout the rest of the poem we are shifted through four centuries of metrical history, and it is only through the presence of these concessions to tradition that the purely modernist texture of the free verse sections can begin to signify. Eliot inscribes what Jakobson calls 'poetic evolution', the 'shifts in the hierarchy' within a single text. *The Waste Land* unsettles the protocols of naturalisation. In order to make sense of the stylistic and referential complexities of a text we need to identify (or in reader-response parlance 'construct') a speaking presence and it seems that Eliot's poem refuses to allow the unstructured and diverse patterns of signification to come to rest upon a stable moment of fusion between contact, context, message or code. But there is a unifying element that allows us to situate the text as the creation of a speaking presence who can only be the anxious, erudite poet of the early 1920s. Who else would be able to display such an authoritative command of the types of line–syntax relationship developed from Shakespeare to the free verse revolution? Read the text carefully and you will find that not only are there echoes of blank verse technique, the irregular ode, the quatrain and the heroic couplet; there are also permutations of all four categories of free verse method. I use the term 'permutations' because no single device remains immune from some form of infusion from some other element of the modernist or pre-modernist *langue*.

In section III, 'The Fire Sermon', one part begins as an echo of the Imagist pattern of structure determined by impression.

> The river sweats
> Oil and tar
> The barges drift
> With the turning tide
> Red sails

But gradually, perhaps addictively, the speaker begins to allow the poetic *langue* – in this instance a very irregular rhyme scheme – to impose upon the impressionistic fragments.

> Wide
> To leeward, swing on the heavy spar.
> The barges wash
> Drifting logs
> Down Greenwich reach
> Past the Isle of Dogs.

The poetic line is the 'dominant', the organising principle of the text, something from which the speaker seems unable or unwilling to detach himself. The two lines that were rewritten by Pound, echoing the juxtaposed pattern of 'In a Station of the Metro',

> Unreal City,
> Under the brown fog of a winter dawn   (60–1)

reemerge almost as a refrain,

> Unreal City
> Under the brown fog of a winter noon   (207–8)

> . . .

> Falling towers
> Jerusalem Athens Alexandria
> Vienna London
> Unreal   (374–7)

In each case the ability of the line to isolate and stabilise fragments of thought, memory and mediation against the incursions of anarchic multi-signification becomes evident.

MODERN AND POSTMODERN FORM

The Waste Land can be regarded as the first self-conscious exploration, though certainly not the first instance, of that elusive and friable concept, the postmodern. Limitations of space do not permit a full discussion of the postmodern: it seems to mean different things to architecture theorists, literary critics, political commentators and practically anyone with anything to say about the twentieth century. But mercifully the enclosed field of poetry and linguistics allows us a more confident grip upon its function as a means of classifying the structure and function of a text. I'll begin with a general thesis: the postmodern poem involves the acknowledgement and the deployment of devices and functional premises drawn from the recognised archetypes of modernist and pre-modernist form.

If we are to test this thesis against alternative perceptions of twentieth-century literature we must start with an implicit paradox. In short, the modernist and the postmodern poem are the same thing. The most obvious and explicit break with traditional form involves a total rejection of the conventional elements of the double pattern, but the single feature which had once been the organising principal of these elements, the line, is maintained. No other aesthetic genre, linguistic, visual or musical, involves the same degree of formal continuity. True, modernist fiction will usually make some concession to the organising principle of the sentence, and abstract, surrealist or post-impressionist paintings often share with their traditional predecessors a hierarchical disposition of units, colours or shapes, but none can claim to have transposed a formal element which is so regular, persistent and influential upon the broader signifying patterns of the artefact as the modernist/postmodern poem's deployment of the tension and interdependence between syntax and the line. We have so far identified four types of free verse technique whose common feature is their foregrounding of the syntax–line relationship. In what follows we will examine how these stylistic types are deployed in poems that have been variously categorised as modernist, pre-modernist, anti-modernist and postmodernist. In short we will use this abstract framework of documentation in an attempt to identify a synthetic but nonetheless recognisable denomination of the 'modern'. It would be wise to remind ourselves of what these four techniques involve and allocate names to each.

1 The dominant syntagm. Line division is secondary to the more dominant pattern of syntax.

2 The isolated line. The line operates as an enclosed syntactic and thematic unit.
3 Innovative tension. The line functions as an axis between shifting patterns of interpretation, while making few concessions to the conventions of regular form. The visual–acoustic, static–temporal tension is particularly important.
4 The stylistic precedent. Concessions are made to the mainly acoustic elements of the conventional pattern, often, though not exclusively, as stable a counterpoint to syntactic, semantic, thematic and deictic discontinuities.

The following poems and extracts will deploy one or a combination of more than one of the above as a significant element of their structural and functional identity. Our use of these stylistic models will be supplemented by references to the broader aesthetic and historical context of the poem.

I

He disappeared in the dead of winter:
The brooks were frozen, the airports almost deserted,
And snow disfigured the public statues;
The mercury sank in the mouth of the dying day.
What instruments we have agree
The day of his death was a dark cold day.

Far from his illness
The wolves ran on through the evergreen forests,
The peasant river was untempted by the fashionable quays;
By mourning tongues
The death of the poet was kept from his poems.

But for him it was his last afternoon as himself,
An afternoon of nurses and rumours;
The provinces of his body revolted,
The squares of his mind were empty,
Silence invaded the suburbs,
The current of his feeling failed; he became his admirers.

Now he is scattered among a hundred cities
And wholly given over to unfamiliar affections,
To find his happiness in another kind of wood
And be punished under a foreign code of conscience.
The words of a dead man
Are modified in the guts of the living.

But in the importance and noise of to-morrow
When the brokers are roaring like beasts on the floor of the
    Bourse,
And the poor have the sufferings to which they are fairly
    accustomed,
And each in the cell of himself is almost convinced of his
    freedom;
A few thousand will think of this day
As one thinks of a day when one did something slightly unusual.
What instruments we have agree
The day of his death was a dark cold day.

II

You were silly like us; your gift survived it all:
The parish of rich women, physical decay,
Yourself. Mad Ireland hurt you into poetry.
Now Ireland has her madness and her weather still,
For poetry makes nothing happen: it survives
In the valley of its making where executives
Would never want to tamper, flows on south
From ranches of isolation and the busy griefs,
Raw towns that we believe and die in; it survives,
A way of happening, a mouth.

III

Earth, receive an honoured guest:
William Yeats is laid to rest.
Let the Irish vessel lie
Emptied of its poetry.

In the nightmare of the dark
All the dogs of Europe bark,
And the living nations wait,
Each sequestered in its hate;

Intellectual disgrace
Stares from every human face,
And the seas of pity lie
Locked and frozen in each eye.

Follow, poet, follow right
To the bottom of the night,

With your unconstraining voice
Still persuade us to rejoice;

With the farming of a verse
Make a vineyard of the curse,
Sing of human unsuccess
In a rapture of distress;

In the deserts of the heart
Let the healing fountain start,
In the prison of his days
Teach the free man how to praise.

W. H. Auden's, 'In Memory of W. B. Yeats' is as much about the stylistic revolutions of the previous half century as it is about Yeats's life. It is effectively a distilled history of nineteenth–twentieth-century poetic form, played backwards. Section I is governed chiefly by the conventions of 1, section II deploys 4, and makes concessions to 3 and section III returns us to the trochaic, ballad form of Blake's *Songs*. But Auden offers us more than simply a display of technical skill. Pay particular attention to how the relation between the metonymic–syntagmatic and metaphoric–paradigmatic poles (crucial to Jakobson's distinction between the prosaic and the poetic) responds to or perhaps controls the shifts in metrical pattern. Most of section I involves a kind of double metonym: the parts of a landscape, perhaps a nation, ('forests', 'rivers', 'squares', 'cities', 'provinces') are listed rather than juxtaposed, and this discursive progress is paralleled by a similar part–whole synecdoche in which the physical and cultural elements of Yeats's presence ('his illness', 'his body', 'his mind', 'the words') are enumerated. The progressive, combinative nature of the syntagm seems to dominate both elements of the double pattern – the discourse is consecutive, prosaic, and syntax controls the duration and positioning of the unmetrical lines. In section II we encounter both an irregular off-rhyme scheme and an iambic undertow, and we also find that the adventurous illogic of paradigmatic similarity and selection begins to replace the contiguous logic of the first section. The relation between poet, poetry, landscape and nation is maintained but now, as Jakobson put it, 'metaphor' not 'metonymy is the line of least resistance'. Poetry is actually part of 'the valley of its saying' and like the river 'it flows' and 'survives', 'A way of happening, a mouth' (mouth of poet, mouth of river). Think back to the poetry–prose relationship in *Measure for Measure*. Prose tends to be organised according to some perceived relation between text, external events and circumstances while poetry gathers these into an enclosed field in which there is a constant interplay between the material elements of the double pattern and its referential function. Something similar happens between parts I and II. The speaking presence in II is effectively recuperating the facts of I as elements of a self-determined artefact. Jakobson: 'The principle of similarity underlies poetry; metrical parallelism of lines, or phonic equivalence of rhyming words prompts the question of semantic similarity or contrast'. By section III the uncertain patterns of metrical and phonic equivalence of II have become fully synchronised with the metaphoric excursions. Yeats is both an object (vessel) and a poet, time is a person, the night is a physical as well as a temporal dimension, verses are farmed, the heart is a desert, temporal existence is a prison. Again the relation between external and existential conditions is maintained but they have now become interwoven with the text; no referential or ideational concept remains immune from the insistent parallelism of rhyme and metrical regularity. Auden would seem to have preempted Jakobson's 1950s thesis that there is a predictable causal relationship between the metrical and phonic density of the text and poetic or non-poetic deployments of syntax and metaphor: roughly summarised, free verse (part I, metonymic) is more prosaic than regular verse (part III, metaphoric). One could argue that the three sections of this poem represent the same text at different stages of composition; as the poem proceeds the tentative, discursive pattern is gradually enclosed within an autonomous self-determined condition of textuality. But it would be wrong to interpret this simply as an anti-modernist, revisionist gesture. To properly understand its significance we need to consider the broader historical and aesthetic context of modernist poetics.

Auden produced his best known early poems during the 1930s. The Imagist revolution had occurred two decades earlier, and figures such as Eliot, Pound and Williams had in various ways been transformed from iconoclasts to icons. In British poetry this period has come to be known as that of the Auden generation, whose most celebrated members were Auden's contemporaries at Oxford – Louis MacNeice, Stephen Spender and C. Day Lewis (see Tolley, 1975). To generalise further would be to obscure the rich complexities of this 'next stage' of modernism, but two issues should hold our attention. Firstly, the poets who began writing in the late 1920s and 1930s were the inheritors of a literary tradition that included modernism, and as a consequence they felt able to draw both upon the stylistic innovation of their immediate predecessors and upon pre-modernist conventions. Secondly, the poets of this period initiated a change in the functional conditions of post-1900 poetry. Early modernist writing, particularly poetry, centred upon the individual consciousness as a means of perceiving, recording and communicating experience while remaining largely immune from the imperatives of order, judgement, classification or rational objectivity. The poetry of the thirties began to forge more tangible links between the individuality of the speaking subject and the broader social, political and existential conditions that the speaker shared with the implied reader – consider how Auden's 'In Memory . . .' uses deictic clues to situate the condition of speaker and hearer as inhabitants of a continent on the brink of war. These two factors – stylistic eclecticism and a desire to reestablish poetry as a platform for social and political comment – resulted in compositional pressures that have effectively dominated British poetry between the 1930s and the 1980s. In short, how can the poet balance the availability of a rich and diverse repertoire of patterns, techniques and stylistic devices against the attractions of unfettered individuality? Is it the duty of the poet to set aside the drive toward innovation in favour of a new and specifically modern form of accessibility and relevance? The two poets who represent the most divergent engagements to these questions are Philip Larkin and Dylan Thomas.

Consider the opening stanza of Thomas's 'When, Like a Running Grave':

When, like a running grave, time tracks you down,
Your calm and cuddled is a scythe of hairs,
Love in her gear is slowly through the house,
Up naked stairs, a turtle in a hearse,
Hauled to the dome,

The relative adverb 'When' introduces the complex explanatory clause of the first line, and we are uncertain if the unfolding situation will involve the specific circumstances of when time will track you down like a running grave or whether time will always track you down like a running grave. This uncertainty is not resolved; rather it is further complicated by a montage of syntactic and semantic discontinuities. What exactly is your 'calm and cuddled'? The semantic pattern of a 'scythe of hairs', 'Love in her gear', 'naked', 'hearse', suggests perhaps a tension between sensual, physical images and death. Perhaps. The poem extends Eliot's precedent in

'Prufrock', and extends it beyond any acceptable balance between intrinsic and imposed coherence. Read the rest of the poem and if you can disclose a pattern of syntactic and referential continuity you are, I believe, deceiving yourself. The potential for self-deceit is provided by a complex and admirably precise formal pattern. Each stanza consists of four roughly iambic decasyllabic lines, followed by a quattro-syllabic coda. These are held together by a system of alliterative/assonantal off-rhymes, binding each stanza into a discernable pattern of a bbb a. Without this concession to regularity the poem would be meaningless. The reader is literally bounced from one point of metrical and phonic foregrounding to the next and this is the only formal pattern upon which an attempt at naturalisation can be based: the conventional has effectively replaced and overridden the cognitive dimension of the double pattern. Read 'After the Funeral', 'Fern Hill' and 'Do Not Go Gentle into That Good Night' and consider how Thomas's method of 'baring the device' of versification (category 4) operates as a replacement for the ordinary functions of syntactic and semantic coherence.

Thomas was not the only British poet to make extravagant use of Eliot's early precedent – see also the work of W. R. Rodgers – but by the late 1940s he had become the most conspicuous target for a new generation of British anti-modernists. Novelists, poets and critics such as Amis, Wain, Larkin, Enright, Davie and Conquest would eventually come to be classified by literary historians as members of 'The Movement' (see Blake Morrison's study, 1980). These writers were a more determined and more confident manifestation of the Auden generation. In 1955 Donald Davie published *Articulate Energy. An Inquiry into the Syntax of English Poetry*, and this could stand as a disguised and sophisticated manifesto for the Movement poets: 'In free verse and in Dylan Thomas's complicated metrical stanzas the articulation and spacing of images is done by rhythm instead of syntax' (126–7). What was needed, Davie implied, was poetry that restored the syntagm as the anchor, the thread of stability against which metrical and referential excursions could be counterpointed. This would not necessarily involve the outright rejection of categories 1–4 – free verse and experiment were still permissible – but the syntagm was the vital channel through which the poetic might communicate with the non-poetic world of ordinary language and experience.

The following is Philip Larkin's 'An Arundel Tomb':

Side by side, their faces blurred,
The earl and countess lie in stone,
Their proper habits vaguely shown
As jointed armour, stiffened pleat,
And that faint hint of the absurd –
The little dogs under their feet.

Such plainness of the pre-baroque
Hardly involves the eye, until
It meets his left-hand gauntlet, still
Clasped empty in the other; and
One sees, with a sharp tender shock,
His hand withdrawn, holding her hand.

They would not think to lie so long,
Such faithfulness in effigy
Was just a detail friends would see:
A sculptor's sweet commissioned grace
Thrown off in helping to prolong
The Latin names around the base.

They would not guess how early in
Their supine stationary voyage
The air would change to soundless damage,
Turn the old tenantry away;
How soon succeeding eyes begin
To look, not read. Rigidly they

Persisted, linked, through lengths and breadths
Of time. Snow fell, undated. Light
Each summer thronged the glass. A bright
Litter of birdcalls strewed the same
Bone-riddled ground. And up the paths
The endless altered people came,

Washing at their identity.
Now, helpless in the hollow of
An unarmorial age, a trough
Of smoke in slow suspended skeins
Above their scrap of history,
Only an attitude remains:

Time has transfigured them into
Untruth. The stone fidelity
They hardly meant has come to be
Their final blazon, and to prove
Our almost-instinct almost true:
What will survive of us is love.

The poem adheres to the complex stanzaic formula of iambic, octo-syllabic lines, rhyming a bb c a c, but the syntax maintains the unforced yet consistently ordered pattern of detail and reflection that one would expect from the prose of a literary journal. How do these two elements of the double pattern intersect? The first three stanzas are dominated by the speaker's description of the details of the tomb. Note how the enjambments operate as a form of metasyn-tax, and cause a subtle tension between what Benveniste calls *his-toire* (an impartial account) and *discours* (the intervention of the speaker). In stanza 2 the 'eye' of the experiencer and the ideational 'eye' of the reader are 'hardly involved' by the plainness of the monument: does this mean that the perceived image demands neither intellectual nor emotional involvement? This uncertainty intensifies as we encounter 'still'. The gauntlet is both 'still' (static) and is 'still/Clasped' (temporal). In the next line 'and' would at first seem to continue the listing of the parts of the object, but after the line break '*histoire*' is merged with '*discours*'. Is the 'sharp tender shock' ours, or is it something that we imagine might have inspired the original conception of the effigy?

At one level the dominant pattern is metonymic, the syntagm allowing the speaker to list each part of the perceived object, but when the syntagm makes tangible contact with versification, the sense of language as in some way affecting and modifying the impar-tiality of the visual register (the beginnings of metaphor) becomes evident. In stanzas 4–7 the perceptual focus shifts from the object to the reflections of the speaker, and crucially the same subtle interface between the referential and the purely poetic dimensions of the text is maintained. In the closing stanza the verb phrases disclose on one level a decisive, factual certainty that echoes the earlier listing of visual objects: 'Time *has* transfigured them into untruth', 'The stone fidelity . . . *has* come to be their final blazon', 'What *will* survive of us is love'. But there are also echoes of the ways in which effects which register as elements of the linguistic and emotional presence of the speaker can interfere with the impersonal progress of the syntagm. What they are 'transfigured into', what they have 'come to be', what they 'prove' are all qualified by a pattern of hesitations and uncertainties foregrounded by the tension between syntagmatic progression and the line.

It would be wrong to categorise this poem as simply a return to pre-modernist convention. In various ways it involves all four categories of syntax–line interaction. Its syntactic excursions recall Thribb and Williams's 'This Is Just To Say' (1), while the subtle shifts between progress and stasis recall 'Spring and All' (3). Its metrical regularity is as persistent as in Eliot's 'Whispers' (4). We can also discern echoes of Pound's 'In a Station' (2), as single, isolated lines and images assimilate and modify preceding and succeeding statements (note the closing lines of stanzas 6 and 7). It is the archetypal postmodernist poem. The syntax embodies the informal progress of the free verse poem and foregrounds the specificity of the speech act and the presence of the experiencer, while the persistent regularity of the stanza distances this particular speech act from non-poetic discourse.

THE CLASHING OF CODES: A DEFINITION OF MODERNISM

To trace all the points of intersection between modernist poetics and contemporary literary and interpretive theory would require another book. Instead, I shall propose a basic formula which might help readers to organise their own investigations, and which can be tested against poems already discussed, those listed in the Exercise section, and texts of your own choice. Modernist poetry involves what I shall term the clashing of codes.

The isolation of distinct categories of the structural and functional condition of a text is the common feature of practically all forms of literary/linguistic method. The classic example is Barthes's identification of five codes in *S/Z*, but in most instances of localised close reading or broader interpretive debate we encounter a bipolar opposition. In this study the double pattern has functioned as our keynote, and in every other element of linguistic and critical practice binary doubling is endemic: speech and writing, signifier and signified, deep and surface structure, noun phrase and verb phrase, *langue* and *parole*, poetry and prose, text and context, metonym and metaphor, linguistic and non-linguistic, literary and non-literary . . . The list could continue. Identifying these binary relations and tensions is not too difficult but problems arise when we attempt to construct homologies (persistent and verifiable relations between one opposition and another) and hierarchies (the identification of the dominant and the subsidiary code). Is poetry always metaphoric and prose metonymic? Does literary writing always subordinate context to text? With regular verse form we are provided with a relatively stable model against which we might test homologous relations. It is the continuous and intensive interplay between the two parts of the double pattern that enables Jakobson to construct a minutely detailed plan of what the sonnet is and how it discharges meaning. But in modern poetry the fundamental opposition between the two elements of the double pattern is discernable but persistently resistant to broader homologous correspondences. Is a particular free verse line a component of syntax (thus shifting the text toward the referential, non-poetic realm of signification) or does it subvert and effectively dominate the progress of syntax (thus shifting the text toward the enclosed specificity of the poetic function)? Is the use of irregular correspondences between metre and syntax (Eliot and Thomas) an attempt to sustain the cultural eminence of the poetic or an admission that twentieth-century poetry invokes the binary code that underpins our analyses of poetry from the sixteenth to the twentieth century (syntax and line) but thereafter sends our familiar system of homologous relations into a bewildering cycle of disappointments, missed connections and revisions? Try out the following experiment.

Literary theorists often draw up two columns of binary oppositions to illustrate the structural and functional relations of a particular text (see the metaphor–metonymy columns in Chapter 5, pp. 134–5). Choose a modern poem and first identify the structural tension that to you seems to be its most prominent feature. For 'Whispers of Immortality' you might identify metrical regularity versus referential incoherence; for 'Spring and All' you might isolate speech (the unstructured progress of the syntagm) versus writing (the static presence of the line). Then go on to identify other oppositions that are within or at least addressed by the text. You will, I believe, find that it is difficult to maintain a regular and stable distinction between the horizontal and vertical axes of the columns. For example, with 'Whispers of Immortality' you might identify:

tradition	innovation
metre	syntax
the past	the present
poet	persona
textual	referential
langue	*parole*

Such a diagram is useful in so far as it documents those elements of the text that normally enable us to naturalise it; to describe how it works and what its effects are intended to achieve. But in this case difficulties arise in the shift from documentation to naturalisation. Does metrical regularity (tradition) guarantee the commanding presence of the poet? Or does the bizarre referential collage (innovation) compromise and decentre this presence and turn the poet into an element of the text?

So how do we make sense of modernist poetry? Roland Barthes in *S/Z* provides a useful distinction between modernist and traditional writing by associating the former with the *scriptible* (writerly) and the latter with the *lisible* (readerly) text, and this opposition could be claimed as the archetype for later manifestations of reader-response theory – particularly in Fish's and Culler's discussions of free verse. Roughly summarised, a scriptible text is that which demands the participation of the reader in the production of meaning while its lisible counterpart involves a straightforward transference of effects to a more passive reader. One could argue that Wordsworth's 'The Idiot Boy' is far more lisible than scriptible in the sense that we are fully informed of who the characters are, what they do and of the emotional effects of these activities. Eliot's 'Prufrock' is scriptible in that we remain constantly uncertain about the spatio-temporal circumstances of the speech act, and we are consequently obliged to speculate on how the text works and what it means – in Barthes's terms we become the co-writers of the text.

A non-literary analogy could be found in what happens when we encounter the utterance of a child or a non-English speaker. Our linguistic competence enables us to invoke a deep structure for what might be an ungrammatical statement and provide a 'correct' surface structure. Substitute literary for linguistic competence and in most instances a very similar process occurs in our response to the scriptible or difficult modernist poem (think back to Gross's naturalisation of Pound). Just as we draw upon our awareness of the conventions of the *langue* in order to comprehend an incorrect non-literary utterance, so with a modernist poem that fails to satisfy the usual expectations of formal or referential coherence we draw upon our experience of how lisible, traditional texts work. But is this the proper way to deal with modernist texts? When we correct or make sense of non-literary statements we make two implicit assumptions: first that there is an abstract norm against which we might judge deviant statements; second, that the act of deviation from this norm is unwitting, the result of incompetence. The problem with modernism is that the poet consciously and deliberately violates the norm of literary conventions: the indefinable nature of the free verse line and discontinuities of reference and syntax are purposive strategies. So if we impose a 'correct', normative structure upon modernist poems, make sense of or demystify them in accordance with our familiarity with traditional texts, we are doing a grave injustice to the purpose and intended effect of the artefact. An equivalent process in the visual arts would be the retouching of a picture by Picasso or Dali to make the figures and objects more recognisably 'real' and comprehensibly connected. Is it possible to find an alternative to the usual methods and objectives of naturalisation (usually termed 'closure') that in some way respects the modernist text's deliberate and purposive act of removal from the norms and conventions of tradition?

I have only half explained Barthes's concept of scriptible texts. These, he argues, demand the active participation of the reader in the production of meaning but this cooperative enterprise is, in conventional terms, an inconclusive, interminable process. We make connections between formal features, identify codes and oppositions, locate precedents in other texts. But we do not, in accordance with the usual objectives of naturalisation, bring this process to a conclusion and confidently state that 'Eliot means . . .'. Instead the activity of reading is interactive rather than interpretive or normative. The binary oppositions that we identify in Eliot's or Williams's texts are verifiably present but they are in a constant and unresolvable state of tension and uncertainty which would be reflected in our critical analysis. The sort of critical writing produced by such an assumption is usually categorised as poststructuralist and has drawn angered responses from critics and theorists who believe that unless criticism 'makes sense' of the text it cannot properly be regarded as criticism. For example in *Ferocious Alphabets* (1981) Denis Donoghue calls poststructuralists (De Man, Derrida, Bloom, Hartman, Barthes) 'graphireaders', 'From GREEK *graphos*, writing. Hence the graphireader deals with writing as such and does not think of it as transcribing an event properly construed as vocal or audible'. Traditional naturalisation is practised by 'epireaders', who 'read and interpret – the same act – in the hope of going through the words to something that the words both reveal and hide. Epireaders say to poems: I want to hear you. Graphireaders say: I want to see what I can do, stimulated by your insignia' (151–2).

As the disagreement between Jakobson and Riffaterre demonstrates (see Chapter 3, pp. 85–92) reading and interpreting poems are by no means 'the same act'. When we naturalise or 'epiread' a poem we have to strip the text of its immediate, multi-dimensional effects, and it could be argued that in criticising poems, particularly modernist poems, we should acknowledge the copresence of epireading and graphireading (a pairing roughly equivalent to Barthes's lisible and scriptible). In short we should balance the element of 'going through the words' or making sense of them – no text is entirely impenetrable – against our admission that some element of the relation between form and substance, effect and meaning is constantly shifting and uncertain. For example Gross could have qualified his imposition of Pound's 'missing grammar' with the admission that he can never be entirely certain of what is missing; in our reading and interpreting of Williams's 'Spring and All' we can make valid claims as to the poem's status as an impressionistic record of a perceptual experience but we should also acknowledge that the tension between the static visual text and its spoken form is persistent and irreconcilable.

I shall close with a definition of modernist poetry which draws together a number of issues already raised.

Modernism and more specifically modernist poetry, represents the terminus of literary history. All subsequent and forthcoming developments – postmodernism included – are extensions, mergers or revivals of established modernist and pre-modernist precedents. In making this claim I do not rule out the possibility that poems to come will possess a sufficient degree of originality, stylistic and thematic brilliance, to earn them the title of classics of their period. What I do claim is that formal experimentation has reached, to borrow a phrase from popular culture, the final frontier. In the eighteenth or nineteenth centuries the poems by Eliot, Thomas, Gomringer and Williams discussed above would not have been accepted as poems – or they would have been treated by the more tolerant as engaging eccentricities. They would have violated the accepted conventions of the poetic *langue*. The strange and deviant patterns embodied by these texts have now become part of the readjusted poetic *langue*. Further adjustments cannot and will not occur. How do I know? Consider the premise established at the beginning of this study – the double pattern. Poetry, whatever else it might be or say, can only be accepted as poetry if it supplements the organisational framework shared by all other linguistic genres with a continuous pattern of effects drawn primarily from the material, non-signifying element of language, and we have reached the limits to which this relationship can be pressed. The line can now consist of a single letter (see e. e. cummings); it need not even follow the linear progress of the syntagm (see concrete poetry); it can be organised around patterns of pure sound which defy syntactic or lexical coherence (see the poems of Edith Sitwell or Robert Lax). My point is that in the early decades of this century poets could move beyond precedent and consequently disrupt the conditioned expectations of the competent reader, but today a precedent can be found for any form of modernist innovation and if the reader is interested, an essay, book or thesis can be provided to inform us of the best way to naturalise this phenomenon.

Pure innovation might be a thing of the past but there is one elusive and compelling question that demands the attention of critics and literary historians. The double pattern at once defines poetry and foregrounds the paradoxical nature of poetic writing. It involves limitless tensions and cooperations between the referential function of language – what it does – and the material identity of its sounds and shapes – what it is. The rules and conventions that govern this relationship have, from Shakespeare to e. e. cummings, been extended, amended, revised and abandoned, but the relationship endures. Why? All poems, irrespective of their concessions to or violations of the norms of formal regularity or referential coherence, draw the reader into the poet's experience of two compositional imperatives involving a constant interplay between tangible patterns of phonemes and graphemes and the less tangible and very personal visions that can be disclosed by these signs. Poetry is, and has always been, the form that consciously and deliberately obscures the distinction between language and whatever exists beyond language. The possibility that linguistic and pre-linguistic experience are inseparable and mutually dependent dimensions of the human condition has held centre-ground in recent poststructuralist–deconstructionist controversies, but the tenacious attraction of the double pattern for writers and readers of poetry provides us with a much more engaging perspective on this question. Language is not simply a means of mediating our condition; it is part of our condition and poetry allows us to experience rather than just ponder this relationship: signifier and signified, sign and substance become persistently interchangeable elements of a process. What a poem means can never finally be detached from what a poem is. Auden:

> For poetry makes nothing happen: it survives
> In the valley of its making . . .
>   it survives,
> A way of happening, a mouth.

Exercises

THE USA

The formal eclecticism of Eliot, Auden and the Movement had its American counterpart, particularly in the work of Hart Crane and Wallace Stevens. Both maintain an allegiance to the parallelism of the double pattern, rarely allowing the disjunctions of categories 1–4 to disturb the reader's sense of a speaker in control of his linguistic material and mediating pre-linguistic events, images and responses (see Gross, 1964, Chapter 8).

The principal difference between the US and British modernist traditions exists in the continuation in the United States of the innovative techniques and objectives of Imagism (see Gefin's *Ideogram*, 1982, for a detailed account). Poets such as Zukofsky, Duncan, Creeley and Olson all sought to construct a transparent poetic medium. Charles Olson's essay 'Projective Verse' (1950) is a chaotic yet intriguing reengagement with the ideal of poetry as pure expression, uncontaminated by syntactic and metrical rules: 'The line comes (I swear it) from the breath . . . for only he, the man who writes, can declare, at every moment, the line its metric and its ending – where its breathing can come to, termination' (p. 19). Test Olson's manifesto against his *Maximus Poems*, and pay particular attention to how his line divisions disrupt syntactic continuity and open the text to the imposition of normative patterns of coherence. Note also how the poems of Olson, Creeley and Duncan engage with categories 1 and 2 of the line–syntax model.

The following is from Olson's 'Letter 13' of *Maximus Poems*:

> I have this sense
> that I am one
> with my skin
>   Plus this – plus this:
> that forever the geography
> which leans in
> on me I compell
> backwards I compell Gloucester
> to yield, to
> change
>   Polis
> is this.

BARING THE DEVICE

In various ways modernist poetry makes concessions to the registers and patterns of regular verse: Williams often foregrounds the inter-face between the line and syntax while disrupting conventional expectations of how the line is formed. Eliot and Thomas draw upon familiar patterns of sound and metre as a counterpoint to syntactic and referential discontinuities.

The most intriguing instance of modernist variation juxtaposed with pre-modernist structure occurs in the sonnet. Read the follow-ing sonnets.

(i)   e. e. cummings's number 4, from 'Sonnets Realities'.
What effect is created by cummings's foregrounding of the sonnet structure – the most potent symbol of the codes, devices and expec-tations of traditional form – while maintaining the half punctuated, barely grammatical pattern of non-literary discourse?

> when you rang at Dick Mid's Place
> the madam was a bulb stuck in the door
> a fang of wincing gas showed how
> hair, in two fists of shrill colour
> clutched the dull volume of her tumbling face
> scribbled with a big grin. her sow-
> eyes clicking mischief from thick lids.
> the chunklike nose on which always the four
> tablets of perspiration erectly sitting.
> – If they knew you at Dick Mid's
> the three trickling chins began to traipse
> into the cheeks 'eet smeestaire steevensun
> kum een, dare ease Bet, an Leelee, an dee beeg wun'
> her handless wrists did gooey severe shapes.

(ii)   Number 2 from the 'Funeral Music' sequence of Geoffrey Hill's *King Log*.
The sonnet is unrhymed. Does Hill substitute the *contre-rejet* (ten-sion between the pause at the line ending and syntactic progress) for the conventional rhyme scheme?

> For whom do we scrape our tribute of pain –
> For none but the ritual King? We meditate
> A rueful mystery; we are dying
> To satisfy fat Caritas, those
> Wiped jaws of stone. (Suppose all reconciled

By silent music; imagine the future
Flashed back at us, like steel against sun,
Ultimate recompense.) Recall the cold
Of Towton on Palm Sunday before dawn,
Wakefield, Tewkesbury; fastidious trumpets
Shrilling into the ruck; some trampled
Acres, parched, sodden or blanched by sleet,
Struck with strange-postured dead. Recall the wind's
Flurrying, darkness over the human mire.

WHAT IS A FREE VERSE LINE?

For linguistics the most problematic challenge is offered by category 3 of the line–syntax relationship. Williams has shown (particularly in 'Spring and All') that the practices of identifying deep and surface structures can be unsettled when the poem leaves us uncertain about the points at which phrases and clauses terminate and reengage.

(i) The following is section VII, 'The Corn Harvest', from Williams's *Pictures from Brueghel*. Try to work out why phrases and words (such as 'perhaps' and 'carelessly') seem to disrupt the progress of the syntagm. Is Williams attempting to reproduce, with linguistic signs, the blendings of shapes and objects and the consequent ambiguities of visual art (it is a poem about a painting)?

Summer!
the painting is organized
about a young

reaper enjoying his
noonday rest
completely

relaxed
from his morning labors
sprawled

in fact sleeping
unbuttoned
on his back

the women
have brought him his lunch
perhaps

a spot of wine

they gather gossiping
under a tree

whose shade
carelessly
he does not share the

resting
centre of
their workaday world

(ii)   The following extracts are from 'Burnt Norton', one of Eliot's
Four Quartets. Consider how the line operates, not according to
some abstract metrical formula, but as a metasyntactic unit. Do the
line divisions construct patterns of meaning that are not merely
breaks in the syntagmatic chain? (Compare them with Thribb's piece
(p. 159) and Williams's 'This Is Just To Say'.)

Footfalls echo in the memory
Down the passage which we did not take
Towards the door we never opened
Into the rose garden. My words echo
Thus, in your mind.

(Section I)

Words move, music moves
Only in time; but that which is only living
Can only die. Words, after speech, reach
Into the silence. Only by the form, the pattern,
Can words or music reach
The stillness, as a Chinese jar still
Moves perpetually in its stillness.

(Section V)

(iii)   The following is an extract from Auden's 'Musée des Beaux
Arts'. Note how the verb phrases shift between equivocation and
certainty ('may/Have', 'must have', for example). Does the relation
between the irregular rhyme scheme, the lines and syntax underpin
this referential effect? Why, given there is no persistent accentual–
syllabic pattern, is 'green' separated from 'Water'? (Remember that
it is 'about' a painting).

In Brueghel's *Icarus*, for instance: how everything turns away
Quite leisurely from the disaster; the ploughman may
Have heard the splash, the forsaken cry,
But for him it was not an important failure; the sun shone
As it had to on the white legs disappearing into the green

Water; and the expensive delicate ship that must have seen
Something amazing, a boy falling out of the sky,
Had somewhere to get to and sailed calmly on.

VISUAL POETRY

The following is part 9 from cummings's *No Thanks*. Read it aloud,
read it silently, and consult Jakobson's definition of visual and linguistic effects (9–11; 170). Can it be argued that the total signifying
effect of the poem is only discernible when it is perceived visually
and audibly? Does this visual–acoustic precondition operate in our
reading of any of the above poems by Milton, Williams, Eliot and
Auden?

```
o  pr
      gress verily thou art m
      mentous superc
      lossal hyper pr
      digious etc i kn
      w & if you d

      n't why g
      to yonder s
      called newsreel s
      called theatre & with your
      wn eyes beh

   ld The
              (The president The
              president of The president
              of the The) president of

              the (united The president of the
              united states The president of the united
              states of The President Of The) United States

              Of America unde negant redire quenquam supp
      sedly thr
          w
            i
              n
                g
                a
                  b
                    aseball
```

Appendix

Using the double pattern and the sliding scale as an interpretive framework for poems

The double pattern and the sliding scale (see Chapter 1 and Glossary) are terms I have coined to provide a practical focus for the vast and disparate methodologies of linguistics and literary criticism. The following is a brief guide, with examples, to how these concepts can be used in the interpretation of poems. It is effectively a summary of the methods used in the book.

(i)   Begin by distinguishing the two elements of the poem's double pattern. The conventional element is the easiest to identify and name (blank verse, free verse, the ode, the couplet, etc.). The cognitive element (syntactic structure, coherence and deviation) should be dealt with in relation to this.

(ii)   Consider whether, in the process of understanding (in formal terms naturalising) the poem, the conventional or the cognitive element of the text is its most prominent or problematic feature. For example, in Dylan Thomas's 'When Like a Running Grave' the patterns of metre and rhyme (conventional) are far more regular and prominent than their syntactic or referential counterparts (cognitive), while in Shakespeare's blank verse the cognitive element (syntax and speech pattern) seems to dominate convention (blank verse).

(iii)   Examine how the interactions between the two elements of the double pattern affect our broader understanding of the intention of the poet, and our classification of the poem within a particular type or genre. Does the tension between cognitive and conventional elements make it more or less difficult to reconcile our experience of the text with the imagined circumstances of the speech act? In short, is the text easy or difficult to understand? Can we identify a predictable causal relation between the transparent or refractory nature of the text and its classification as Augustan, Romantic, modernist, etc.?

(iv)   Draw up a diagram of the sliding scale.

cognitive   conventional
referential   ←——————————→   textual
real world   poetic world

In your consideration of points (i), (ii) and (iii) use this as a means of recording your impressions of how the text works. The following are examples of how to use the diagrams, with texts drawn, respectively, from chapters 2–6. Try out this method with texts from the Exercise sections or poems of your own choice.

Donne's 'The Flea' This poem indicates the immediate circumstances of the speech act but sets up a tension between this imagined situation and the complex internal devices of the text, which are contrived and unspontaneous.

Sliding Scale
cognitive   ←— — —'The Flea'— — —→   conventional
referential   ←————————————→   textual
real world   poetic world

Conclusions: 'The Flea', like many other metaphysical (early seventeenth-century) poems, exists at the centre of the sliding scale and foregrounds the condition of poetry as caught uneasily between the referential purposes of non-poetic discourse and the enclosed and uncertain functions of the purely poetic.

Pope's 'The Rape of the Lock' This poem distances the speaker both from the situation of the narrative and from the means of narration. The heroic couplet allows us to distinguish more clearly between speaker, events narrated and medium.

Sliding Scale
cognitive   ←'The Rape of the Lock'   conventional
referential   ←————————————→   textual
real world   poetic world

Conclusions: Pope and most other Augustan poets move poetry toward the discursive, functional purpose of the essay and other non-poetic discourses.

Coleridge's 'Kubla Khan' This poem marginalises the referential/

cognitive dimensions of the double pattern by creating an independent system of relations within the complex metrical and sound patterns of the text.

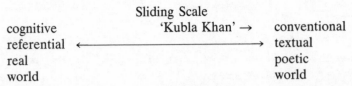

Conclusions: Coleridge and most other Romantic poets focus attention upon poetry as an independent *langue*, a system of conventions and devices, separate from the structural and functional conditions of non-poetic discourses.

Browning's 'My Last Duchess' This poem foregrounds both the immediate circumstances of the speech act and the status of the text as poetic (enjambed couplets) while not permitting any serious tensions between the two.

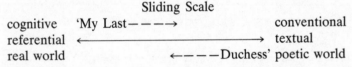

Conclusions: Browning and most other Victorian poets achieve a balance between the two elements of the double pattern by at once situating the text within the real world of non-poetic discourses while maintaining a persistent but unprovocative concession to the conventional features of the poetic.

Eliot's 'The Love Song of J. Alfred Prufrock' This poem effectively destabilises the interpretive framework of the double pattern and the sliding scale. We can identify a speaker but we are never certain of his circumstances or the situation of the speech act. We are also uncertain of whether the conventional, textual patterns (line division and rhyme scheme) are a token of immediacy and spontaneity or of the poet's imposition of an, albeit irregular, formal framework upon a chaotic collage of deictic features.

Sliding Scale

cognitive	←⁻The→	←Love Song→	conventional
referential	←	→	textual
real world	←of→	←J. Alfred Prufrock'→	poetic world

Conclusions: Eliot's 'Prufrock', like most other modernist texts, draws upon stylistic precedents from the established poetic *langue* and assembles these in a disorientating and unprecedented manner.

Glossary

binary oppositions
A basic analytical tool of linguistics and structuralism. Founded on the assumption that language is a differential structure of signs and that the most basic distinction is binary (e.g. good-bad, right-wrong, yes-no, etc.); and extended as a method of analysing the way in which texts, ideologies and modes of perceptions are structured. See chapter 6, pp. 189–91.

blank verse
The iambic pentameter without rhyme. The basic verse form of sixteenth–seventeeth-century drama (see chapter 2, pp. 31–40 on 'Shakespeare'), which became an accepted non-dramatic form only after Milton's precedent in *Paradise Lost* (see chapter 3, pp. 76–85).

cognitive – conventional
The cognitive dimension of language refers to our most fundamental level of comprehension (a.k.a. linguistic competence). The term can only be properly understood in relation to its opposing conventional dimension. For example, when we read and understand the statement, 'I am Richard', we generally focus upon its signifying structure as pronoun, verb and name (cognitive) but if a statement has a prominent rhythmic pattern, uses rhyme or alliteration, or is divided typographically into distinct lines, we are also obliged to take into account its conventional structure, i.e. those elements that are self-evidently poetic. See S. R. Levin's 'The Conventions of Poetry' (1971), and Chapter 1, pp. 15–16.
　　See also the 'double pattern' and the 'sliding scale'.

cohesion
This is fundamental to our perception of how texts are organised. In prose, cohesion is governed by the relation between syntactic units, particularly when something is designated specifically by a predicate or referring expression ('John', 'my mother', 'the house') and thereafter referred to as 'he', 'she' or 'it'. In poetry this relationship is complicated by a second level of organisation dividing the text into lines, couplets or stanzas. See Birch (1989) and Halliday and Hasan (1976), and Chapter 3, pp. 69–76.

competence – linguistic and literary
Linguistic competence is what enables us to relate instances of linguistic usage with the rules and conventions which govern usage. Literary competence involves the adaptation of this event-instance relationship to the particular conventions, rules and precedents of literary writing. For example a competent reader of poetry will recognise metre, sound pattern and line division as elements of a specifically poetic grammar. See also '*langue*' and '*parole*', and 'reader-response criticism'.

contact
A subdivision of context (see Jakobson's diagram of the communicative circuit, chapter 1, pp. 26–8). The contact code refers to the means by which the message is delivered from addresser to addressee (spoken, written, sung, books, handwritten notes, etc.). Each of these will be affected by context. For example our expectations of the spoken message at a poetry reading will differ from our expectations of a political oration.

context
Two principal meanings: (i) The immediate or situational context. This is important in interpreting poems. It is the situation of the poem as speech act which the reader constructs from the evidence within the text (see 'deictics'); (ii) The historical context. This involves the broader network of linguistic, social and behavioural conventions that influence the construction of the text. For example, to understand the term 'the Romantic poem' we also need to appreciate the cultural, political and social conditions of the early nineteenth century (see 'functional – structural').

A third type is the intertextual context. This is ahistorical and refers to the *langue* of poetic writing. For example Wordsworth's 'Tintern Abbey' invokes the broader stylistic context occupied by

Milton's 'Paradise Lost' (both are in blank verse). See chapter 1, pp. 25–30. See also 'contact'.

contre-rejet

A term used most productively by Hollander (1975). It refers to the double effect created when a line division cuts into the deep structure of a sentence, often appearing to at once close and re-engage with the pattern of meaning. For example, Williams's,

> with dead, brown leaves under them
> leafless vines

See chapter 6, pp. 164–73 on 'Williams and Visualism'.

conventional

See 'cognitive'.

couplet

The most basic form of stanza, rhyming aa, bb, etc. The heroic (ten syllable) and octosyllabic (eight syllable) couplet are the most widely used forms. See chapter 3 *passim*.

deconstruction

Deconstruction is an extension of the linguistic theories of Saussure. Saussure suggested that language is not so much a medium that allows us to reflect or mediate reality but more an autonomous sign system of relations in which to some extent we construct reality. For example the difference between two words is conventionally regarded as a representation of the difference between two elements of reality, physical or mental. Deconstruction (founded by Derrida) holds that the differential relation between signs is what enables us to construct and stabilise the differential nature of physical and mental existence. To deconstruct a text is to demonstrate how by relying upon the differential structure of language, it subverts its own claims to reflect or mediate pre-linguistic reality.

Poetry offers itself as an attractive test-case for literary deconstructionists because it foregrounds the unstable relationship between the autonomous, material, differential nature of language and its idealised function as a transparent medium (see the 'double pattern'). In short, some poems appear to be self-deconstructing texts, because they are as much about language as they are a means by which language reflects reality. See Chapter 2, pp. 46–7, Chapter

3, pp. 89–92, Chapter 4, pp. 118–28, 'The Ode and Deconstruction'. See also Culler (1982).

deep structure – surface structure
The deep structure of a sentence is the abstract, underlying pattern that links its surface structure (the actual sentence) with the rules and conventions of language. This system has been adapted by metrists to account for the tension between the abstract metrical pattern of a line (deep structure or verse design) and the more variable spoken pattern which might sweep across line divisions (surface structure or verse instance). See Traugott and Pratt (1980) for the syntactic method and Attridge (1982) for its metrical counterpart. See Chapter 3, pp. 78–81 on '*Paradise Lost*'. See also '*contrerejet*'.

deictics – deixis
Deixis is the study of the part or parts of language (the deictic features) that allow us to establish the context of the speech act – the orientational features of the text. The identification of deictic features is particularly important in the criticism of poetry because the poem (unlike the reported speech acts of a novel or a play) is rarely attended by external evidence of its spatio-temporal or social context. See Traugott and Pratt (1980) and see Chapter 2, pp. 40–5.

double pattern
The defining characteristic of poetic language. A double pattern is discernible when a linguistic structure draws upon the normal organisational imperatives of language (syntax, grammar etc.) and creates patterns comprised of the material constituents of language (phonemes, graphemes, rhythmic and metrical patterns). This binary doubling also incorporates, respectively: cognitive and conventional functions; syntax and the line; referential and poetic functions; functional and structural conditions. See Chapter 1, pp. 1–8. See also the 'sliding scale'.

experiencer
The experiencer is the animate being inwardly affected by a state or a pattern of events, whose speech act is a subjective record of these. Benveniste's concept of *discours* (subjective record) involves the foregrounding of the presence of the experiencer, while *histoire* (objective record) involves the distancing of the state or the events

reported from the presence of the experiencer. See Traugott and Pratt, and see Chapter 4, pp. 115–17 on 'Blake'.

Formalism
The collective title given to a number of mostly Russian and Eastern European linguists and literary critics, whose seminal work was done in the first two decades of this century. The Formalists, more than any other literary-critical school, emphasise the necessary and cooperative relationship between literary and linguistic studies. Their objective of defining in abstract terms the structure and effects of poetry corresponds with that of the Anglo-American New Critics of the 1930s–1950s, except that the former maintained that the empirical study of linguistic and poetic data would explain factors such as aesthetic quality, while the latter remained coyly enigmatic regarding the mysterious nature of 'literary art'. Formalists referred to in this study include Jakobson (Chapter 1 and *passim*), Bakhtin (Chapter 2), Ingarden (Chapter 2) and Propp (Chapter 4). See Erlich (1965).

free verse
The most important innovative development in twentieth-century poetic form. Free verse disrupts or rejects the conventional regular and irregular forms of the double pattern. The only common feature of all free verse poems is the existence (in various conditions of cooperation, conflict or tension) of syntax and the line. See Chapter 6 *passim*.

functional – structural
The functional condition of a text is determined by what it is meant to achieve and by the circumstances which substantiate this objective. For example the functional purpose of a washing machine guarantee is straightforward, while the function of literature, poetry and prose, is not so easy to define. To properly understand the function and the functional objectives of texts we should consider their structural condition: the salient technical or stylistic features of a text that allow us to identify categories such as poetic or prosaic. The principal problem with poetry is the specification of what its stylistic features actually do. See Chapter 2, pp. 58–61.

grapheme
The visual equivalent of the phoneme: the shape or appearance of the character on the page. See Chapter 6, pp. 164–73.

iambic pentameter

The most consistently employed metrical pattern in post-sixteenth-century English poetry. The iambic pentameter consists of ten syllables, with a basic stress pattern of weak-strong, weak-strong. There are variations upon this formula, and the most sophisticated methods of documenting these have been developed by the so-called 'linguistic metrists'. See 'deep structure – surface structure' and Chapter 1, pp. 22–3.

langue – parole

These terms were used by Saussure to account for the relationship between language as a system of rules and conventions (*langue*) and individual instances of linguistic usage (*parole*). This distinction underpins the broader twentieth-century phenomenon of structuralism (see Culler, 1975). The meaning or status of an individual speech act or text (*parole*) is largely determined by the broader system or structure (*langue*) from which it is drawn. See also 'deep structure – surface structure' and 'competence – linguistic and literary'. The poetic *langue* supplements the normal rules of syntax and semantics with specifically poetic elements such as metre, line division and rhyme, and each poem (each poetic *parole*) can only be properly understood in terms of this system (*langue*) of poetic conventions and devices.

See also the 'double pattern'.

metaphor

The comparing or contrasting of two or more linguistic elements in relation to a pre-linguistic impression, experience or fact. The simile (a type of metaphor) involves a comparison which announces the self-evident intervention of the speaker/writer ('is like'), whereas the most prominent type of literary metaphor suggests a natural or immanent resemblance ('is').

The most widely used method of analysing a metaphor is to divide it into tenor (the intended effect) and vehicle (the means by which this effect is achieved). For example in Wordsworth's 'I Wandered Lonely as a Cloud', the tenor is the condition of wandering and loneliness while the vehicle is the image of the cloud.

Regarding poetry, Jakobson (1960) has distinguished between metaphoric and metonymic elements of language. The metonymic function involves a less violent disturbance of the relation between language and perceived reality. For example, we might refer to cars as wheels or to training shoes as runners. In short metonymic usage involves the substitution of a part or a function for the whole. Metaphor involves a more extreme shift from one level of meaning and context to another: John Donne, for instance, transposes a fleabite with sexual intercourse. Jakobson regards the metonymic as the function which underpins prose and the metaphoric as that which underpins poetry.

In terms of syntactic structure, metaphor involves the foregrounding of the paradigmatic axis (a.k.a. the selective or associative); for example, the use of the verb 'flew' instead of 'walked'. Metonymy shifts the balance toward the syntagmatic axis (a.k.a. the contiguous, or combinative) in which there is a more logical correspondence between tenor and vehicle. For example, 'paced' instead of 'walked'.

The most problematic distinction is between poetic and non-poetic metaphor. Jakobson claims that poetic metaphor involves an interaction between the effect of the metaphor and its embedding in patterns of versification (metre, rhyme, alliteration, assonance, line division, etc.). See Chapter 1 on 'Jakobson'. See also Hawkes (1972) and Leech (1969).

metonym
See 'metaphor'.

metre
In specific terms metre refers to the measurement of a poetic line by the number and the stress, pitch and accentual value of its syllables. In a more general sense the term refers to the practice and study of poetic form, a sphere also referred to as prosody, metrics and versification. These constitute the conventional dimension of the double pattern. The best bibliography and reference guide to the 'science' of metre and versification is Brogan (1981), and recent studies include Fraser (1970), Easthope (1983) and Attridge (1982). See Chapter 1 *passim*.

naturalisation
In basic terms, when we naturalise a poem we explain it, translate its effects into the more familiar terms and conventions of non-poetic language. The principal problem for linguists and critics is whether, when naturalising a poem, we simplify and unjustly rationalise its complex multi-dimensional pattern of effects. See Chapter 1, pp. 17–21, 'Naturalisation' and Appendix.

ode
The most flexible and irregular type of rhymed pre-modernist verse. Its structure consists of strophes which, unlike the stanza, permit almost limitless variations of rhyme scheme and metrical pattern. To complicate matters, more regular stanzaic poems are sometimes called 'the ode on . . .'. See Chapter 4 on 'The Ode and Deconstruction'.

paradigm – syntagm
See 'metaphor'.

phonetics – phonemes
Phonetics is the study of sounds in language, a phoneme indicating a particular class of similar sounds. In poetry phonetics relates specifically to effects such as rhyme, assonance and alliteration. See Chapter 4, pp. 127–8 on 'The Ode and Deconstruction'.

reader-response criticism – reception theory
This type of criticism involves a shift in emphasis from the relation between the projected author's intention and the text toward the relation between the text and the expectations, affiliations and inter-pretive competence of the reader. With poetry, reader-response criticism is applied mainly to the type of text (particularly modernist) which unsettles regular patterns of form or syntactic, referential coherence. The reader is consequently obliged to impose structures and patterns of coherence upon formless texts, and to draw upon his/her awareness of the poetic *langue* in order to achieve this (see 'competence – linguistic and literary').

See Chapter 1, pp. 13–17 and Chapter 6 *passim*, particularly 'The Clashing of Codes: A Definition of Modernism'.

reference – referential
The kind of meaning whereby an expression or speech act designates real-world entities or states (as opposed to 'sense' which indicates the lexical, word–meaning relation irrespective of context or usage). In poetry the opposing term is 'textual' which indicates patterns and effects (metre, rhyme etc.) whose relations with one another are determined as much by the internal structure of the text as they are by a relation between text and predicated meaning. 'Referential' and 'textual' are terms that correspond closely with 'functional' and 'structural'. See Chapter 4, pp. 120–8 on 'The Ode and Deconstruction'.

See also the 'double pattern' and the 'sliding scale'.

rhyme
Similarity or identity in sound. Prior to *Paradise Lost* the use of rhyme in non-dramatic English poetry was a prescribed convention because it was thought that metre alone would not enable the hearer to distinguish between the line and syntax. Prior to free verse, blank verse was the dominant unrhymed form.

The principal interpretive questions are whether rhyme always produces a counterpattern of meaning (focusing upon the semantics of the rhyme words), whether it functions only as a supplement to punctuation, or as a merely decorative sign of the poetic. See Chapter 3 on 'Rhyme, the Superreader and the Superpoem' and Wimsatt (1944).

semantics
The relation between sign (word) and meaning. There is an important distinction between lexical semantics (the meaning of individual words) and sentence semantics, which refers to the relation between the meaning of a word and broader signifying structure of the sentence. See Traugott and Pratt (1980), and Chapter 4, pp. 111–14.

sliding scale
A means of measuring the relationship between the two elements of the double pattern. At one end of the scale we place the cognitive–referential dimension (syntax–paraphrasable meaning) and at the other the conventional and textual dimension (metre, sound pattern, line division – the structural–textual elements). A text which foregrounds the former (see 'Browning', Chapter 5 or 'Pope', Chapter 3) shifts toward the end of the scale that is closest to the referential functions of non-poetic discourse. A text which foregrounds the latter (see 'Hopkins', Chapter 5 or 'Thomas', Chapter 6) shifts toward the end of the scale that is furthest from non-poetic discourse and which involves a dense proliferation of devices drawn from the specifically poetic *langue*. See Chapter 1, pp. 16–17 and Appendix.

sonnet
Arguably the most complex metrical formula in English. The two most commonly used versions are the Shakespearean (rhyming abab cdcd for the octave, and efef gg for the sestet) and the Petrarchan (rhyming abba abba for the octave and cdc dcd for the sestet). Irregular or unrhymed sonnets have been used in modern poetry (see Chapter 6, pp. 196–7). The sonnet differs from the stanza in

that the latter is an organisational unit of the poem while the former is a complete text. See Chapter 1, pp. 12–13 and Chapter 2, pp. 48–52).

speech acts
A linguistic act performed to accomplish some communicative goal, such as commanding, promising, stating, naming or influencing the addressee emotionally or ideologically. The most prominent form of the poetic speech act is the lyric in which the hearer is addressed directly and drawn into the context of the utterance. See Searle (1969).

speech – writing
The most obvious distinction between speech and writing involves, respectively, what is spoken and heard and what is written, printed and read on the page. But there are two more complex designations: (i) The poststructuralists (see Culler, 1982, on Derrida) regard speech as the idealised medium for truth and sincerity (the speaker is always verifiably present) and writing as a more powerful, autonomous structure in which the speech act is subservient to an intertextual collage of pre-existing texts and utterances (see Chapter 3, pp. 89–92); (ii) In some poetry, particularly blank and free verse, the relation between the spoken and the written text becomes uncertain. What we see on the page might not correspond with what we hear, and the consequent tension is an element of the double pattern. See Bradford (1993) and Chapter 6, pp. 164–73 on 'Williams and Visualism'.

the stanza
Roughly translated (from Italian) 'stanza' means 'room' – in short a designated space within which a linguistic pattern can operate. The line length can vary but the crucial unifying feature of the stanza is the rhyme scheme. The most basic form of stanza is the couplet (aa bb), the next the quatrain (rhyming ab ab). See 'sonnet'.

structure
See 'function'.

superreader – superpoem
The superreader is a term coined by Riffaterre to account for the type of reader who maintains a commanding, omniscient perspective

on all of the complex internal structures of the poem (see 'reference – referential'), and on the relation between the situational context of the speech act and its broader historical and cultural circumstances (see 'context'). In short the superreader is the informed and competent critic. The superpoem refers to the vast framework of devices, effects and contexts surveyed by the superreader. See Chapter 3, pp. 85–92 on 'Rhyme, the Superreader and the Superpoem'.

surface structure
See 'deep structure – surface structure'.

syntagm – paradigm
See 'metaphor'.

syntax
Syntax refers to the sentence structure of language, and the sentence is the fundamental organisational unit of language. The two concepts most widely used to document syntax or sentence structure are clause and phrase: a clause is effectively the most basic sentence, containing its own subject and predicate, and some sentences contain two or more clauses; a phrase (most significantly noun phrase and verb phrase) enables us to account for the hierarchy of a sentence, in particular whether it is dominated by noun or verb. See Traugott and Pratt (1980).

In poetry syntax represents the organisational element of the cognitive part of the double pattern (with metre/versification as its conventional counterpart). Particular attention should be given to the interactive relationship between syntax and metre. Grammatical deviation (grammar being the rules that determine correct or incorrect syntax) in traditional poetry will often be compensated for by metrical regularity.

Metasyntax refers to the effect achieved when conventional features (such as line division) control or subordinate the normal structures of non-poetic syntax (see 'Williams and Visualism', Chapter 6, pp. 164–73). A related term is grammetrics, which refers to a cooperative relation between syntax and metre (see 'Blank Verse in the Eighteenth Century', Chapter 3, pp. 81–5).

See Chapter 1 *passim*, 'double pattern', 'sliding scale' and 'Appendix'.

tenor
See 'metaphor'.

text
See 'context'.

textual
See 'reference – referential'.

vehicle
See 'metaphor'.

writing
See 'speech – writing'.

Bibliography

If a reprint is referred to, this will be the edition cited in the main text.

Abrams, M. H. (1953) *The Mirror and the Lamp. Romantic Theory and the Critical Tradition*, Oxford: Oxford University Press.

Armstrong, Isabel. (1978) ' "Tintern Abbey": From Augustan to Romantic', in *Augustan Worlds: Essays in Honour of A. R. Humphries*, ed. J. C. Hilson, M. M. B. Jones and J. R. Watson, Leicester: Leicester University Press.

Arnold, Matthew. (1888) 'The Study of Poetry', in *Matthew Arnold. Selected Prose*, ed. P. J. Keating, London: Penguin (1970).

Arnold, Matthew. (1950) *Poetical Works*, ed. C. Tinker and H. Lowry, London: Oxford University Press.

Attridge, Derek. (1982) *The Rhythms of English Poetry*, London: Longman.

Auden, W. H. (1966) *Collected Shorter Poems 1927–1957*, London: Faber.

Bakhtin, Mikhail. (1968) [1940] *Rabelais and His World*, Cambridge, Mass.: MIT Press.

Bakhtin, Mikhail. (1973) [1929] *Problems of Dostoyevsky's Poetics*, Ann Arbor: Michigan University Press.

Barthes, Roland. (1975) *S/Z*, tr. R. Miller, London: Cape.

Belsey, Catherine. (1980) *Critical Practice*, London: Methuen.

Benveniste, Emile. (1971) *Problems in General Linguistics*, Miami: Miami University Press.

Birch, David. (1989) *Language, Literature and Critical Practice. Ways of Analysing Text*, London: Routledge.

Blake, William. (1966) *The Complete Writings*, ed. G. Keynes, London: Oxford University Press.

Bradford, Richard. (1988) 'Milton's Graphic Poetics', in *Re-Membering Milton. Essays on the Texts and Traditions*, ed. M. Nyquist and M. Ferguson, London: Methuen.

Bradford, Richard. (1992) *Silence and Sound. Theories of Poetics from the 18th Century*, New Jersey and London: Associated University Press.

Bradford, Richard. (forthcoming 1993) *The Look of It. A Theory of Visual Form in English Poetry*, Cork: Cork University Press.

Brogan, T. V. F. (1981) *English Verification 1570–1980. A Reference Guide with a Global Appendix*, Baltimore: Johns Hopkins University Press.

Brooks, Cleanth. (1947) *The Well-Wrought Urn*, New York: Harcourt & Brace.

Brown, Laura. (1985) *Alexander Pope*, Oxford: Basil Blackwell.

Browning, Robert. (1970) *Poetical Works*, ed. I. Jack, London: Oxford University Press.

Chatman, Seymour. (1956) 'Robert Frost's "Mowing": An Inquiry into Prosodic Structure', *Kenyon Review*, 18, 421–38.

Chomsky, Noam. (1957) *Syntactic Structures*, The Hague: Mouton.

Cockin, William. (1775) *The Art of Delivering Written Language; or, an Essay on Reading*, London: no pub.

Coleridge, S. T. (1969) *Poetical Works*, ed. E. H. Coleridge, Oxford: Oxford University Press.

Culler, Jonathan. (1975) *Structuralist Poetics. Structuralism, Linguistics and the Study of Literature*, London: Routledge & Kegan Paul.

Culler, Jonathan. (1982) *On Deconstruction. Theory and Criticism after Structuralism*, London: Routledge.

cummings, e. e. (1972) *Complete Poems 1913–62*, New York: Harcourt, Brace, Jovanovich.

Cushman, Stephen. (1985) *William Carlos Williams and the Meanings of Measure*, New Haven: Yale University Press.

Davie, Donald. (1955) *Articulate Energy*, London: Routledge & Kegan Paul.

Derrida, Jacques. (1973) *Speech and Phenomena: and Other Essays on Husserl's Theory of Signs*, tr. D. B. Allison, Evanston: Northwestern University Press.

Derrida, Jacques. (1977) *Of Grammatology*, tr. G. Chakravorty Spivak, Baltimore: Johns Hopkins University Press.

Derrida, Jacques. (1981) *Positions*, tr. Alan Bass, London: Athlone Press.

Donne, John. (1971) *The Complete English Poems*, ed. A. J. Smith, London: Penguin.

Donoghue, Denis. (1981) *Ferocious Alphabets*, London: Faber.

Dryden, John. (1666) Preface to *Annus Mirabilis* in Ker, I, p. 15.

Dryden, John. (1668) 'Essay of Dramatic Poesy' in *Essays of John Dryden* (1926), ed. W. P. Ker, Vol. I, Oxford: Oxford University Press.

Easthope, Anthony. (1983) *Poetry as Discourse*, London: Methuen.

Eliot, T. S. (1917) 'Reflections on *Vers Libre*', in *Twentieth Century Poetry* (1975) ed. G. Martin and P. N. Furbank, Milton Keynes: Open University Press.

Eliot, T. S. (1919) 'Tradition and the Individual Talent', in *Twentieth Century Poetry* (1975) ed. G. Martin and P. N. Furbank, Milton Keynes: Open University Press.

Eliot, T. S. (1921) 'The Metaphysical Poets' in *Oxford Anthology of English Literature* (1973) Vol. III, ed. Kermode, Hollander, Bloom, Price, Trapp and Trilling, London: Oxford University Press.

Eliot, T. S. (1969) *The Complete Poems and Plays*, London: Faber.

Empson, William. (1961) [1930] *Seven Types of Ambiguity*, London: Penguin.

Enkvist, Nils, E. (1973) *Linguistic Stylistics*, The Hague: Mouton.

Enright, D. J. (1980) *The Penguin Book of Light Verse*, London: Penguin.

Erlich, Victor. (1955) *Russian Formalism. History–Doctrine*, The Hague: Mouton.

Faulkner, Peter. (ed.) (1986) *A Modernist Reader*, London: Batsford.

Fenollosa, Ernest. (1919) *The Chinese Written Character as a Medium for Poetry*, ed. Ezra Pound, in *Prose Keys to Modern Poetry* (1962), ed. K. Shapiro, New York: Harper & Row.

Fish, Stanley. (1980) *Is There A Text In This Class? The Authority of Interpretive Communities*, Cambridge, Mass.: Harvard University Press.

Fowler, Roger. (1966) 'Structural Metrics', *Linguistics*, 27, 49–64.

Fowler, Roger. (1971) *The Languages of Literature*, London: Routledge & Kegan Paul.

Fowler, Roger. (1975) *Style and Structure in Literature*, Oxford: Basil Blackwell.

Fowler, Roger. (1981) *Literature as Social Discourse*, London: Batsford.

Fowler, Roger. (1986) *Linguistic Criticism*, Oxford: Oxford University Press.

Fraser, G. S. (1970) *Metre, Rhyme and Free Verse*, London: Methuen.

Fussell, Paul. (1965) *The Rhetorical World of Augustan Humanism*, Oxford: Clarendon Press.

Gascoigne, George. (1575) 'Certayne Notes of Instruction concerning the Making of Verse or Rhyme in English . . .', in *The Complete Works of George Gascoigne* (1907–10) ed. J. Cunliffe, Cambridge: Cambridge University Press.

Gefin, Laszlo (1982). *Ideogram: Modern American Poetry*, Milton Keynes: Open University Press.

Gleckner, Robert F. (1957) 'Point of View and Context in Blake's Songs', in *English Romantic Poetics* (1975) ed. M. H. Abrams, London: Oxford University Press.

Graves, Robert, and Riding, Laura. (1925) *Contemporary Techniques of Poetry, A Political Analogy*, Hogarth Essays No. 8, London: L. & V. Woolf.

Greimas, A. J. (1966) *Semantique Structurale*, Paris: Larousse.

Gross, Harvey. (1964) *Sound and Form in Modern Poetry*, Ann Arbor: University of Michigan Press.

Halle, Morris, and Keyser, Samuel J. (1971) *English Stress: Its Growth, and Its Role in Verse*, New York: Harper & Row.

Halliday, M. A. K. (1973) *Explorations in the Function of Language*, London: Edward Arnold.

Halliday, M. A. K. (1978) *Language as Social Semiotic*, London: Edward Arnold.

Halliday, M. A. K., and Hasan, R. (1976) *Cohesion in English*, London: Longman.

Hartman, Charles O. (1980) *Free Verse. An Essay on Prosody*, Princeton: Princeton University Press.

Hawkes, Terence. (1972) *Metaphor*, London: Methuen.

Hawkes, Terence. (1977) *Structuralism and Semiotics*, London: Methuen.

Hendricks, W. O. (1967) 'On the Notion beyond the Sentence', *Linguistics*, 37, 12–51.

Herbert, George. (1961) *The Poems*, ed. H. Gardner, London: Penguin.

Hollander, John. (1975) *Vision and Resonance. Two Senses of Poetic Form*, London: Oxford University Press.

Hopkins, Gerard Manley. (1953) *Poems and Prose*, London: Penguin.

Hulme, T. E. (1938) 'A Lecture on Modern Poetry', in Michael Roberts *T. E. Hulme* (1938), London.

Ingarden, Roman. (1973) *The Literary Work of Art*, tr. G. G. Grabowicz, Evanston: Northwestern University Press.

Jakobson, Roman. (1935) 'The Dominant', in *Readings in Russian Poetics : Formalist and Structuralist Views* (1971) ed. L. Matejka and K. Pomorska, Cambridge, Mass: MIT Press.

Jakobson, Roman. (1957) 'Shifters, Verbal Categories and the Russian Verb', in *Selected Works* (1971) Vol. II, The Hague: Mouton.

Jakobson, Roman. (1960) 'Closing Statement: Linguistics and Poetics', in *Modern Criticism and Theory* (1988) ed. D. Lodge, London: Longman.

Jakobson, Roman (1964) 'On the Relation between Visual and Auditory Signs', in *Language in Literature* (1987) ed. K. Pomorska and S. Rudy, Cambridge, Mass.: Belknap/Harvard University Press.

Jakobson, Roman, and Halle, Morris. (1956) *Fundamentals of Language*, The Hague: Mouton.

Jakobson, Roman, and Jones, L. G. (1970) 'Shakespeare's Verbal Art in 'The "Expence of Spirit" ', in *Language in Literature* (1987) ed. K. Pomorska and S. Rudy, Cambridge, Mass.: Belknap/Harvard University Press.

Jakobson, Roman, and Levi Strauss, C. (1962) 'Charles Baudelaire's "Les Chats" ', in *Language in Literature* (1987) ed. K. Pomorska and S. Rudy, Cambridge, Mass.: Belknap/Harvard University Press.

Johnson, Samuel. (1779) 'Milton' in *Lives of the English Poets* in *Oxford Anthology of English Literature* (1973) Vol. II, ed. Kermode, Hollander, Bloom, Price, Trapp and Trilling, London: Oxford University Press.

Jones, Peter. (ed.) (1972) *Imagist Poetry*, London: Penguin.

Jordan, John E. (1976) *Why The Lyrical Ballads?*, Berkeley: University of California Press.

Keats, John. (1973) *The Complete Poems*, ed. J. Barnard, London: Penguin.

Kenner, Hugh. (1972) *The Pound Era*, London: Faber & Faber.

Kiparsky, Paul. (1975) 'Stress, Syntax and Metre', *Language*, 51, 576–616.

Kiparsky, Paul. (1977) 'The Rhythmic Structure of English Verse', *Linguistic Inquiry*, 8, 189–247.

Lanz, Henry. (1931) *The Physical Basics of Rhyme: An Essay on the Aesthetics of Sound*, Stanford: Stanford University Press.

Larkin, Philip. (1988) *Collected Poems*, ed. A. Thwaite, London: Marvell.

Leavis, F. R. (1949) *Revaluation: Tradition and Development in English Poetry*, London: Chatto & Windus. Section on 'Shelley' rpt. in *English Romantic Poets* (1975) ed. M. H. Abrams, London: Oxford University Press.

Leech, Geoffrey. (1969) *A Linguistic Guide to English Poetry*, London: Longman.

Levin, S. R. (1971) 'The Conventions of Poetry' in *Literary Style. A Symposium*, ed. Seymour Chatman, London: Oxford University Press.

Lodge, David. (1977) *The Modes of Modern Writing. Metaphor, Metonymy and the Typology of Modern Literature*, London: Edward Arnold.

Lowell, Amy. (1920) 'Some Musical Analogies in Modern Poetry', *Musical Quarterly*, 6, 127–57.

Lowes, John Livingstone. (1927) *The Road to Xanadu: A Study in the Ways of the Imagination*. The most recent edition was published in 1978 by Pan Books, London.

Marvell, Andrew. (1971) *The Poems and Letters*, ed. H. M. Margoliouth, Vol. I, Oxford: Clarendon.

Mayo, Robert. (1954) 'The Contemporaneity of the *Lyrical Ballads*, in *Lyrical Ballads. A Selection of Critical Essays* (1972) ed. A. R. Jones and W. Tydeman, London: Macmillan.

Milton, John. (1968) *Paradise Lost*, ed. A. Fowler, London: Longman.

Milroy, James. (1977) *The Language of Gerard Manley Hopkins*, London: Andre Deutsch.

Morris, William. (1966) *Collected Works*, London: Longman.

Morrison, Blake. (1980) *The Movement*, Oxford: Oxford University Press.

Norris, Christopher. (1983) *The Deconstructive Turn. Essays in the Rhetoric of Philosophy*, London: Methuen.

Olson, Charles. (1950) 'Projective Verse' in *Selected Writings of Charles Olson* ed. Robert Creeley, New York: New Directions.

Olson, Charles. (1987) *Collected Poems*, Berkeley: University of California Press.

Pater, Walter. (1910) *Appreciations*, London: Macmillan.

Peirce, C. S. (1931–58) *Collected Papers*, ed. C. Hartshorne, P. Weiss and A. W. Burks, Cambridge, Mass.: Harvard University Press.

Pope, Alexander. (1939–69) *Twickenham Edition of the Poems*, 12 vols, ed. J. Butt, London: Methuen.

Price, Martin. (1964) *To The Palace of Wisdom: Studies in Order and Energy from Dryden to Blake*, Garden City, New York: Doubleday.

Priestley, Joseph. (1777) *A Course of Lectures on Oratory and Criticism*, London.

Ramsey, Paul. (1968) 'Free Verse: Some Steps Toward a Definition', *Studies in Philology*, 65, 98–108.

Rice, John. (1765) *An Introduction to the Art of Reading with Energy and Propriety*, London.

Ricks, Christopher. (1963) *Milton's Grand Style*, Oxford: Oxford University Press.

Ricks, Christopher. (ed.) (1987) *The New Oxford Book of Victorian Verse*, Oxford: Oxford University Press.

Riffaterre, Michael. (1966) 'Describing Poetic Structures: Two Approaches to Baudelaire's "Les Chats" ', *Yale French Studies*, 36–7, 200–42.

Ruskin, John. (1903–12) *The Works of John Ruskin*, London: George Allen.

Saussure, Ferdinand de. (1959) *Course in General Linguistics*, tr. W. Baskin, New York: McGraw-Hill.

Searle, John. (1969) *Speech Acts: An Essay in the Philosophy of Language*, Cambridge: Cambridge University Press.

Shakespeare, William. (1965) *Measure for Measure*, ed. J. D. Lever, London: Methuen.

Shelley, Percy Bysshe. (1970) *Poetical Works*, ed. T. Hutchinson, London: Oxford University Press.

Shuster, George N. (1940) *The English Ode from Milton to Keats*, New York: Columbia University Press.

Solt, Mary Ellen. (ed.) (1968) *Concrete Poetry. A World View*, Indiana: Indiana University Press.

Sprat, Thomas. (1908) 'The History of the Royal Society', in *Critical Essays of the 17th Century*, ed. J. E. Spingarn, Oxford: Clarendon Press.

Steiner, Wendy. (1982) *The Colors of Rhetoric. Problems in the Relation Between Modern Literature and Painting*, Chicago: Chicago University Press.

Stankiewicz, Edward. (1961) 'Poetic and Non-Poetic Language' in *Poetics – Poetyka – Poetika*, ed. D. Davie, Warsaw: Polish Scientific Publishers.

Tennyson, Alfred. (1992) *Selected Poems*, London: Penguin.

Thomas, Dylan. (1971) *Collected Poems*, New York: New Directions.

Thomson, James. (1981) *The Seasons*, London: Oxford University Press.

Tolley, A. T. (1975) *The Poetry of the Thirties*, New York: St Martins Press.

Tomlinson, Charles. (1986) *Collected Poems 1951–81*, Oxford: Oxford University Press.

Trager, George L., and Smith, Henry Lee Jnr. (1951) *An Outline of English Structure*, Studies in Linguistics Occasional Papers no.3, Norman, Oklahoma: Battenburg Press.

Traugott, E. C., and Pratt, M. L. (1980) *Linguistics For Students of Literature*, New York: Harcourt, Brace, Jovanovich.

Trilling, L., and Bloom, H. (eds) (1973) *Victorian Prose and Poetry*, London: Oxford University Press.

Wesling, Donald. (1980) *The Chances of Rhyme: Device and Modernity*, Berkeley: University of California Press.

Williams, William Carlos. (1991) *Collected Poems Vol. I 1909–39*, New York: New Directions.

Williams, William Carlos. (1991) *Collected Poems Vol. II 1939–62*, New York: New Directions.

Wimsatt, W. K. (1944) 'One Relation of Rhyme to Reason', in *The Verbal Icon* (1954), Lexington, Kentucky: University of Kentucky Press.

Wimsatt, W. K., and Beardsley, M. C. (1959) 'The Concept of Metre: An Exercise in Abstraction', *PMLA*, 74, 585–98.

Woodring, Carl. (1970) *Politics in English Romantic Poetry*, Cambridge, Mass.: Harvard University Press.

Wordsworth, William, and Coleridge, S. T. (1963) *Lyrical Ballads*, ed. R. L. Brett and A. R. Jones, London: Methuen.

Wordsworth, William. (1984) 'The Oxford Authors', ed. S. Gill, Oxford: Oxford University Press.

Index

Note: A number of terms and concepts are used so frequently in this study that it would be impractical to include them in the index. For brief definitions and references to prominent uses in the text please refer to the glossary. For example: deictics, double pattern, metaphor, metonymy, metre, natural-isation, rhyme, sliding scale.

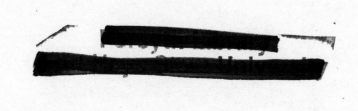